THE
STRANGE
FILES

THE
STRANGE
FILES

J.C. BRUCE

The Strange Files

Copyright © 2019 J.C. Bruce

ISBN: 978-1-7347848-0-0 (Hardcover); ISBN: 978-1-7342903-0-1 (Paperback)
ISBN: 978-1-7342903-1-8 (eBook)

Library of Congress Control Number: 2019920429

This is a work of fiction. Names, characters, places, and incidents are a product of the author's imagination. Locales and public names are sometimes used for atmospheric purposes. Any resemblance to actual people, living or dead, or to businesses, companies, events, institutions, or locales is completely coincidental.

Book design by Damonza.com
Website design by Bumpy Flamingo LLC

Published by Tropic ⚇ Press in the United States of America.

First printing edition 2019

Tropic ⚇ Press LLC
P.O. Box 110758
Naples, Florida 34108

www.Tropic.Press

BOOKS BY J.C. BRUCE

The Strange Files

Florida Man: A Story From the Files of Alexander Strange

Get Strange

Strange Currents

To Sandy Bruce

"News is history shot on the wing. The huntsmen from the Fourth Estate seek to bag only the peacock or the eagle of the swifting day."
— **Gene Fowler**, 1890-1960
American journalist, author, and playwright

Fearless Poodle Saves Baby

By Alexander Strange

Phoenix Daily Sun

There are countless stories of firefighters, police, and other humans who have saved pets from harm.

Three weeks ago, Tempe firefighters axed their way through a blazing apartment roof to free a greyhound trapped in the burning building. These heroic first-responders will be honored tomorrow at the annual PETA gala for their heroism.

But sometimes roles are reversed. Vanessa Moreau, who moved here from Argeles-sur-Mer, France, was walking her six-month-old standard poodle, Coco, at Buffalo Ridge Park when she spotted a pack of coyotes stalking a young woman and an infant who were enjoying a picnic lunch. Ms. Moreau, terrified for the mother and child, unleashed her puppy.

"Coco, she went *des fous*," she told police.

Translated from the French: Coco went crazy.

The poodle charged the coyotes. She barked, and nipped, and chased, and finally drove them away. She gave the young woman time to grab her baby and run to the safety of her car.

Witnesses confirmed the account. One caller told me, "I could see a German shepherd or maybe a pit bull attacking like that, but a poodle? It was five against one. I take back everything I've ever said about the French."

Phoenix police have prepared a special commendation medal for Coco. She will be named an honorary member of the Arizona Law Enforcement Police Dog Association. PETA, too, will honor the puppy, giving Coco a "Heroic Dog Award." Translated to the French: *chien heroique.*

STRANGE FACT: The poodle—the national dog of France—is

an excellent hunter and retriever. And coyotes, however wily, distinguish themselves from other canines and humans—the French included: They mate for life.

Weirdness knows no boundaries. Keep up at www.TheStrangeFiles.com. Contact Alexander Strange at Alex@TheStrangeFiles.com.

CHAPTER 1

THE LEGGY BLONDE strode through the newsroom like she owned the place and stepped into my office. As she leaned over the desk, her hair fell forward, and she swept it away revealing sparkling diamond earrings that matched the rocks around her neck. She wore a low-cut black cocktail dress, tight fitting, that showed off her lissome figure. But it was her eyes that drew my attention. They were cobalt and rimmed in red, as if she would begin crying at any moment.

"Geez, Mom, you all right?"

Her brow furrowed. "I thought we agreed not to call me that. I'm not *that* much older than you, Alexander."

She had me by at least fifteen years, but no question she looked younger than her age.

"Well, you are my stepmother."

Her name was Sarah and she was newly wed to my Uncle Leo—Maricopa County Superior Court Judge Leonard D. Strano to you. Leo adopted me after my mother—his sister—drowned in a cave during a sit-in to save an endangered species of spider.

So, any of Leo's succession of wives qualified as a stepmother. Sarah was the latest, *Numero Cinco*.

"Please, Alex," Sarah said, her voice strained. "There's a problem and Leonard said you'd help."

I stood and motioned her to the guest chair in my small and cluttered office. It was nine o'clock at night and the newspaper was deserted. The *Phoenix Daily Sun* was an afternoon paper, one of the last PMs in the country, and most of the reporters and editors had gone home. I was working my once-a-month graveyard shift monitoring the police scanner and rolling when something exciting broke loose—fires, gunplay, alien sightings, that sort of thing. All the writers took a turn, columnists like me not exempted.

"Talk to me, Sarah," I said. "What is it?"

"Freddie."

"Fred? What's wrong?" Fred is Sarah's Papillon. He's a tiny black and white furball with a smile that would melt an editor's heart. He resembles a collie shot by a shrink ray, but with oversized ears like silky butterfly wings. Hence the breed's name: Papillon is French for butterfly.

"Freddie's missing."

"He got out?"

She paused for a moment and took a deep breath. "Yes, he got out. And it's probably my fault." Her voice cracked a little. She rubbed her eyes. Her pink fingernails matched her lipstick. The diamond on her wedding ring sparkled under the fluorescent light.

"I left the house this afternoon to go to the hairdresser. Then I drove straight away to a PETA banquet at the convention center. Leonard didn't want to go." She rolled her eyes. "Imagine that. Anyway, I had my phone turned off and missed his call. Just got the message. That's why I came by."

I waited a beat, giving her time to finish her story, but she just stopped, going internal, thinking who knew what? I prompted her: "Leo called and said what?"

"That when he got home, Freddie was gone."

"And Fred was there when you left?"

"Yes, I fed him then let him out to tinkle."

"Tinkle?"

Her brow furrowed again. "What? Is that the wrong word? What would you like me to say?"

"Tinkle is a fine word. Fred tinkled. Then what?"

"Then I grabbed my purse and left."

"You said it might be your fault."

"Leonard's furious with me. This isn't the first time."

"The first time Fred got loose?"

"No, the first time I forgot to close the garage door, the side door, all the way. The lock, sometimes it doesn't, uh, doesn't…"

"Engage?"

"Yes. The thingie…"

"The latch?"

"Yes, that, it gets stuck, and one day when Leonard came home from work the door wasn't closed all the way. Breeze must have blown it open."

"And you think that's how Fred ran away?"

She shrugged. "I'm afraid so."

"OK, Sarah. How can I help?"

She took a moment to compose herself.

"Leonard told me to come here. That you could make flyers with Freddie's picture. I've got a photo. She pulled a cell phone from her purse and showed it to me. Fred was staring straight at the camera, his mouth open, his little pink tongue dangling out. "Can you download it and make copies?"

I pulled out a wad of tissues from one of my desk drawers and handed it to her. She offered a weak smile and dabbed her eyes.

"I'm sorry," she said. "It's been a difficult day."

"Your dog running off, that will do it. Let alone enduring a PETA banquet."

She reached over and grabbed my forearm and squeezed. "Thank you." A friendly gesture, but unusual. For the most part, she was shields-up around me. Distant. And perhaps I wasn't Mister

Enthusiastic after Leo returned with Sarah from Vegas three months ago to break the news he was hitched again.

I'd been crashing at Leo's place since taking this job at the newspaper, and it had been fun hanging with him. We'd been working our way through his immense collection of old movies and detective novels. Leo wasn't just my adoptive father, he was my best friend. But I knew for some time I needed to find my own place, and with his new wife it was time for me to pack up. Still, it was a bit awkward.

Sarah emailed me the picture of Fred, and I knocked out a brief bit of text to go with it, including a phone number to call. In half an hour, she walked out of the newsroom with a handful of flyers.

It seemed a fool's errand. Fred's dog tag would have contact information engraved on it. A bigger worry, which I didn't mention to her, were predators. Packs of wild dogs and coyotes had been prowling neighborhoods, and there had been several reports of vanishing pets. Poor little Fred wouldn't stand a chance out in the wild.

Leo's yard, like most in upscale Phoenix neighborhoods, was enclosed—six-foot-high stuccoed brick. And Leo's front porch was defended by a wrought iron gate that Fred couldn't squeeze through. Even if Sarah had left the side door of the garage open, it led to a fenced yard. Unless the gate had been left open, too. What else could it be?

It was a good question, but I didn't have time to dwell on it. After Sarah left, the police scanner began squawking about a burglar trapped in a chimney at a home in Paradise Valley. I grabbed my backpack and took off. The address was on Hogahn Drive, Barry Goldwater's old neighborhood.

When I got there, two firefighters were on the roof trying to extricate him, their efforts brightly illuminated by a searchlight from a hovering helicopter. Didn't help matters that the perp was, to be kind, a bit over his ideal body mass index. Maybe he thought if Santa could do it, he could, too. I shot several photos as they pulled him free. Was he grateful? Did he thank the brave first responders? Did he summon his reindeer? Nah. He pushed one of the firefighters out of the way, then slid down the tiled roof and jumped off—right onto an enormous prickly pear cactus. You could hear his screams on Mars.

By the time I filed my story and pictures it was 5 a.m., Leo's invariable time to rise and shine. He would be in his kitchen brewing coffee, then he would retrieve the morning newspaper off his patio. He'd have the paper read cover-to-cover before Sarah even stirred.

I looked out the newsroom windows. Still dark, but the sun would soon paint the tip of Camelback Mountain in golden hues. A couple of copy editors drifted in and began sorting the overnight news, including my story.

I was beat, but figured I should volunteer to help with the search for Fred. Sarah might appreciate the gesture; Leo, hard to tell. Fred was part of the Sarah package—he came with her when they got hitched. To my certain knowledge, Fred was the first animal to set paws in Leo's house. My uncle is not what you would call a pet person. He's not much of a people person, for that matter.

I punched his number on my cell phone and he answered after the first ring.

"Hey, Leo, what's the word on Fred?"

There was a pause, and I could hear Leo take a sip of coffee.

"Yeah, that's a complication."

"Complication?"

"Sarah's frantic. She only got to sleep a couple hours ago. She's guilt-ridden. I haven't summoned the courage to tell her how he really got out."

"What does that mean?"

"It means I haven't told her that I think Fred ran out of the house when the burglars ransacked my study."

CHAPTER 2

CREATURES OF HABIT are the easiest to stalk, and Leo was, without a doubt, one of those predictable critters. One of the county's most successful trial lawyers before his appointment to the bench, he was regarded as the most rigid jurist in Maricopa County. A rite of passage for young attorneys was to be "Stranoized" for daring to suggest a change in the court's calendar. It was an ass chewing never to be forgotten.

So I was confident His Honor would emerge from chambers precisely at five p.m., not a minute earlier, nor later. Ordinarily, he would then traverse Patriot's Square to Kelso's Saloon for a bit of late afternoon restorative, his invariable after-work routine. But today would be different, I assumed, given our terse morning phone conversation.

"See me after work," he commanded when I pressed him on the burglary. So I was awaiting Leo in the busy corridor outside Courtroom 331, a huntsman of the Fourth Estate ready to bag my prey.

I checked my watch. It was time.

"Hello, Your Lawfulness," I said as the door marked "Private" swung open and Leo strode into the hallway and turned toward the bank of elevators. "Punctual and predictable as ever."

"I'm not predictable," he snapped. "I'm reliable. There's a difference."

It was a running courthouse joke that Leo didn't get a hard-on without scheduling it in his docket. Nobody had the courage to share that with him, of course, and it certainly wouldn't be me. But I enjoyed needling him.

Immaculate in one of his trademark off-white suits and a western string tie, Uncle Leo turned to confront me. He ceremoniously whipped off his horn-rimmed glasses and thrust his prominent proboscis in my face. We stood schnoz-to-schnoz for a moment, me flat-footed, looking down, he on his tip-toes, looking up, pressing his beak into mine. I fought back a snort. Leo worked hard on this badass routine. It served him well on the bench. But I knew better. And he knew I knew.

"You're still in my courthouse and that sounds like contempt to me." He winked and expected me to wink back, my role in our little exchange of banter. But I wasn't in the mood.

"Leo, we need to talk about the puppy in the room. What's up with Fred? And the burglary? And why are you keeping Sarah in the dark?"

"Walk with me."

With that, he turned and resumed his beeline to the elevators. "Your Tortness," I said. "Seriously?" I sprinted past him, hit the down button, and blocked the elevator door, which opened behind me. "Come on, give."

He shook his head. "Hold the 'vator. Got something to mail."

Leo propped his ancient alligator briefcase on a knee, raised the lid, and extracted an envelope that he had addressed in his signature green ink. He dropped it into the postal chute in the elevator bank, taking his time as if this were an act that required intense concentration. A drop of sweat beaded on the tip of his nose. Odd. You could hang bacon in the courthouse.

The open briefcase slipped from his knee and dumped his planner and other papers onto the tile floor. "Dammit," he sputtered.

I stepped away from the elevator to help him, but he brushed me back with a wave of his hand. "I got it. The latch on this goddamned thing's been broken for years. Why I never replaced it's beyond me. Come on, let's get out of here."

"Kind of clumsy in your old age," I said as we stepped into the elevator.

"Don't you know it's politically incorrect to make fun of people in ill health?"

"You sick?"

"Kind of you to notice."

"Whatcha got?"

"Dropsy."

I groaned. "Seriously, Leo, you OK? You're dripping wet."

"I'm fine, I'm fine. Had to run an errand a few minutes ago. Across the street. Still haven't cooled off."

I found myself sweating, too. I don't do well in confined spaces. Leo noticed and patted me on the shoulder.

The elevator bell dinged and the door opened to reveal the sprawling courthouse lobby. Leo steered us away from the Jefferson Street exit toward the East Courthouse wing. It saved a few steps and kept us in the blessed confines of air conditioning for an extra minute or two. We passed a clutch of courthouse employees yakking in the corridor. They halted their chatter as we walked by. "Your honor," a couple of them intoned. Leo nodded. None of them said boo to me.

"I called the house today, tried to reach Sarah about Fred, but she didn't call back."

"Busy packing. She's flying to Salt Lake tonight."

"Sarah's leaving? Now?"

He stopped and studied me for a moment.

"She doesn't know what I'm going to tell you."

This wasn't the first time Leo had confided in me to the exclusion of one of his wives.

"Well, as long as you can afford the alimony payments."

He scowled. "It's not like that."

"Then why haven't you told her?"

"I don't want her tangled up in this, but I do need *your* help."

"My help and not Sarah's?"

"She's got family issues. Something to do with one of her sisters. I don't want her burdened with this."

Sarah was Mormon. Probably had a big family, but I wasn't sure. Until they eloped to Las Vegas, she was the judge's secretary—or, in courthouse parlance, judicial assistant. With Leo's history of serial monogamy, who could keep up with his wives' bios? And our relationship wasn't what you would call warm. Her showing up at my office asking for help was a huge departure from her normal behavior. But normal seemed to be on vacation.

"It can't wait, her trip to Salt Lake?" I asked Leo. "What about Fred?"

Leo shook his head. "She wanted to cancel her flight, but I insisted. It's better if she leaves town. I told her a little dog like Fred could never survive a day in the desert anyway. That she had to accept the fact that he's gone."

"You didn't."

"I did."

"You're just a ray of sunshine, you know that?"

"Keep up."

We lumbered along a bit, Leo forcing an aggressive pace. He pushed open the glass courthouse door and we were engulfed in the volcanic heat. I slipped on my Oakleys. It was mid-August and the high for the day was forecast to hit 107. With all the concrete and blacktop, though, the temperature spiked even hotter downtown.

The square was crowded with workers making their way from their offices to parking lots and watering holes. A slight breeze kicked up the skirt of a pretty young woman on our left. Leo and I looked and caught each other in the act.

We passed an Asian couple wearing surgical masks—tourists, no doubt terrified by the news of the Ebola outbreak in Chicago. TV and the internet had hyped the epidemic out of proportion and people were jittery even out West.

"Leo, about Fred?"

"What about it?"

"He. Not it. Fred's a guy. Like us."

He gave me the stink eye. "Fred's *cojones* are long gone."

I tried a different tack. "How'd the burglars get in?"

"Through the side door on the garage. It was open."

"Sarah told me. She was afraid she didn't close it properly."

"I've thought about that. I was annoyed at first. But it wouldn't have mattered. The burglars would have gotten in some other way if she hadn't."

"And the burglars. They were looking for something in your study?"

"Yes."

"And did they find it?"

"It wasn't in the study."

"That's not an answer."

"I know. You want answers, meet me at the house at three o'clock tomorrow. We're talking to a guy who can help clear this up. And if I'm right, you'll have a hell of a story to tell."

"What story?"

"Don't start on me. Tomorrow. Three o'clock. In the meantime, let's drink."

I couldn't leave it at that. "But you called the cops, right?"

It was a stupid question. If he hadn't told Sarah, he wouldn't have called the police. Leo didn't hesitate to show his disdain. I got the look that lawyers appearing before his bench dreaded, right before they were Stranoized.

"Tomorrow," he said.

I shut up and plodded along with him to Kelso's. Leo had put answering my questions on his to-do list for tomorrow. No force of nature, and no nattering nephew, could change that.

Creatures of habit can be such a pain in the ass.

CHAPTER 3

ARCTIC CHILL WASHED over us as we stepped into Kelso's. The saloon's tables were decoupaged with headlines from the *Arizona Republic*, my paper, and others. Famous front pages covered the walls: "Man Lands on the Moon," "Nixon Resigns," and my favorite— "Ride Sally Ride"—celebrating the launch into space of NASA's first female astronaut. Elsewhere in the bar were remnants from newspaper history: an ancient Smith Corona typewriter, wood cases filled with lead type, green eyeshades hanging from hooks over the bar and, the centerpiece of the establishment, an ancient Linotype machine. The decorating scheme was a tribute to a dying industry, a veritable newspaper museum complete with booze.

Jake Kelso had been a political reporter for the *Republic* before he was laid off a few years before. He opened the bar in partnership with a notorious local madam, Michelle "Stormy" Sheetz, who had been forced out of the escort business during one of the city's periodic vice crackdowns. Today, Kelso was resplendent in white shirt and bow tie. His black bar apron bulging under the pressure of his prodigious midsection, he was writing the day's drink special on a blackboard— *Betrayal of Minsk*.

We walked over to say hello.

"What's this *Betrayal* thing?" I asked.

Kelso beamed. "My late cousin, John, in Austin, he invented it. You substitute rum for vodka in a screwdriver. Get it? Russian vodka betrayed by rum?" He was bobbing up and down, so excited to reveal his secret.

"Genius."

Leo and I moved down the bar and commandeered the last two empty stools. Across the saloon sat my boss, Edwina Mahoney, the *Sun's* managing editor, chatting with a couple of the newspaper's senior editors. A brief smile crossed her lips as she spotted us. I waved. At a booth near the back door, a gaggle of *Phoenix Daily Sun* staffers was huddled in hushed conspiratorial conversation. I made a mental note to annoy them before I left.

"Leo, what the hell's going on?"

"I know you're worried. Wasted energy."

"You just gonna leave me hanging?"

"That's what hanging judges do."

"You suck."

"Fine way to talk. Have a drink."

"Can't. Gotta blow this pop stand in a few minutes."

"What's the rush?"

"Got a meeting at the TV station."

"Aren't you ashamed, working with the talking dogs?"

Leo disdained the blow-dried set. Most of what passes for news on local TV is crap, of course—if it bleeds, it leads. Now the newspaper wanted me to team up with the station for an early morning program. They'd shoot video of me doing interviews for my column, *The Strange Files*, and we'd cross-promote and help each other grow audience. That was the theory.

"The new owner of the paper, he's into media convergence," I said. That earned me a perplexed look. "That's jargon for newspapers and TV stations covering stories together."

Leo snorted. "What's next? Cats and dogs doing the horizontal bop?"

"Hey, it could work."

"Don't get me wrong, nephew, I think you're the pips, but I predict your new owner—what's his name, Wormhole? —will be out of business and you'll be selling pencils on a street corner before you can say 'stop the presses.'"

The new owner of the *Phoenix Daily Sun* was Francis Van Wormer. His first act as the new owner was to convert the paper from morning to afternoon publication, even though most PM papers had gone the way of the dodo bird. Then he scuttled the Sunday edition in favor of a beefed-up Saturday paper. In his youth, he had worked in Canada while dodging the draft during the Vietnam War, and they never published on Sundays in the Great White North. Good enough for the Saskatoon *Star-Phoenix*, good enough for the *Phoenix Daily Sun*, he reasoned.

Owning a newspaper of his own had been a lifelong fantasy since repatriating to these United States. Newspapers were cheap, and he had a pile of cash. He'd made a fortune as a big-time K Street lobbyist in Washington, D.C., which was still his day job.

"I ever tell you about Wormhole's first and only day at the paper?" I asked Leo.

He shook his head.

"So he calls this staff meeting. We're all gathered around. And he starts by saying, and I quote, 'It may be fatalistic that I began my newspaper career at the *Star-Phoenix*, and now I am here. But you have my word that this newspaper, like the great bird for which this city is named, will rise from the ashes of its failing history.'"

"Fatalistic?" Leo asked.

"Yeah. You and Abby Conwest should form a club."

"Who's she?"

"Our copy desk chief." I nodded in her direction at the table across the barroom where the *Sun* staffers I spotted earlier were huddled.

"So get this. Conwest interrupts Wormhole and says, 'Kismet.' And Von Wormer turns to her and says, 'Kiswhat?' And Conwest says, 'The word you're searching for is kismet or karma, not fatalistic.'

And Von Wormer, at this point, he's got this panicked look, like the zombies are attacking, and he says, 'Kismet, karma, what the fuck difference does it make?' And that's the last we've seen of him. He did a 180, stormed out of the newsroom."

I nodded toward my boss, Edwina Mahoney, at the other end of the bar. "He only talks to her, now. From his office in Washington."

Leo shook his head. "I hear his nose is so far up the President's ass he can't take a dump without unplugging Wormhole first."

"Maybe. Anyway, me partnering with KPX-TV, that's his latest brainstorm on how to improve what he likes to call 'the product.'"

"Product, huh? That's what newspapers are now? Products?"

"Don't get me started," I said. And I definitely did not want to talk about the ethical implications of having an owner who was also a political lobbyist. Then again, the *Washington Post* was owned by the founder of Amazon. At the rate newspapers were circling the drain, even I could be a newspaper owner one day. With a staff of me, myself, and I.

Kelso walked over to take our drink orders. "Everything strange over here?" he asked.

"I'm always Strange."

Kelso cackled. It was the same routine every time. Uncle Leo wasn't the only creature of habit.

The judge ordered his usual, a Coors Light.

"A rum and Coke for you?" Kelso asked. It was my go-to ethanol delivery system.

"Not now, Jake. Can't linger. Just keeping tabs on His Verdict, making sure he stays out of trouble."

As Kelso turned to pour the beer, Leo's attention was captured by the TV over the bar. I looked up to see video of medics carrying a GI on a stretcher, the latest scenes from the "police action" in Uganda.

"What do you make of that?" Leo asked.

"I don't understand how we so quickly linked those Ebola deaths in Chicago to jihadists in Africa. How many countries we going to invade in the name of fighting terrorism?"

"How many countries are there?'

"Careful, Big Brother might be eavesdropping."

Leo nodded. "The Man's testicles are everywhere."

"You mean tentacles."

Leo tipped his beer glass in my direction. "Them, too."

Leo had obsessed over government snooping ever since he ruled against the Defense Department's efforts to build a "detainment facility"—read that, another Guantanamo—at the old air base, Williams Field, in Mesa, a suburb east of Phoenix. The city had filed a lawsuit to block the construction of the prison, and Leo granted a temporary injunction. He ruled that the U.S.A. Patriot Act—and by extension the new Guantanamo—was unenforceable in Arizona because the eavesdropping provisions of the Act amounted to an illegal "taking" of privacy, a kind of property right. He also challenged the propriety of the construction contract being awarded to Ravenous Unlimited Global Holdings, previously run by the current director of Homeland Security.

Rather than fight it, the Administration pulled an end-run and cut a deal with a local Indian tribe to build the prison on "sovereign" reservation land, outside the jurisdiction of pesky state judges. Construction had been completed and the first detainees were en route from Africa.

Leo had his fifteen minutes of fame. He spent a week fielding interviews with the likes of Steven Colbert, Rachael Maddow, and Bubba the Love Sponge. But ever since, he was convinced he was being watched.

Kelso returned with Leo's beer. "You know why drinkin' Coors is like making love in a canoe?" he asked.

I shook my head.

"It's fuckin' near water."

I groaned. Kelso cackled. Then he looked over to Leo expectantly. It was a ritual and Leo never disappointed, his stock of terrible jokes a bottomless pit.

"Got a new one for you, Jake," Leo said. "There's good news and bad news." He didn't pause to ask Kelso which he wanted to hear first. "The bad news is the Martians have landed."

"What's the good news?"

"They eat politicians and piss gasoline."

Kelso snorted and Leo slugged down half his beer. Then he swiveled in the barstool to face me. "Tell me about this new assignment of yours. Who they teaming you up with?"

"She's new to the station. From Vegas."

"Showgirl?"

"No, Leo, she's not a showgirl."

"Good looking, though. Right?"

"Leo, that all you think about?"

"You got something better?"

I could have said yes, how about we talk about Fred. Or what's up with Sarah and her family? Or, are you serious, your house was burglarized, can we talk about that? But after the years I've lived with Leo, I've learned when to fold 'em.

On my way out, I stopped by the table filled with *Sun* staffers. The paper's editorial cartoonist, Garreth DePutron, was holding forth.

"So here's the idea: Super Dude."

DePutron hadn't directed the remark to anyone in particular, but it clearly annoyed Elmore James. "Nice going, Garreth," he said. "Once again you've slipped off to la-la land."

DePutron took another pull on his *Betrayal of Minsk* and persisted: "Super Dude from the Planet Claptrap. He wears a boa instead of a cape."

Harold Ponitz, also seated at the table, frowned. "If we could exit the Phantom Zone, your colleagues have a serious proposition to discuss with you," he said in his crisp New England accent, a sharp contrast to James' surly western twang.

A broad grin stretched across DePutron's freckled face. He looked up to see me lurking over the back of their booth and winked.

The "serious proposition" over which DePutron's colleagues fretted concerned an effort to unionize the editorial staff of the newspaper. Representatives of the Newspaper Guild had flown into town the previous evening and there had been a discreet off-site meeting. A select handful of newsroom employees were solemnly sworn to secrecy. Oaths of confidentiality were exchanged. Handshakes shared. Vows taken. But within minutes of the meeting's conclusion, of course, everyone on the staff knew about it.

I understood why the Guild might make a run at the *Sun* given the ownership turmoil and the uncertainty that breeds. But this was Arizona, where popular sentiment held that Barry Goldwater in his dotage had turned into a left-wing sellout. Unions were anathema. Besides, newspapers all over the country were laying off staff.

Elmore James was a reporter, a veteran unburdened by ambition, who had covered the police beat for seventeen years. He was one of those guys who smelled of alcohol even when he wasn't drinking on the job. He had a pockmarked face, drooping eyelids, and a hairline that receded to form a point, like the prow of a battleship. He combed it straight back using God knows how many gallons of petroleum byproduct to keep his few remaining follicles pasted in place. Think Bella Lugosi without the charm.

Ponitz was nearing retirement age. He worked in the newspaper's library. It used to be called the morgue, but that was too gothic for current sensibilities. Now it's the News Research Department. A slight, precise man, Ponitz spent most of his time doing tedious database analysis. I'd rather have a colonoscopy.

Abigail Conwest was a giant of a woman—almost my height—with a penchant for colorful dresses, pearl necklaces, and high heels. An Amazonian June Cleaver. In a newsroom in which slovenly appearance was *de rigueur*, her formality of dress set her apart from *hoi polloi*, as if her physical stature were an insufficient delimiter. After all, she was no mere ink-stained wretch like the rest of us, she was the newspaper's Copy Desk Chief, and she embraced her role as the guardian of the newspaper's rules of style with the fierceness of a praetorian. Every word of every story that passed through her hands would be sanitized through the filter of *Strunk & White* and the *Associated Press Stylebook*. There would be no passive phrases nor parenthetic expressions unenclosed by commas. Errors of syntax would be excised; "which" was transformed to "that" unless preceded by a comma. And all participial phrases at the beginning of sentences would correctly refer to their grammatical subjects or hell would be paid. She was a walking Dull-o-matic machine who could render the most creative piece prosaic. She was feared and hated by the staff. And she was blinded by literalism. Some years earlier, a newly elected governor had decided to celebrate his inauguration by holding three galas around the state—one each in Phoenix, Tucson, and Flagstaff—as opposed to the usual single shindig at the state Capitol. Conwest wrote a headline on the story that read:

GOVERNOR HAS THREE BALLS

She didn't understand why that caused such a ruckus. As far as I knew, she still hadn't cleared up the confusion she had created over karma and kismet, either.

What struck me at that moment, though, was her new wig, a platinum Dutch boy job that looked a size too small for her head.

"Nice do," I said.

Conwest gazed up at me and smiled, revealing a set of choppers stained amber by too many years of coffee and coffin nails.

"Thank you," she preened. "It's slenderizing, don't you think?"

"Absolutely," I lied.

James rostered at me, a challenging look in his eyes. "You catch all that earlier, kid?"

I looked down and smiled. "I wasn't eavesdropping, Mr. James. But did I overhear something about the Newspaper Guild and boas?"

DePutron laughed. "They're trying to sell me on the Guild. But I'm trying out my idea for a new comic strip. He'll have a big "D" on his chest."

"Super Dude abides, huh?"

"You got it!"

"I like that idea better than the Guild."

I actually had nothing against unions as a philosophical matter. And owners like Van Wormer practically begged to be organized. But it was obvious the newspaper was in desperate financial shape. That's how Van Wormer was able to buy it on the cheap. And when the ship you're aboard starts taking on water, your job is to bail—as hard as you can—not waste time debating what sized bucket you should have.

All we had to do was pull together, pitch in. Teamwork. That was the key.

"You can leave now, Strange," James said. "This is a private meeting.

So much for teamwork.

CHAPTER 4

I SLIPPED BEHIND the wheel of my maroon Chrysler Sebring convertible, which I'd bought from Uncle Leo—notwithstanding some unusual upholstery stains—and pulled out of the *Sun's* back lot. The seatbelt warning light blinked at me like a spasmodic Cylon. I ignored it.

The gas bag on the radio was saying the anti-terror campaign in Uganda was heating up as American "military advisers" were closing in on the newly discovered uranium deposits near the Congolese border. It was important these deposits stay out of the hands of terrorists, we were told. The Centers for Disease Control remained clueless about the cause of the Ebola virus outbreak in Chicago, although the Administration continued to blame the outbreak on Ugandan terror cells.

Not all the news from this latest overseas expedition was disheartening, though. It had led to a revival of the Uranium Savages' classic hit, "Idi Amin Is My Yard Man." See, you can always find some good no matter how glum the news. You just have to look.

National news gave way to local. Forest rangers were struggling to contain a wildfire that had broken out north of Phoenix in the Tonto National Forest. A thirty-five-year-old Glendale man was being held on manslaughter charges after shooting his wife with a .22-caliber rifle. He claimed he was trying to punch a hole in his wall to run a cable to his TV. And a Tempe bank heist was foiled when the robber's cell phone battery exploded, setting him on fire. That report was a verbatim rip-off of one of my columns. The radio pukes were always stealing newspaper material.

Alice Cooper came on playing *Novocain* and I turned the radio off. Not that I don't like Alice. It's just that music gives me earworms and I find myself rewriting the lyrics in my head. I'm told it's a mental disorder.

Bit of trivia: Alice is not his real name. He was born Vince Furnier. He started his first band when he was a high school student right here In Phoenix. They called themselves the Earwigs. Later the Spiders. They took the band to Los Angeles and settled on Alice Cooper. And Vince adopted the name for himself thereafter. I knew all this because I have an interest in people named Alice. It was my mother's name. And for a very short time, mine. But that's another story.

It's a short drive from downtown to uptown where KPX-TV was housed in a nondescript stucco block. The station's actual broadcast tower was across the city atop the rumpled shoulders of South Mountain, which sprouted dozens of antennas, like a rocky bull bristling with banderillas.

The western sky was darkening and the queen palms along the road were swaying in a rising breeze. A yellow Mustang was hugging my rear bumper, another idiot who fantasized he was a NASCAR driver. I'd nagged about tailgaters in my columns, comparing them to butt-sniffing dogs. I changed lanes, then grabbed my notebook off the passenger seat as he passed me and scribbled his license plate: MSAGRO. I was building a list of vanity plates for a column. Why people paid extra for them was beyond me. Then again, maybe if I had one I could remember my tags. You could put a gun to my head and I couldn't tell you.

The entrance to the television station loomed on my left, flanked by two giant saguaros. I pulled into a Visitors Only slot and as I did my cell phone buzzed. Caller ID showed it was Dani Vaquero, the reporter I was meeting.

"Twenty-four hours a day, seven days a week, this is Alexander Strange," I said.

"No shit? *The* Alexander Strange!" There was a lilt of *Español* in her accent.

"Is this the incomparable Dani Vaquero?"

"Incomparable? That good?"

"Just like Dejah Thoris."

"Who? Whatever. Listen, the reason I'm calling, we gotta postpone our meeting."

"Dude, I'm in the parking lot."

"If you're in the lot, look west and you'll see why. My crew, we're driving to Buckeye. Got to get there before the haboob."

"Whose boob?"

"Not boob. Haboob. Dust storm."

I stepped out of my car and looked across the parking lot. She was right. A gigantic wall of dirt was bearing down on the Valley. Never heard it called a haboob before. Always just called them sandstorms.

"You wanna try to get together next week?" I asked.

"How about breakfast? Tomorrow?"

I had to meet with Leo, but I also had to eat. No reason I couldn't do both. I jotted down her address next to the odd license plate in my notebook.

"Say, got any idea what this means?" I spelled out MSAGRO.

"Huh?"

I spelled it for her again. She was quiet for a moment, and I feared I'd once again come off too obscure, too weird. Dejah Thoris? What's wrong with me? Like everybody should have grown up reading Edgar Rice Burroughs.

My cell phone erupted in laughter. "What's so funny?"

"It's backwards," Dani said. "Reverse the spelling." She hung up.

ORGASM.

Clever. I reflected for a moment about how she laughed when she figured it out. Then I imagined other ways I might get her to laugh. Then I thought I'd better stop thinking about that.

I glanced at the horizon before stepping back into the car. The sun was becoming obscured by the approaching storm, a premature sunset, as if a dark amber veil were being been raised between the city and the sky. A tumbleweed bounced along the asphalt parking lot. Before long, standing outdoors would become an instant dermabrasion treatment.

I decided to drive back to my apartment in Tempe. Try to get there while there was still enough visibility. Then, maybe, a Cuba Libre, perhaps some online poker if we didn't lose power.

My cell phone vibrated. It was a text message from the paper.

NEED VOLUNTEERS TO COVER THE STORM. CAN YOU HELP?

So much for my quiet evening at home.

It was a dismal ending to a disappointing day. I got nothing out of Leo about the burglary nor our mysterious meeting tomorrow. Fred was still missing and my appointment with Dani had been interrupted by, of all things, the weather.

Another of Mother Nature's annoying ironies: August 18, and once again there was a storm. It was on this date that my mom crawled into a cave in Austin, Texas, to prevent developers from bulldozing the habitat of an endangered species of spider. Within hours of her sit-in, a monstrous storm submerged the Hill Country in more than a foot of rain, ending her life and, for anyone knows, the arachnid's, too. Sadly, no spider powers conferred to her orphaned son.

Dust-up over Sandstorm, er, Haboob

By Alexander Strange

Phoenix Daily Sun

The sandstorm that blew through Phoenix Friday may have wreaked havoc on airline traffic, but it was a boon to the bars and restaurants at Sky Harbor.

Stranded travelers swarmed Taberna del Tequila, Four Peaks Brewery, the Copper Plate and other hangouts waiting for the dust to settle—literally.

Sitting beside a window facing the tarmac, a husband and wife, Robert and Shirley Munson from Santa Barbara, were engaged in a spirited conversation when a reporter approached their table shopping for quotes from passengers whose flights had been delayed.

"Settle an argument for us, would you, kid?" Robert Munson asked.

"Now, Bob," his wife tried to intervene.

"No, seriously. Just tell us. What do you call this? He raised a cocktail in the direction of the sand-blasted window.

"Well," the reporter said, "offhand, I'd say it was a Manhattan."

Shirley burst out laughing. Robert shook his head in disgust. "Not the drink, kid, that, out there, all that yellow stuff blowing around."

"What about it?"

"I say it's called a sandstorm," Shirley said. "Bob says it's a dust storm. What do you say?"

"It's a haboob. Everybody knows that."

STRANGE FACT: Haboob, a word invented to describe the ferocious dust storms in the Sudan, isn't the only Arabic word commonly used in English. Others include assassin, caliber, candy, harem, hazard, mattress, syrup, and zero.

Weirdness knows no boundaries. Keep up at www.TheStrangeFiles.com. Contact Alexander Strange at Alex@TheStrangeFiles.com.

CHAPTER 5

WRITING ON DEADLINE and growing up with Leo made me neurotic about the clock, and now I was running late. Dragooned into covering the sandstorm the night before, I ended up at Sky Harbor interviewing dozens of cranky airline passengers whose trips had been delayed or canceled. I thought I might run across Leo and Sarah, but our paths didn't cross. By the time I returned to the office and filed my story and a short column, it was nearly midnight.

Now I was stuck behind a crypt-hugger at the wheel of an ancient silver Cadillac Seville doing forty-five in the passing lane of the Lori Piestewa Freeway. It used to be called the Squaw Peak Freeway, but that had become intolerable—both for demeaning females of Native American persuasion and the indelicate inference to their anatomy—so it had been renamed for the first American Indian killed in the Iraq war.

I flashed my headlights at the Caddy to no avail. I could barely discern a fluff of white hair over the top of the car's headrest. Although most of the snowbirds had long since migrated back north for the summer, the city was still overrun with retirees killing time until their dirt naps. I suspected they enjoyed driving the rest of us crazy, puttering along and crossing multiple lanes of traffic without warning.

Revenge of the Codgers. I glanced at my watch. It was ten thirty. Hope Dani didn't mind a late breakfast.

I picked my iPhone off the passenger seat to punch in her number, but the battery was dead. I'd stupidly left it in the car when I got home from the airport last night. I reached down to plug it into the charger, but while I was fiddling with it, I missed my exit.

Moron!

I eased into the next exit lane, left the freeway, then re-entered heading back in the direction I had just come from. The view isn't much driving north, uphill, but as I turned south, downtown Phoenix sprawled across the horizon below, its glass and steel skyline glistening in the morning sunshine as it erupted from the shimmering valley floor. The overnight rain trailing the sandstorm had cleared the air of the usual "brown cloud" of smog, and the view of the city was spectacular.

A chain gang was plucking litter from the right-of-way. As I sped past, I noticed they were all women. The sheriff was a real criminal justice pioneer. One of his first acts when elected had been to confiscate all the male inmates' county-issued boxer shorts and dye them pink, ostensibly to cut down on theft when the inmates were released. Then he moved large numbers of prisoners—and, later, illegal immigrants— from the air-conditioned comfort of the county jail into tents in the middle of summer when the mercury routinely topped 100 degrees. Then came the chain gangs. An equal-opportunity law enforcement officer, female chain gangs were his latest innovation. I wondered if they wore pink underpants, too.

Dani's condo, six blocks off the expressway, was in a complex called Roadrunner Estates. There were no estates, just modest two-story units all painted the same shade of coral. I parked the Sebring curbside, top down. As I closed the car door, I found myself once again annoyed by the indelible yellow stains on the maroon cloth upholstery.

A few years ago, a previous Mrs. Strano—*Numero Cuatro*— had persuaded Leo to move from Mesa to upscale Scottsdale. Two enormous olive trees graced the front yard of crushed red granite.

Unbeknownst to *Numero Cuatro*, the trees disgorged a shower of venomous pollen every spring that wreaked havoc with the sinuses and dusted everything nearby in a layer of saffron powder. Blissfully ignorant that this life-long practice would be viewed with disfavor, the olive trees continued their reproductive ritual while *Numero Cuatro's* maroon convertible was parked, top down, beneath their exfoliating limbs. This was an error of Darwinian proportions.

Numero Cuatro would have nothing to do with the Sebring after that. Hence the "screaming deal" offered me by my uncle. I should get a vanity plate that reads CAVEAT EMPTOR. Leo, too. Six months later, *Numero Cuatro* split. She got the cash from the sale of the Mesa house; he got an upside-down mortgage. The olive trees got chopped down.

I was reflecting on that history as I approached Dani's condo. There was no answer to the buzzer at her front door, so I followed a flagstone pathway to the side of the townhouse. I pushed open the white aluminum gate and continued along the path to a small concrete patio. The sliding glass doors were unlocked.

The living room opened into a kitchen and dining area. Magazines and newspapers were strewn across the couch and coffee table. Dishes were overflowing the sink. Dani might be a looker on the set, but she was a slob in her personal life. On the other hand, the newspapers and magazines were an encouraging sign. She didn't get all her information from the tube. I'm pretty fastidious myself. Don't function well with clutter. Like uncle, like nephew.

"Anybody home," I shouted.

Nothing.

I walked over to a stairway leading to the second floor and yelled again.

"Hey, Dani, you up there?"

"Alex, that you?" a voice floated down.

"Yeah. Sorry about running late. It was a long night."

Dani came into view at the top of the stairs. She was a vision in skin-tight yoga pants and a halter top. She was barefoot, and I noticed that her toenails were fire engine red. My eyes traced their way upward. The halter-top exposed a tan, flat tummy and the tantalizing curve of her hips. Her lipstick matched her nails. Her long black hair framed the perfect oval of her face, but that face had a troubled look.

"I didn't expect to see you, what with the news," she said.

"What news?"

"*Dios mio*. You haven't heard? Isn't Judge Leonard Strano your uncle?"

My heart skipped a beat.

"Yes."

"We just broke into our morning programming. We're not sure what's going on, but he may have been shot."

CHAPTER 6

BLUE AND WHITE Scottsdale PD cruisers blocked the entrance to Jackrabbit Court, where Leo and Sarah lived. Yellow crime-scene tape stretched to the street blocking rubberneckers and the media. Three television vans with their satellite masts erect lined the curb. Neighbors mingled outside the barricade gossiping with one another. A TV reporter was doing a talk-back to the Channel 3 studio. A few yards away, a guy from Dani's station was interviewing a woman who was saying something about her nephew finding spent cartridges in the street. Closer to Leo's house, Elmore James from the *Sun* was talking to a cop I knew.

"James, what's up?"

He turned to look at me and ran a hand through his oily hair. "Strange. Glad you're here. I could use a quote. Strano was your uncle, right?"

"Was? You saying Leo's dead?" I felt myself breaking out in a sweat.

"Don't know his condition," James said. "The neighbors told me he was Care-Flighted out of here. Police won't say if he was shot. Police, in fact, haven't said shit." He gave the cop a hateful look.

The officer was Sgt. Brett Barfield. We'd met when I did a column about his painful recovery from a gunshot wound, an uncommon occurrence in tony communities like Scottsdale. He had invited me to join his weekly poker game. A few weeks earlier, he helped me debunk a scam artist who claimed to have invented a car wax that rendered vehicles undetectable to police radar.

"About that quote?"

"James, you don't need to talk to me. I heard a TV puke interviewing a neighbor lady over there. Said her nephew found some bullets in the street."

"Bullets?"

"Yeah, over there."

Elmore James scurried off like a lizard after a bug. I didn't know he had any hustle left.

"What can you tell me?" I asked Barfield. "Is my uncle OK?"

"He took a nasty fall."

"Was he shot?"

"No. But he was shot at."

"Jesus."

Barfield looked around to see who might be watching, then turned back to me.

"My partner—you've never met; name's Susan Valdez—we took the 10-33 and were the first to arrive."

"Who called it in?"

"His wife, Sarah."

"Sarah's here?" That was a surprise. Guess she didn't fly out last night because of the sandstorm.

Barfield nodded. "When we got here, the judge was convulsing in the courtyard. He was making croaking sounds and grabbing his crotch through his bathrobe. I thought at first he might be suffering from a stroke or something."

"A stroke?"

He shook his head. "That's not it."

Barfield said Sarah was on the patio trying to comfort him. "She couldn't hear us at first, the burglar alarm was so loud. The gate was locked and we couldn't get it. Finally, she opened it. When I approached the judge, I asked him if he was in pain."

He pulled a small notebook out of his shirt pocket.

"His exact response was, quote: 'Fugginkiddenme. Geditoffme. Geditoffme,' unquote."

"Get what off him?"

Barfield shook his head. "He kept grabbing his crotch yelling, "Mydickmydick."

"You putting me on?"

"No, man. He was suffering."

Barfield said he and Valdez tried to keep Leo calm. "We checked him for any visible injuries. He'd smacked his head, but there was no arterial bleeding, no protruding bones. At first, I thought he might have fallen through the living room window, but then I noticed most of the glass was inside the house."

Barfield said it was then that he spotted the pockmarks in the stucco. There were three of them in a shallow arc beginning about two feet up the wall and ending next to the shattered window.

"I asked him if he'd been shot, but I couldn't understand a word. He was delirious."

"Is that what set off the alarm?" I asked. "The glass breaking?"

"Yeah, we were curious about that, too, since the judge was already outside and the door was open. Mrs. Strano told us the burglar alarm was off, but the glass-breakage detector is separate, installed by the original owner, and it's always on."

"That's right. I remember Leo talking about that when I lived here."

Barfield said the rescue chopper landed in the parking lot of the Mormon church two blocks away, and medics wheeled Leo out to the chopper. That must have been something to see. Leo hates flying. Barfield said he was screaming all the way until they stashed him inside the bird.

"So, he wasn't shot," I said. My stomach was in knots and I

could feel myself sweating. My heart went ker-thunk. A premature ventricular beat. Not fatal, just scary. I get them when I'm stressed.

"No," Barfield said. "But he was in a lot of pain from something."

"Where's Sarah?" I asked.

"Inside with the lieutenant."

"Can I can get past this tape and talk to Sarah?"

"What tape?"

I heard Elmore James yelling behind me. I turned and he was waving his notebook over his head. "Hey, I could still use a quote. Don't forget your friends."

Define friends.

A clot of uniformed officers, detectives, and lab technicians blocked the front door, so I aimed for the garage, hoping to enter the house through the entryway to the kitchen. The garage door was open. Leo's car was inside; Sarah's was missing. Maybe they left it at the airport.

A uniformed officer was stationed in front of the garage, and he challenged me.

"I'm family."

The cop looked at my driver's license. Before he could say anything, I said: "Yeah, I know, different last names."

"Strange?"

"Very. Look, Leonard Strano is my adoptive father. His wife, Sarah, is inside. She'll vouch for me, OK?"

"Follow me. But don't touch anything."

We entered the kitchen through the garage. A pot of coffee on the counter looked untouched. Knowing his unwavering habits, Leo's next destination after brewing coffee would have been the gated front courtyard where a copy of the *Republic* would be awaiting him just inside the wrought-iron fence. It would have been dark. Someone who knew his routine could easily have lain in wait.

The uniform escorted me through the kitchen to the living room. Sarah was seated on the couch by the fireplace talking to another woman. Sarah was wearing a pink satin bathrobe, her shapely, tan legs crossed, her arms folded tightly across her chest. She was staring at the floor.

"Sarah, how's Leo?" I asked.

Her head snapped up. "Alex?"

"About Leo? How bad?"

Before Sarah could respond, the woman on the couch next to Sarah rose and stepped between us, frowning at the uniform who let me in.

"You're Alexander Strange," she said. It was a statement, not a question. "I recognize you from your picture in the newspaper." She extended her hand. "Lieutenant Warren."

I took her hand and shook it. Firm grip. She wore a navy blue suit with a white silk blouse open at the throat. She was slender and tall, six feet, only a few inches shorter than me. Her short, dark brown hair showed fine threads of gray. She peered up at me over the top of a pair of amber-framed bifocals.

"Hello, lieutenant. Can you tell me what condition my uncle is in?"

"I believe there will be a presser later this morning," she said, her voice firm, like her handshake.

"I'm here as a family member," I said.

"Judge Strano is your uncle, is that what you said?"

"He adopted me when my mother died. So, legally, he's my adoptive father."

Something in her eyes changed. She blinked and she cocked her head a bit. "I see."

From her reaction, I thought we might have connected. Maybe she lost her mom. Maybe she, too, was adopted. Maybe…

"Lieutenant, we have a problem."

She jerked her head in the direction of a detective standing in front of Leo's study.

"What is it?"

"Door's locked."

Lt. Warren turned to ask Sarah a question, maybe about a key to the room, but I intervened. "You searching this place?"

"It's a crime scene."

"Lieutenant," I said, keeping my voice as calm and reasonable as possible. "That door leads to the private office of a sitting Superior Court judge. Leo brings work home. A lot. Are you sure you want to enter that room? Without a warrant?"

Out of the corner of my eye, I could see Sarah staring at me. I dared not turn to her. She had no clue that Leo's office had been burglarized or she would have already mentioned it to the police.

Warren paused and gave me a curious look. "What are you saying?"

"Hey, lieutenant, personally, I don't care. But if Leo has case files or other court documents in that room... I mean, you want to take responsibility for contaminating a criminal case or something?"

She looked at me for a moment, so I blundered on.

"Hey, you're an officer of the court, so you would know better than me. Just saying..."

Warren turned to Sarah again. "Mrs. Strano, do you have any objection to our searching your husband's office?"

It's at moments like this that I wish I had studied mental telepathy instead of journalism. I looked at Sarah. She was ignoring me.

Read my mind.

"Do what you have to," she said.

"Go ahead," Warren told the detective.

"You want me to break the door down, lieutenant?" the detective asked. He was leaning against the door frame, his Glock on his left hip, a concerned look on his face.

"You can't be serious," I said. I turned to Sarah. "Leo will have a fit if someone breaks down the door to his office and starts rooting around there."

Before Sarah could react, Lt. Warren held up her hands. "Mrs.

Strano, do you have reason to believe anyone made their way into your house, that anyone could be in your husband's office?"

Before Sarah could answer, I butted in again. "Lieutenant, Sarah had to open the gate to let the police in."

Sarah's head bobbed up and down. "That's right."

"Fine," Warren said. "We'll revisit this later."

She turned to me.

"We're trying to determine what happened here and we are gathering evidence, as you can see." She nodded in the direction of a technician prying something—a bullet, I presumed—from the back of a built-in bookshelf that housed Leo's massive movie collection. Hope they didn't notice how many of those DVDs were pirated. Wouldn't that be perfect? Somebody tries to wax Leo and, instead, he goes to the slam for copyright violations. The technician tossed a couple of shattered jewel cases on the floor. The *Casablanca* DVD had been torn in half by the impact of the bullet. We wouldn't be playing that one again, Sam.

I had tried to convince Leo that he didn't need all those DVDs any longer. That everything he could possibly watch could be downloaded on demand. But he wouldn't hear of it. Maybe now he would.

I turned back to the detective. "If my uncle wasn't shot then why was he choppered out of here?"

"He was in convulsions," Sarah said. "I found him on the patio. He was writhing, and I couldn't make out a word he was saying. There was glass everywhere, and leaves, and the alarm was going off...."

"ENOUGH!"

With Lt. Warren's outburst, the entire house went quiet. Technicians, detectives, and uniforms froze in place.

The uniform who escorted me in broke the silence. "He said he was family, lieutenant. I figured you might want to talk to him."

Warren gave him the hairy eyeball then turned to me.

"When did you last see or speak to Judge Strano?"

"Yesterday. Around five. We were going to meet again today at three."

"Is that so?" she said. "Why?"

Idiot.

I didn't know what the mysterious meeting was about, but if Leo hadn't called the cops—nor told Sarah—about the burglary, I wasn't going to spill the beans, either. Not until I knew more about what was going on.

"Personal business," I said.

She didn't press what the "personal business" was. But then she asked, "Did the judge say anything to you that would lead you to be concerned for his safety?"

"Leo never mentioned being worried about his safety," I said. That was accurate, but not the whole story, of course.

Why was I being evasive? Because Leo had been evasive with me. I had no clue what he had gotten himself into. But until I talked to him, I was going to keep the little I knew close to my vest.

"I have a few more things to discuss with Mrs. Strano and then we'll be taking her to the hospital, Lt. Warren said. "I'm afraid I am going to have to ask you to step back outside." She signaled the uniform to escort me out.

"Sarah, will you be all right?" I asked.

She nodded but said nothing. She hugged herself even more tightly.

"Sarah, how about I take you to the hospital?"

She looked up, cocked her head, and dropped her hands to her lap. "Yes, please."

Lt. Warren frowned. This was not in her playbook. Easy to understand: What cop would want her one witness to a shooting spending time with a journalist?

"Let me ask you a question," she said. "Is it likely you will be covering this story for the newspaper?"

It was a fair question. "Not sure."

"All right. If it turns out you bump into anything useful, please give me a call." She handed me her business card.

I took it. Her first name was Janice.

"Lieutenant, will you be taking Mrs. Strano to Good Sam or may I?"

"We can all go in my car. Look for us outside in twenty minutes."

The uniform escorted me out the front door and across the patio where Leo had been found by officers Barfield and Valdez. The red brick of the patio's floor was buried under a mat of leaves blown onto the porch from the storm the night before.

August is Arizona's stormy month—the Monsoon Season—as sodden air from the Gulf of California pushes its way into the desert. Spectacular lightning displays, terrifying thunderclaps, violent winds, and brief showers were the norm. The gusts stripped the Eucalyptus, oleander, acacia, and mulberry trees of their foliage, littering neighborhoods with leafy debris. Leo's patio had become a virtual botanical garden of fallen flora.

Crime scene investigators were poking at bullet holes in the stucco with dowel rods, calculating the angles of entry. My escort grabbed my elbow and scooted me away from the techies and through the gate.

Elmore James was waiting for me on the other side of the police tape.

"Find out anything?" he asked.

"Not much. I'm told he wasn't shot, but shots were fired. Why he was hauled off to the hospital, I don't know. I'm on my way over there in a few minutes. Give me your cell number and I'll call you if I learn anything useful."

James wrote the number in his notebook, tore off the bottom half of the page, and handed it to me. I shoved it into a pocket of my cargo shorts.

"You hanging around?" I asked.

"Nah, I phoned in my story while you were inside. I made up a quote for you. You'll like it."

"Here's a quote for you: You're fired."

"Yeah. Yeah. Obviously, I didn't. Could have used one, though, you being Strano's kin. As it stands, the story's paper thin. The *Repulsive's* going to own this."

The *Sun* was dark—that is, it didn't publish—on Sundays, so the *Arizona Republic* (the *Repulsive* to those of us at the *Sun*) wouldn't have to worry about what the competition might print until Monday afternoon. We'd post updates on the Web, of course, but on paper, we were toast. That moron, Van Wormer, and his decision to cancel the Sunday edition would be the death of the paper. I think he got it right in his speech to the staff: his plans *were* fatalistic.

James trudged off, and I looked around the neighborhood. I heard a voice across the street calling to me. "Hey, Mr. Strange." It was Bevin Darcy. Friendly kid. Carrot top.

"Hey, Bevin, what's up? Pretty scary stuff, huh?"

"No kidding. I was watching Pokemon when it happened."

"So, you heard the shots?"

He shook his head. "Nope. Just the alarm. A policeman asked me the same thing. I told him about finding the bullets."

"You found some bullets?"

"Yeah, they were in the street right here," Bevin said. "I picked them up, but my aunt made me give them to the cops."

"Your aunt?"

"Yeah, she's housesitting while mom and dad are away. She's real nice."

"I see. The officer you gave them to, he still here?"

"No, he left. He came over and said goodbye and asked me how to spell my last name. I told him, too. D-A-R-C-Y. No E."

"Well, about those bullets, Bevin. How many were there?"

Bevin was looking at his shoes and fidgeting. He shot me a sideways glance and held up the palm of one hand, fingers splayed, and the index finger of his other hand. "Six. But don't tell."

"Why's that?"

The boy hesitated and looked over his shoulder to see if anyone was watching before he answered. "Can you keep a secret?" he asked.

"Sure."

He dug into the front pocket of his pants and pulled out a balled fist. He opened it to reveal one of the spent cartridges he'd found on the street. "I kept one," he whispered.

I bent down to examine his prize. "Sweet. But you know what? I hate to tell you, this is evidence. You could get in trouble."

"You promised not to tell."

"Oh, I won't, but I don't think it's a good idea for you to keep it, either. Tell you what: Why don't you let me have it and I'll make sure the police get it without knowing you swiped it, OK?"

He closed his fist around the cartridge and jammed his hand back into his pocket.

"I didn't swipe it. I found it. Finders keepers."

"I know, Bevin, but sometimes the cops aren't very understanding about these things. I'm sure if you told your mom, she'd insist that you turn it over. Right?"

He looked defiant. "My mom's not here."

Stubborn kid. "Your aunt, then. Should we go and ask her?"

He shook his head.

"Bevin, what if we do this," I said, my turn to look over my shoulder. Two of the TV vans had pulled out, as had one of the police cruisers that blocked the street. The neighbors were returning to their houses. "I'll take it and make sure you don't get in trouble, and when the police are done with it I'll see if I can't get it back for you. I'll give it to that nice officer you met. Does that sound fair?"

"I have to?"

"Afraid so, but I'll make it up to you. Say, I'll bet I could score a couple of Diamondbacks tickets. Do you think your mom—I mean, your aunt—would let me take you to a game?"

Bevin's face lit up. "Thanks, Mr. Strange."

"You can call me Alex."

"No way. Mom says I got to treat grownups with respect."

Tricking the kid didn't make me feel very grown-up, much less worthy of respect. I pocketed the shell and ruffled his mop of red hair.

"Say, Bevin, you haven't seen Fred roaming the neighborhood, have you?" I pointed to the flyer taped to the light pole by his house.

"Oh, Freddie?"

"He's missing."

His mouth formed a big "O." Then he looked away.

"What is it, Bevin?"

He looked at his shoes. Again.

"Spill it."

"I found Freddie. He seemed lost. So, I brought him inside."

"Fred's inside your house now?"

He nodded.

"Oh. My. God. That's epic. And your aunt, she's OK with that?"

He looked away. "I haven't told her yet exactly. He's in my room."

I knelt down and grabbed Bevin by his shoulders. "Thank you so much, Bevin."

I glanced back toward Leo's house and saw Sarah and Lt. Warren emerging. "Bevin, I have to go. Could you please keep an eye on Fred until we get this sorted out?"

His little head bobbled up and down. "You bet, Mr. Strange."

"Give this to your aunt," I said, handing him one of my business cards. "If she has any questions, tell her to give me a call."

Odd that Fred showed up right after the shooting. I wondered where he had spent the night. Poor little guy must have been terrified. He certainly hadn't wandered far. Or maybe Bevin hadn't told me the whole story. He was showing a sneaky side.

But I'd been sneaky, too. I had no intention of turning the spent cartridge over to the police. Not yet, anyway. My curiosity was aroused. That was a lot of shots fired. Amazing they didn't find their mark. Would the cartridge provide a clue to the shooter's weapon and would that be useful to know? Harold Ponitz might be able to help answer that question.

Of course, what I knew about this sort of stuff I learned from reading John Sandford and watching NCIS. I wasn't an investigator. Still, what could it hurt?

CHAPTER 7

I SLID INTO the back of the unmarked car, a beige Ford Police Interceptor. The interior was divided like a squad car, the back seat a paddy wagon, except these were real seats, fabric, not the plastic benches in the cruisers. Lieutenants in the Scottsdale Police Department weren't often called upon to haul around druggies and winos with their blood and barf. Nothing but the finest in automotive upholstery for the white-collar criminals of Scottsdale. I tried the door handle. Locked. A Plexiglas wall shielded the occupants of the front seat from the undesirables in the rear. That made it impossible to talk to Sarah. Score one for the lieutenant.

But I wanted to at least let her know that Fred had been found. I tapped on the Plexiglas. "Good news. Fred is OK."

Sarah shook her head and cupped her ear, letting me know she couldn't hear. Lt. Warren cranked the car's engine, and I could see her turning up the volume of her police radio. I'd have to let Sarah know when we got to the hospital.

I appraised both women through the clear divider. Sarah, riding front seat shotgun, had donned a mauve cotton shift. She turned to glance at me through the Plexiglas. She had brushed her locks and done something with her eyes. She wore her hair shoulder length. It bounced when she walked, unlike Lt. Warren's, which was short, a professional cop cut. Sarah had a small, powder-blue overnight bag on her lap. Leo's things, I assumed.

I wondered what must be going through Sarah's mind. Her husband hospitalized. Her house riddled by bullets. Her dog missing—or so she still assumed. Even though we weren't close, I felt a strong sense of responsibility to help her and Leo through this. It was me, Leo, and now, Sarah. And Fred. That was my tribe. It wasn't much in terms of numbers, but it's all I had. I never knew my dad. Nor my grandparents. My mom had died pointlessly, trying to save a bug, for crying out loud. I didn't want to fail at doing my part to preserve the little bit of family I had left.

Why Sarah was leaving town, or had tried to split, seemed odd. Especially with her dog missing. Not that I didn't believe Leo's story that she had family issues. It's just that with Leo's matrimonial track record, wives blowing town on the spur of the moment wasn't without precedent.

Sarah and Leo weren't a promising match, in my opinion, what with their age differences. Not that anyone, let alone Leo, ever asked me for my advice on matrimonial matters. I'd only discovered Leo and Sarah were an item right before they ran off to Vegas to get hitched. Which might seem weird, but you have to understand: Leo never, ever talked about his romantic relationships. To no one. Including me. I asked him once about his reticence. His answer: "I'm a gentleman."

I'd do anything for my uncle, but I couldn't help but wonder if Sarah's trip to Salt Lake involved more than Leo had said. Was their marriage in trouble, despite Leo's denial? And I was puzzled about Sarah's reaction when I told Lt. Warren about the meeting with Leo that afternoon. She clearly had no idea her house had been broken into the night before. When I saw Leo, I needed to get that cleared up.

I pulled out my iPhone, partially charged during the trip from Dani's to Leo's, and noticed I had several missed calls. Most were from the newspaper, but the one that grabbed my attention had arrived at five in the morning. Only person I knew up at that hour was Leo. I tapped the voicemail button and the scroll bar indicated a message was being played, but there was no sound. I looked and saw the phone was on silent mode. I switched the sound back on and replayed the message, the phone to my ear so it could not be overheard through the Plexiglas:

"Nephew. Take care when you come over this afternoon. I got a call last night after you left Kelso's. Said he was the guy who ransacked my study." There was the sound of a door opening. It had to be Leo stepping outside to get the newspaper. He continued talking. "Said if I didn't turn over what he wanted, and right away… Jesus!…" Then a clatter, the phone hitting the bricks, I guessed, then the blare of a burglar alarm. Then the recording died.

I looked up, but neither Lt. Warren nor Sarah seemed aware of what I had just heard. I played it again.

Holy shit!

I sat paralyzed for a few minutes, barely aware of the passing scenery outside the car's windows, not thinking, not feeling, just numb. Eventually, my mental hard drive rebooted and I looked back down at the phone. I punched in the number for the *Sun's* newsroom.

"City Desk," came the monotone answer. I recognized the voice of one of the interns, a student at Mesa Community College. Bright kid. Planned to transfer to Arizona State in the fall. Hoped to work his way into a full-time slot at the newspaper, if it was still around when he graduated.

"Hey, Eduardo, this is Strange. Who's on the desk today?"

"Besides yours truly, that would be our esteemed copy desk chief filling in today. I'll put her right on."

"Wait!" I shouted into the phone, but it was too late, I was already on hold. The last person in the newsroom I wanted to talk to was Abigail Conwest. I needed help, not advice on punctuation. I ended the call, then dialed again.

"Morgue."

"Harold, this is Strange. I was hoping I might catch you."

"Night and day, the News Research Department never sleeps. Actually, I'm here making copies of Guild propaganda at the insistence of our colleague Mr. James. But let me drop everything I'm doing for the good of the order and ask how I may be of service to you."

"You don't sound very enthusiastic."

"Not at all. I'm at your command."

"No, I mean about the Guild. I assumed you were one of the ringleaders."

"My dear Alexander, I have been in the employ of this here newspaper for twenty-four years under, now, three different ownerships. In less than six months I will turn sixty-five and, thus, be eligible for retirement. I figure I'm bulletproof, so I'm happy to assist in this noble, if foredoomed, effort, but I have no personal stake in the matter inasmuch as all this will soon be a receding image in the rear view mirror of my life."

"That's what I like about you, Harold, you're a man of few words. Listen, I need some actual research ASAP." I was taking a bit of a risk with a cop in the front seat, but the police radio was squawking and Sarah and the lieutenant were engaged in muffled conversation on the other side of the Plexiglas. I cupped the cell phone: "What do you know about bullets?"

"Well, you may recall that before deciding to commit journalism for a living, I spent my formative years in the service of our great nation, specifically in Southeast Asia, where, among the many useful skills I acquired was an acquaintanceship with munitions. What do you need to know?"

"I've got a spent shell casing I need to identify," I whispered, peering through the Plexiglas screen to see if the question had attracted Lt. Warren's attention. She was listening to something Sarah was saying, paying me no heed. "Think you can help?"

"Should be a matter of no great effort. Bring it in and we'll see what we can discover. Got some reference books that might be useful if I don't recognize it or it's not on the Internet. I'll be here for the next few hours."

"Thanks. I've got to run over to Good Sam, then I'll be by the office."

"What's at Good Sam?"

"Guess you haven't heard. Uncle Leo was rushed there this morning. Looks like someone tried to shoot him."

"Uncle Leo?"

"Judge Leonard D. Strano. I'm his nephew."

"Oh, yes. Sorry. Didn't put two and three together. Look, I hope everything's all right. I'll stick around until I hear from you."

Lieutenant Warren swung the car into the emergency room entrance and parked at the curb. I tapped at the Plexiglas window behind her head.

"Don't forget about me."

The detective opened her door without so much as a glance toward the back seat and stepped around the car to the passenger side. She opened Sarah's door and extended her hand to her. After helping Sarah out of the car, the lieutenant took Sarah by the elbow and guided her toward the ER, never looking back my way. I might as well have been invisible.

"Hey, this isn't funny," I shouted, pounding on the window.

Sarah heard that and turned, a befuddled look on her face. But the detective placed a hand on her back and ushered her into the hospital.

"Crap!"

How hard would it be to kick the window out of the car? I smacked the window again.

Suddenly, there was a guy rapping on it with his knuckles. He opened the door. "There a problem?"

I leaped from the car and smacked into a mountain. Picture a young Charles Barkley, maybe 25 pounds heavier but no fat. Now picture him in chinos and a t-shirt, add a silver earring in the left ear and a belt buckle of matching silver the size of a Fiat. I had collided with Morrison Hawker—or as his friends call him, Mohawk—a former Sun Devils fullback who could have gone pro but for a run-in with the NCAA over gambling. He was Uncle Leo's bailiff.

You may have seen Hawker on TV: He's shown up, if only briefly, on the World Poker Tour. Never made the final table; never got the bracelet. But he was a gamer. We were standing too close for comfort. He must have bathed in the cologne he was wearing, which was suffocating. I'm nearly six-four, but he had me by another four inches and a heck of a lot more body mass. Still, I pushed him away to give myself some breathing room. It wasn't easy.

"Jesus, didn't David *kill* Goliath?"

"Don't believe everything in the Bible," he said. "Especially the New Testament."

You'd expect a guy with his build to have a deep baritone—you know, Darth Vader—but the words came out in a near-whisper and high-pitched—think Clint Eastwood on helium. Something about getting punched in the throat when he was a kid. Or so he said. I was thinking steroids.

"Did you see that?" I sputtered. "Locked me in this Ford shit box. What the hell's the matter with her? It's a hundred and ten. You can get arrested for leaving a dog in a car on a day like this."

"Maybe she likes dogs better. Maybe she allergic to tes-tos-ter-rone."

"You think?"

"If it walks like a duck…"

"Goddammit, that's discrimination."

"Prejudice is a bitch."

"Mohawk, you here for Leo?"

"Yeah. Heard on the radio. Came right away. Checked on the judge when I got here. He's out of the ER. Phoenix PD's got his room guarded."

"Can we get past the cops, see how he's doing?" I asked.

"Sure. You family."

We turned toward the emergency room entrance. I was tempted to key Lt. Warren's ride, but thought better of it.

"It was the Old Testament, by the way."

Hawker turned, unsure, wondering what the fuck? He had this interesting way he crinkled his forehead that made creases all the way up his shaved head like a chocolate Shar-Pei.

"David and Goliath."

CHAPTER 8

A UNIFORMED PHOENIX cop was guarding Room 402 when Hawker and I arrived at the nurse's station. I stepped toward the door, expecting a hassle, but as I approached, a short, olive-skinned doctor in a white hospital coat bustled out.

"Excuse me," I said. "I'm here for Judge Strano. Can he receive visitors?"

The doctor looked up from the chart he was holding and a broad grin spread across his face. "Alexander Strange," he said. "The police officer from Scottsdale said to expect you. I read your column. I'm Dr. Rostami. I am very pleased to meet you. I enjoyed your articles exposing the Stealth Car Wax fraud. I would love to talk to you about that sometime as my brother-in-law was an investor." He laughed—more a bark that ended in a cough. "I'm sorry," he said, "but you see my brother-in-law and I have issues. Long story. Family feud. I know it is a terrible thing to take pleasure in someone else's misfortune, but if you knew that horse's ass you'd understand. Excuse my French."

"French?"

"Ha! Good catch. I must remember I am talking to a journalist."

"Anyway, Dr. Pastrami, I wonder if you could tell me about my uncle?" I made a move to skirt past him to the door to Leo's room.

"Rostami, with an "R. He pinched my elbow and guided me back toward the nurse's station. "Your uncle is sleeping right now," he said. "I have him sedated for the pain. Most unusual injury, I must say. Never seen anything like it before. Fortunately, we have an ample supply of antivenin here at the hospital."

"Antivenin?"

"He was stung by a scorpion. First on his foot, which I imagine is why he fell. Then in a most unusual location. The antivenin abated the convulsions almost immediately. Amazing how fast it works. But the discomfort from the stings must be excruciating. Terrible."

"Where else besides his foot was he stung?" I asked, growing impatient.

"On the glans penis."

"The what?"

"The head of his penis."

"*Leo was stung on his dick?*" I might have been shouting.

"Yes. There are no visible indications, but there never are. Puncture is too small. I wouldn't have believed it if the scorpion hadn't still been in his pajamas. *Centruoides sculpturatas*, the bark scorpion. You can tell by the little hair on its tail."

"What about the gunshots?" I asked the doctor.

"Oh, yes. The police told us that there had been reports of gunfire, but, if that is so, your uncle is most fortunate because he was not hit. However, in addition to the scorpion stings, he has a very nasty break of the temporomandibular joint from his fall."

"The temporo what?"

"His jaw. A break at the joint. Often with a broken jaw, we operate and pin the bones in place to ensure proper alignment of the jaw and teeth, but at the joint there are numerous nerves that pass through that area creating a high danger of nerve damage with an operation. Disfigurement is a risk. Most likely, we will wire your uncle's jaw closed for five or six weeks and let it heal on its own. Unfortunately, our oral surgeon—good man—isn't here right now, so we will immobilize his jaw with bandages until he can see him tomorrow. Meanwhile, we will keep him sedated. The sting from the bark scorpion is agonizing, and in that area of the anatomy it is too gruesome to imagine. Really."

I couldn't imagine. "May I see him, please."

"Most assuredly, if we can persuade this nice police officer to allow you in."

An orderly pushing a gurney glided between us and the doorway to Leo's room. Whoever was on it had seen better days. A sheet covered the body head to toenails. As it slipped by, the door to Leo's room opened and Sarah emerged.

"Alex, I thought I heard you yelling." She was drawn, pale.

After checking my ID, the guard let me pass, which surprised me. I had been prepared to try to bullshit my way in. I was also surprised to discover Sarah alone.

"Where's Matilda the Hun?" I asked. That drew a blank look, so I tried again. "Lt. Warren, she come up with you?"

"She brought me up here, but she got a call. I'm surprised you didn't run into her."

I felt like running over her, but I kept that to myself. The hospital room was standard issue, a double, but Leo had it to himself. His bed was angled upward in a semi-sitting position. The ubiquitous hospital IV stand stood like a metallic sentinel beside the bed and held a clear plastic bag that dripped fluid into a tube leading to his left wrist, taped to the side rail. Leo's chin and the left side of his cheek were scraped. There was a bulge under the sheets at his midsection. Made him look pregnant. Maybe ice packs for his damaged johnson. He was zonked out.

"Looks like he got banged up pretty good," I said.

Sarah plopped down in a visitor's chair, held her head in her hands, and sighed. "I can't believe this is happening. What a nightmare."

She looked exhausted. I stepped over to her chair, bent down and took her hand. She didn't resist. "Sarah, I don't know what's going on, but you know the cops are going to be all over this. Right now, the important thing is that you and Leo are both safe. There's a guard outside the door. If you like, I'll take you home…"

"No! I can't go there."

"Alright, Sarah, OK. I'll take you wherever you want. To a friend's. To a hotel. Whenever you're ready. You name it."

She had been staring at the floor, but she looked up at me, her cobalt eyes rimmed in red. "I wasn't supposed to be here. I was supposed to be in Salt Lake. I didn't want to leave because of Freddie. But Leonard insisted. Now I can't leave, not with him like this."

Fred!

"Hey, I've got some news on that front."

"About Freddie?"

"Yeah. A neighbor found him."

"Oh, my God. Oh, my God. Is he all right?"

"He's fine."

She stood and wrapped her arms around me and squeezed. A lesser man might have winced. "Thank you, Alex. Thank you so much."

"Well, at least all the news today isn't awful," I said.

She nodded. "I've made a decision, Alex. I'm staying in Phoenix. I'm not going to Salt Lake.

"OK. Just let me know where you want to go."

She nodded again and looked up at me. "I want to go home with you."

CHAPTER 9

BEFORE I COULD respond to Sarah, there was a knock at the door. I wasn't sure whether to be annoyed or relieved at the interruption. Two suits stood in the doorway.

"Who are *you?*" the suit on the left demanded, then glanced at the cop standing guard by the door. The uniform played dumb, staring straight ahead. He must not have mentioned my presence in Leo's room.

Left Suit was about five-six, porky and mustached. Right Suit, the older of the two, was lean and nearly six feet. Mutt and Jeff. I knew Right Suit. He had been one of the instructors at the Phoenix Citizens FBI Academy I'd attended. The academy was designed to educate civilians about the ins and outs of the Bureau's activities. I recalled there hadn't been much love lost on the Fourth Estate by Mr. Right Suit. Left Suit, I'd never seen before.

"Alexander Strange," I replied. "And you are…"

Left Suit pushed forward as if to blow past me into the room. I stood firm, blocking the entrance. "Officer," I said to the uniformed cop, "who are these guys?" I knew, but I didn't like Left Suit's attitude. Cops, from federal agents to crossing guards, came in multiple flavors, and at the bottom of the food chain were the officious bullies that Left Suit seemed to personify.

The suits gave one another a quick glance, then, in unison, they reached inside the breast pockets of their jackets and produced matching black leather ID holders. They flipped them open. "FBI. I'm Special Agent Volker," said the short guy on the left. "This is Special Agent Collins."

"I like that," I said, giving them my 200-watt grin, the one I usually saved for first dates. "Volker and Collins. Catchy. Sounds like one of my favorite drinks. Say, can you do that again, that synchronized badging thing? Could be an Olympic event someday."

"Agent Collins, we have a comedian on our hands."

"No, just a punk," Right Suit said, his voice a couple decibels louder than appropriate, like someone talking on a cell phone. "I see you're still a smart ass, Strange."

"It's a genetic defect."

Volker gave Collins a quizzical glance, surprised we knew one another, then turned back to me. "I repeat. What are you doing here?" He hunched his shoulders, ready to rumble. Tough guy. No doubt studied Dragnet reruns to polish his technique.

"I'm Judge Strano's nephew and I'm here with his wife." I slid one of my business cards out of my wallet and handed it to Volker. "But what is the FBI's interest in this?"

Agent Volker made a show of examining my business card, which identified me as a columnist for the *Phoenix Daily Sun*. While he checked out the card, I fished the notebook out of my rear pocket and flipped it open. I could do this flip-open stuff, too. Maybe I'd see them at the Olympics—synchronized badging would kill synchronized swimming.

Volker eyed my notebook warily. "You said you were family."

"Newspapermen have families, too. So why are you guys here? Is taking potshots at a local judge a federal crime these days?" I dug my pen out of my pocket.

Collins stared at me and shook his head.

"Off the record?" I ventured. I closed my notebook hoping that would make the decision easier for him. I hadn't expected to get anything, just wanted to push back a little.

"Mrs. Strano," Collins said, looking past me. "May we come in?"

Sarah nodded and I stepped aside.

Collins reached into his coat pocket and extracted an official looking document. "Mrs. Strano, since your husband is unable to receive service, I am giving you this." He handed her the papers.

"What is it?"

"It is a subpoena to appear before a grand jury investigating the theft of federal property."

"What theft?" I asked.

Collins turned to me. "Lt. Warren of the Scottsdale PD said you might be showing up, Mr. Strange. We'll want to talk to you, too, but at the moment we need to visit with Mrs. Strano."

"Since when did FBI agents become process servers? Thought that was the job of the Marshals."

"What can I tell you, Mr. Strange," Collins said. "It's the weekend."

Like that explained anything.

"Would you mind stepping outside and waiting for us?"

I did mind, but it wasn't a request. But no way was I going to loiter in the hospital corridor waiting for these guys to finish giving Sarah the third degree.

"Gentlemen, I need to run back to the newspaper. You have my number."

"Yes, Mr. Strange," Volker said. "I believe we do have your number."

Now there were two people on the planet calling me mister. Bevin and this fed. I wondered if Volker's mother would also object if I asked him to call me Alex. Then again, mentioning cops' mothers is rarely a constructive conversational gambit.

I started to walk out of the room, but Volker grabbed my shirtsleeve.

"Hey, Clark Kent," he said, "you know the best years in any reporter's life?"

"Tell me."

"The three years he spent in second grade," he snorted, his entire, portly little body jiggling like a bowl of Jell-O.

"That's moronic, Volker."

"Oh yeah? You know who the real moron is?"

"Your mom."

CHAPTER 10

MORRISON HAWKER WAS leaning his hulking countenance against the desk at the nurse's station. The two women behind the counter self-consciously tried not to stare, but it's hard not to look at a guy his size, his bulging pecs and biceps the size of footballs stretching the thin fabric of his t-shirt. He was shaking his head, a sly grin on his face, doing that Shar-Pei thing, his head crinkly. "You a real charmer," he said. "That how you hotshot reporters do it? That how Bernstein recruited Deep Throat?"

"Feds. 'We can neither confirm nor deny.' That's their mantra."

It's not that I don't like cops, exactly. After all, Brett Barfield was a friend. But I have a tendency to get prickly around *all* authority figures. And cops don't like to have their authority questioned. And questioning authority is basically a journalist's job description. So cops and reporters often find themselves on opposite sides of the police tape, both literally and figuratively. And, yeah, to this day, I still wish the police had been more assertive about pulling mom out of the cave during that awful storm in Austin. But that could be unfair. She was a world-class drug user and not always, shall we say, receptive to suggestion.

"Touchy, touchy."

"Sorry. Say, can you give me a lift down to the paper? I left my car over at Leo's."

"No can do," he said, shaking his head and putting one of his giant paws on my shoulder. "Got a date." With that he gave me a wink.

"Anybody I know?"

"Brother I played ball with. He's come out."

"Well, you fellas enjoy yourselves. I'll just hitch-hike back to the office. Don't give me another thought."

"Maybe that lieutenant give you a lift," he suggested. "She just left."

"Yeah, got a picture of that."

I turned to leave. Figured I'd Uber it back to the paper.

"And it was Woodward, not Bernstein," I said over my shoulder.

As I headed toward the bank of elevators, my iPhone vibrated. Caller ID said it was Dani Vaquero.

"Hey, Dani. I'm at Good Sam, just left my uncle's room. Where are you?"

"At the station. I've been assigned to the story. Can you fill me in?"

"Tell you what, I'm stuck at the hospital without wheels. I need to get to the paper. Give me a ride, and we'll talk."

I looked at the elevators and got a brief chill. I hadn't liked the ride up, but I was in a hurry then. No rush now. A red EXIT sign shone a few feet down the hallway, so I took the stairs and walked outside to wait for Dani by the ER entrance.

What had Leo gotten himself into? People were shooting at him, burglarizing his house, and now the FBI was on his ass. The stubborn old coot had left me hanging the night before. Why the hell hadn't he just told me?

"Leo, dude, what the fuck?"

I realized I'd said that out loud and looked around to see if I'd been overheard. A short middle-aged woman in a pink pantsuit was helping an elderly lady in a walker navigate her way toward me, and she stared at me wide-eyed and worried.

"It's OK," I said. "The medication should kick in soon." I walked away from the entrance to put some space between the women and the crazy man talking to himself.

Calm down. Take stock. Think.

With Leo doped up, most of the questions I needed answered would have to wait, starting with what our mysterious meeting that afternoon was supposed to have been about. In the meantime, though, I couldn't sit idle. I stuck my hand in my pocket and felt the shell casing little Bevin had given me. Could it reveal anything useful about the shooter? First stop at the newspaper would be to see what Harold Ponitz had to say.

Then I needed to talk to my boss, Edwina Mahoney. Would she want me to write about this? If I were a news reporter, the answer would be clear—absolutely not. It would constitute a conflict of interest. But a columnist isn't expected to be strictly objective—truthful, for sure— but with a point of view. Edwina might like the idea. But would I?

Maybe at some point. Maybe if everything turned out OK. And Leo was safe. At the moment, though, my first priority was figuring out what the hell was going on.

A gold P.T. Cruiser pulled up to the curb at the hospital entrance. Ugly as an Edsel. At least it didn't have vanity plates. The passenger side window rolled down, and Dani Vaquero was laughing. "Kinda makes a statement, doesn't it? Hop in."

As she started to pull away, I looked out the windshield and came face-to-face with a small fish encased in plastic. It was dangling from her rear view mirror. "Who is this?"

"That's Oscar," she said. "He was my first pet, a Siamese Fighting Fish. When he died I laminated him so he'd always be with me. Say hello to Oscar, Alex."

"Hello, Oscar."

Dani was dolled up. She must have just left the set. She looked spectacular. She'd done something with her eyes, some mascara thing that highlighted them like an ancient Egyptian princess. She turned to me and winked. I felt faint.

I cleared my throat. "Why Oscar?"

"My childhood hero," she said. "Oscar Gordon. You know?"

"From *Glory Road*?"

Her head bobbed up and down. "Yes. My favorite Heinlein novel. I read a lot of science fiction when I was a kid."

"And you never heard of Dejah Thoris?"

"Who?"

"Never mind."

She had the radio on and some blabbermouth was going off on the war in Uganda: "Is it just me being paranoid or is there something smelly about the fact that a company our secretary of Homeland Security formerly ran has major lease holdings in Uganda, where American troops are now?"

Dani turned it off. "Buckle up," she said.

I just shook my head no.

"What? You want me to get a ticket?"

"You get a ticket, I'll pay for it. I have a thing about confinement. I don't even like being in a car, let alone strapped in. It's why I drive a convertible, top down, even in this heat."

She shrugged and pulled away from the curb. "So, Alex, are we working together on this story or what?"

I cleared my throat. "Dani, I've got to run this past my editor. We were assigned to something different. Odds are good I won't be allowed to work on this story because of the conflict of interest I have with my uncle…"

"Conflict? Are you *loco*? You're on the inside. He's your uncle. This is the chance of a lifetime."

"I'm not so sure. It may turn out I would have a *harder* time getting information because of my relationship with Leo. Besides, I don't know if I *want* to work this story. I mean, come on, this isn't just a *story* to me; this is my uncle we're talking about. His life, it's in danger."

"I think you're overreacting," she argued. "Way. I mean, I understand where you're coming from on the personal side of things, *amigo*, but this isn't a conflict of interest. It's not like you stand to gain financially or anything from covering this. And maybe, *posiblemente*, you might be able to get to the bottom of what's happening better than anyone else—maybe even help your uncle." She was annoyed, and her *español* was becoming more pronounced.

"Hey, let's call a truce," I said. "I need to talk to my editor first, get my bearings. In the meantime, I've been to the scene and the hospital, but I'm out of the loop as far as anything from the cops. They hold a press conference yet?"

"Yes, there was a very brief press conference, if you want to call it that. They read a statement and refused to answer any questions. All they said was shots were fired at Judge Strano's house. He wasn't hit, but that he fell and injured himself and is hospitalized and under guard. That's it."

"That's more than I guessed they'd say. Interesting they revealed he hadn't been hit. Maybe the neighbors saw too much to keep that under wraps."

"How about at the hospital?" she asked. "Learn anything there?"

I admired her persistence.

"Yes, I can tell you this much: Leo broke his jaw. Don't know how, exactly, but his chin and cheek are scraped up. He was sedated when I went to visit him, Dani, so I didn't get a chance to talk to him."

"A broken jaw! Thanks." Her accent was fading now that she got what she wanted.

A lot of journalists wrap themselves in the panoply of their jobs to buck themselves up, like cops hiding behind their badges. People who in ordinary circumstances avoid confrontation become belligerent, showing a tough professional veneer masking their more vulnerable personalities. Dani did it, too, it seemed. It would be interesting to discover the real person behind that facade.

As we drove to the newspaper, I found myself second-guessing the decision to share the news about Leo's jaw. But, surely, it would get out soon enough. Now Dani got to advance the story. It cost me nothing, and, consequently, she owed me. It could come in handy. But I sure as hell wasn't going to tell her about the location of the scorpion sting. That would be too embarrassing to Leo, and it wasn't anybody's damned business. Of course, if it had happened to someone besides Leo and I found out about it, I wouldn't be so generous. As noted, I had a conflict of interest.

I was amused by Dani's enthusiasm over such a small scrap of information. The standards for television were so different than for print. This would be a big break for her, but a mere detail, one of many, in a newspaper account. Interesting, sure, but nothing to stop the presses for. Then again, the average story on a TV newscast lasted only 20 seconds. You didn't need too many facts.

She pulled to the curb in front of the newspaper, turned to me, and cocked her head.

"You look like somebody," she said. "The actor. You know, from Star Wars."

"Mark Hamill?"

"No, the good looking one."

"Yoda?"

She laughed. "Get out of here."

"Thanks for the lift, Dani," I said. "Nice to meet your pal Oscar."

"Best pet ever. I don't have to feed him and he doesn't chew on the furniture."

"There's that."

"You got a pet?" she asked.

"No. But I got visitation rights to a Papillon."

"Papillon? Wasn't that a movie?"

"Yeah. With Steve McQueen. His nickname was Papillon. Means

butterfly in French. That's how the breed got its name. They're like tiny collies with big ears like Yoda. Only not green."

"This dog got a name?"

"Fred."

"Fred? Who names a dog Fred?"

"Who names a fish Oscar?"

CHAPTER 11

HAROLD PONITZ, TRUE to his word, was waiting in the newspaper's morgue. I handed him the shell casing I'd liberated.

"I assume we are no longer worried about preserving fingerprints, chain of evidence, or any of the other forensic niceties," he said. Ponitz held the shell up to the overhead light, turned it, then handed it back. "No need to look this up. It's a ten-millimeter Auto cartridge."

"How can you tell so quickly?"

He turned the cartridge in his hand, showing me the base. "10 mm Auto" was stamped there.

"That a common bullet?"

"For some handguns. But it's a powerful load. Hotter than the .45, the .357 Magnum, and certainly the nine millimeter. Not as popular as the others."

"Harold, it looks like multiple shots were fired in an arc. Three hit the wall of the house, the rest burst through the front window. The bullet holes started low then rose toward the right."

"Ah, hah."

"Ah, hah?"

"So, we're not talking about a pistol," he said. "We're talking about an assault weapon. That arc you describe, that's a signature of automatic rifles. They tend to rise as they're fired."

"Translate. You saying it was from a machine gun?"

Ponitz smiled. "Give me a minute. I've got a pretty good idea about this, but I want to check a few things." He gestured to a chair by his desk, and I sat down while he began tapping away at his keyboard.

Even though it was the weekend, the morgue was a flurry of activity as several clerks were busy scanning old newspaper clippings into a machine that converted them into digital files that could be searched by computer. The goal was to get rid of the paper and be all-electronic over the next couple of years. If the paper lasted that long.

Harold looked up from his computer monitor. "What I was curious about was the use of this particular caliber," he said. "Most assault rifles use the .223 millimeter or the 5.56 by 45 NATO rounds." He looked at me to make sure I was following him. In fact, I was, writing it all down even though I was clueless what all those bullet measurements meant.

"You don't see the ten-millimeter Auto used much anymore. It was popular with the feds in the '80s after the big shootout in Miami. But the damned thing has such a kick it lost popularity."

"Big shootout?"

"Yes, in 1986, before you were born, I'd guess?"

"Not even a fertilized egg."

"Ha. Well, a bunch of FBI agents got their asses shot off because they were over-gunned. The Bureau vowed not to let that happen again."

"So, the feds don't use them anymore?"

"Actually, they're still in their arsenal of assault weapons." Ponitz studied his monitor. "Looks like the FBI still has about fourteen hundred MP5 slash tens that fire this round."

"Uh, Harold, forgive me, but what is an MP5 slash whatever?"

"It's a submachine gun made by a German firm, Heckler and Koch. Very reliable. Can be fired single shot, in bursts of three or fully automatic. Most often, you'll see professionals firing it in three-round bursts. You fire off three rounds, correct your aim, then fire another three. As I said, when a submachine is fired, it kicks like any other weapon and it causes the gun to jolt upward and, in the case of the HK, upward and to the right. If you know what you're doing, you fire short bursts then get back on target."

"A pro, you say, wouldn't just blast away on full auto?"

"Not if he cared about hitting what he was aiming at."

"So, these MP5s use this kind of bullet?"

"Most use a nine millimeter round, but the FBI wanted something more powerful so it bought a stockpile of the guns firing the ten-millimeter Auto loads."

"Is that the only gun using these bullets nowadays?" I asked.

"Oh no, you can get Glocks and other handguns using the round. But, like I said, they're just not that popular. Cost more. They're prone to over-penetration."

"Over what?"

"Bullets going through people and hitting other people. Of course, all powerful loads will do that, but the Autos especially so."

"Oh."

"Besides, based on the pattern of bullet holes you described, that suggests an automatic weapon."

"Would it be noisy?" I asked.

"Very. Why?"

"Well, it seems nobody heard any shots fired."

"Hmmm." Ponitz scratched his head and leaned back in his chair focusing on the ceiling for a moment. He turned to me and said, "Well, the shooter must have used a suppressor."

"A whater?"

"Suppressor. They call them silencers in the movies, but that's not correct. They aren't silent."

"How hard would it be to get a suppressor for a gun firing this kind of bullet?" I asked.

"Well, that's the thing. It's possible, of course, but why would anyone go to the expense? Suppressors for 9-millimeter handguns are cheaper and easier to find. And why go to the trouble? Especially if it's an assassination attempt? Hell, I'd use a .22, not a round that could knock down an elephant."

Harold turned back to the monitor and tapped a few more commands on his keyboard.

"This is interesting," he said, "It seems the FBI bought lots of suppressors for its MP5s."

"I suppose it would be a stretch to assume that the weapon used at Leo's belonged to the FBI," I said.

Harold shook his head. "Just because someone is carrying a gold bar doesn't mean they robbed the Federal Reserve. And if I were in the market for an assault weapon, I can imagine many easier ways to obtain one of these than breaking into an FBI weapon's locker."

"But like you said, there are many other weapons with suppressors out there that would be easier to obtain."

"There's that."

CHAPTER 12

ROCK AND ROLL blared from an open door along the short hallway that connected the morgue and the newsroom of the *Phoenix Daily Sun*. I was headed toward my office, but ducked my head in. Garreth DePutron was hovered over his easel, his long, scraggly brown hair falling over his forehead. A life-size Alex Ross poster of the Green Lantern hung on the door. An aging leather loveseat lay buried under a pile of newspapers and comic books. In the opposite corner, by the easel, stood a five-foot-tall plaster-of-Paris Gumby that DePutron had electrified into a floor lamp, attaching a lampshade to its head. It cast an emerald hue over a new painting on the wall: A portrait of a superhero in red and blue tights, wearing a yellow boa and a big "D" on his chest.

"What's that screeching?" I asked.

"Hey," DePutron said, glancing up from his work. He was wearing a pale blue Jimmy Eat World t-shirt, a thin gold chain around his neck with a matching ear stud. *Tres chic.*

"Lemme guess," I said. "This is a recording of someone strangling a cat, right?"

"That's cliché."

"OK, I give."

"Oh, ye of little taste. Do you not recognize the melodious strains of Jesus Chrysler Supercar?"

"I'm auditorily challenged. Why do you listen to this shit?"

"It drowns out the voices in my head," he said, clapping his hands over his ears and shaking his head from side to side.

It was a running bet in the office as to which Garreth DePutron would show up for work any given day. As his musical tastes evolved, so, too, did the corresponding personas he adopted, morphing as he, literally, changed his tune. The previous week, he arrived wearing a suit and bowtie playing Debussy all day long on his office stereo. The week before, it was denim shirts, a black cowboy hat and Garth Brooks. Next week it could be Liberace, Johnny Cash, Snoop Dog—who knew? I'm all in favor of people reinventing themselves, but not even Rube Goldberg could have kept up with this guy.

I peered over the top of his easel. DePutron was sketching an Uncle Sam figure.

"Don't tell me. This has something to do with the Guild."

"It's a recruitment poster," he said, pointing to the drawing. "It'll have an Uncle Sam in the middle, like the Army posters, with big lettering: *I Want You to Join the Guild.*

"Why Uncle Sam?" I asked, turning back toward the door. "Why not Jimmy Hoffa?"

"Hoffa's so yesterday."

"Listen, Garreth, I don't get it. Why are you helping these morons?"

He sniggered. "I'm not," he said. "Come here. Look closer."

I leaned in and realized something was wrong with the image. Then it hit me. It wasn't Uncle Sam's face, but a young Fidel Castro leering out underneath the red, white and blue top hat.

"I'm only pretending to help," DePutron giggled.

I turned to leave and paused to look at the Green Lantern poster again. Something about it looked familiar. Then it hit me.

"Is that George Clooney?" I asked.

DePutron looked up.

"Close resemblance."

I left him to his perverted proselytizing and continued into the *Sun's* main newsroom, a sprawling open space, digs for more than three dozen reporters and as many editors. Desks, computer terminals, and filing cabinets were scattered in no discernable pattern to the uninitiated. A clot of workstations in the center of the room—the City Desk—was where our assignment editor and his staff of assistants labored, sorting through the news of the day and assigning stories to be covered. Abigail Conwest was leaning back in a leather chair talking on the phone, a blue high-heeled shoe resting on the desktop. Her dress, a light green and white striped number, had slipped down her elevated leg, exposing her knee and half of a meaty thigh, an inelegant pose for someone who took her couture so seriously. A police scanner squawked intermittently and competed for attention with the patter of a CNN anchor jabbering about the war on one of the television sets suspended from the ceiling. Across the room, another grouping of workstations, these shaped in a horseshoe pattern, comprised the Copy Desk, where pages were designed and headlines written. Newsroom gossip had it that the copy desk was soon to be eliminated and all of its work outsourced to India.

I had a small office on the far side of the newsroom, a perk that came with being one of the paper's two columnists. That, and since the newspaper's staff was half the size it once was, there were unused workspaces to spare. When I wasn't working on my column, I also wrote a blog, tweeted, and hosted a radio talk-show program once a week at KTAR.

It was the radio gig that prompted the bright lights in management to figure I'd be the right person to partner with the TV station. I could only imagine their logic: He's got the face for radio; let's see if he has the voice for television.

My mind was swirling as I traversed the newsroom: Did the cartridge suggest the weapon used in the shooting belonged to the FBI? Or was that just a coincidence? Was I being paranoid?

What was I supposed to do with Sarah? I could find a place for her to stay. She couldn't go back to her house. I got that. But it would be awkward for her to stay with me. My apartment was an efficiency. I had a fold-out sofa for a bed, and I didn't fancy sleeping on the floor.

Before I could get halfway across the newsroom, a woman's voice called out. "Hey, Alex." It was Edwina Mahoney, my managing editor.

I weaved my way through the disarray of the newsroom to her glass-fronted office and stepped inside. Edwina was at her desk, holding a copy of that afternoon's edition, the banner headline of which read: "Shots Fired at Judge."

"Where you been? We tried calling you all morning."

"Sorry. My battery died."

That earned me an eye roll. "You seen your uncle?" she asked, a look of concern on her face. "How is he? Know what the hell's going on?"

"Yes. Unconscious. Not a clue."

"Unconscious?"

"Yeah, they've got him pretty doped up. For the pain."

Edwina pursed her lips, ran her hand through her ebony hair, and leaned back in her chair. She was wearing bright red lipstick and matching nail polish, which looked good against her dark chocolate skin. She was medium height and a little stout. But I read that women who are overweight live longer—certainly longer than men who mention it.

"All we've got for this story," she said, waving the newspaper, "is that he was shot at, that he was choppered to Good Sam, and that he's under guard," she said. "What do you know that we don't know?"

I sighed. "I'll fill you in, but we have to talk about my role in this. I've obviously got a conflict of interest. Honestly, the reason I'm here is I just wanted to take a few minutes to think about things. And I suppose I could use your advice."

Edwina curled out of her chair, stepped gracefully to the door and shut it. She placed her hands on my shoulders and gave them a little squeeze. Comforting. "You're right, this is a sticky situation for you. Tell me what you're comfortable with and we'll talk about what to do next." Not for the first time, I was impressed with Edwina's good sense and compassion. That was not a universal characteristic of newspaper editors. As the journalist and playwright Gene Fowler once said: "An editor should have a pimp for a brother so he'd have someone to look up to."

Edwina walked past her desk to a small refrigerator and pulled out two bottles of water. She handed me one, then returned to her chair. She adjusted her skirt as she sat, removed her glasses, set them neatly on her desk blotter, and patiently waited for me to begin. I unscrewed the plastic top and drained the bottle. I hadn't realized how parched I was. She just smiled and pushed the second bottle across her desk to me.

I started talking, choosing my words carefully. She had established the ground rules, after all: Talk about what you're comfortable with. I understood that what I actually knew was less important than the questions fermenting in my mind. I decided to stick with the facts, most of them anyway, and save the speculation for later. I laid out a chronology of the day. As I talked, I noticed Edwina studying me. She let me speak uninterrupted, her hands folded atop her desk, her clear, brown eyes focused on me, not straying, nodding at appropriate times during my story. I admired her skillful use of body language, creating a comfort zone for the conversation. She was an active listener. She didn't take notes, but I knew from experience that she would neither miss nor forget any significant detail. In her day, she had been an award-winning reporter.

Maintaining constant eye contact with her while I talked felt artificial, and, as I allowed my vision to stray, I spied my reflection in the circular mirror behind her desk. The mirror was the centerpiece of an elaborate wall hanging. It was framed by wavy fingers of brass, the effect being to create the image of a sunburst, the perfect emblem for the office of the managing editor of the *Sun*. I was embarrassed by my disheveled appearance in the mirror. I hadn't shaved. I'd also forgotten about the ball cap on my head, worn backward, gangsta style, like I was still a teenager or something. Tufts of brown hair hung down over my forehead, pinned to my skull by the cap. I looked absurd, like an overgrown punk who refused to grow up. For crying out loud, I'd soon be thirty.

"Now you know what I know." It was the truth, but not the whole truth. I had omitted the delicate location of Uncle Leo's scorpion sting. That might come out from Leo's blabbermouth doctor, but not from me. I told her about the spent shell casing in my possession and Ponitz's speculation about the weapon. Figured I'd catch hell for that. It was, after all, evidence from a crime scene, and I had brought it into the newspaper.

There was one more thing I should have mentioned but didn't— got wrapped up in storytelling and it only came to mind after I wound down: the mysterious interview that Leo had set up for that afternoon. I glanced at my watch. We were supposed to meet at Leo's at three o'clock, in little more than an hour.

Edwina was quiet for a moment. She unfolded her hands, exposing an ornate gold ring with a ruby in the center. Otherwise, she wore no jewelry. She crossed her legs and her nylons made a silky scratching sound as she did so. She was the only woman I knew who wore hose. A newsroom rumor had it that she was prone to blood clots in her legs. She leaned back in her chair, just a bit. A hint of a smile formed.

"You've spent fifteen minutes telling me everything that happened—well, everything you think you can tell me, anyway—but I've yet to hear the first word from you about your own feelings. Your uncle's hospitalized, he's been shot at, and yet you seem so detached."

"Isn't that what we're supposed to do in this racket, keep our distance?"

"Yes, but good God, Leonard's in the hospital. Aren't you worried about him? Don't you have any feelings?"

How I felt was annoyed that she would ask, but I was more curious about her casual use of my uncle's first name.

"Leonard?"

Her forehead crinkled and she blinked. Twice. "Yes, Leonard. That's his name, right?"

"Sounds awfully familiar."

"Oh, grow up. I've known Leonard Strano longer than I've known you."

"I see."

Edwina cupped her face in her hands, rolled her eyes to the ceiling, and then locked onto mine. "God, you're a pain sometimes."

"You used to cover courts, didn't you, boss? You cover Uncle Leo?"

"Yes, of course."

"You became friends?"

"What of it?"

"How close were you? Are you?"

I was on dangerous ground here. Edwina liked me, but this was bordering on insubordination. But there was something off about this conversation.

"I ought to throw your ass out of my office," she snarled.

"I was just leaving." I rose and turned toward the door.

"Sit the fuck down."

I sat the fuck down.

"All right, wise guy. Yes, Leonard and I have been friends for many years. And, yes, I got to know him when I was covering courts. I admired him. A lot of trial lawyers are just in it for the money. Your uncle was a fighter, sometimes for the worst scum imaginable."

"And..."

"And I suppose, since one of the topics of our conversation is conflicts of interest, I should disclose that he and I once dated. Now. You happy?"

I was neither happy nor sad. Just surprised. I caught my

dumbfounded expression in the mirror behind Edwina's desk and closed my gaping trap.

"Didn't know that, did you? You may also not know that when you applied for a job here, Leonard called and put in a good word for you. He said, nephew or no nephew, you were a gifted writer and I'd be an idiot if I didn't hire you."

"Further proof you're not an idiot," I said. Then smiled, making sure she knew I was joking.

That earned me a smirk.

In fact, I did know Leo had put a good word in for me. I'd asked him to. I was shocked when I landed this job. It was unusual for someone my age to have such a primo assignment.

"Look, Alex. The fact Leonard and I dated, you understand this isn't something I want gossiped about. Leonard has been very discrete over the years. Obviously, from the look on your face."

I started to reply, but she held up her hand.

"Come on, Alex. I'm not just your boss. I'm your friend. It just so happens I'm also Leonard's friend."

Edwina leaned forward in her chair, picked up a ballpoint pen on her blotter, and tapped it on the desk.

"I know Leonard doesn't show his emotions much," she continued. "He's as lousy at that as you are. But if the situation were reversed, I can't help but feel his utmost concern would be your safety."

She paused.

"Shouldn't that be yours?"

"Shouldn't what be mine?" I'd lost track.

"Shouldn't Leonard's wellbeing be your top priority?" she repeated.

"I have no idea where you're going with all this, Ed."

She stopped tapping the ballpoint pen and glared at me. Her left hand rose to massage her earlobe for a moment.

"Let's put it this way," she said. "While I suspect you know more than you've told me, I imagine this is still pretty much a mystery. The police will do their jobs, I'm sure, to keep him safe. But we need to find out what the hell is going on." She took a breath, then continued: "You said earlier that you were concerned about professional ethics and the conflict of interest that you have—we have, I suppose. Well, I'm more concerned about Leonard Strano's life, and I think you should be, too," she said, her voice rising. "That plain enough?"

"If being concerned got anything done, that would be nice. But it doesn't. What are you suggesting?"

She held her breath for a moment then exhaled. A strand of curly brown hair, laced with threads of silver, fell over her forehead and she pushed it away. She massaged her earlobe again. Stress reaction. "I think you are being deliberately obtuse. And, for the record, I resent it. But, just so we're clear with one another, I have no problem with you investing as much time as you need to get to the bottom of this. Whether your efforts result in anything publishable is a secondary concern. That help?"

I rose from my chair and leaned over her desk. "Ed, you know and I know that I'm not an investigative reporter. I write feature columns about weirdos. What makes you think I can do anything to help?"

She frowned. "You've got just as much experience as Bob Woodward had when he brought down Nixon. Sack up!"

Whatever. I turned to leave.

"Alex?"

"Yeah, boss?"

"This is off the subject, but have you done anything to piss off Van Wormer?"

"Not that I know of, why?"

"Oh, it's probably nothing. But I got an email from him asking what you were working on. Very unusual."

That *was* unusual. I'd never said one word to the man.

"Beats me," I said. "Maybe he's a fan."

"No doubt."

I was walking out the door.

"One last thing," she said.

"Yes?"

Edwina paused for a moment, putting on her stern, hard-bitten editor face.

"Give that fucking bullet back to the cops before you get us thrown in jail."

CHAPTER 13

EDWINA MAHONEY'S WORDS still reverberated in my mind as I plopped down at my desk. What was the deal with Edwina and my uncle? How could I have been so unaware of their relationship? Then again, I was clueless about Leo and Sarah, too.

And what the hell was Edwina thinking when she said, "The police will do their jobs…"? What planet was she living on? For all anyone knew, it was a cop who took the shots. Leo hadn't made many friends in law enforcement when he was practicing law. Why would she say such a thing?

Trust no one. If your mother tells you she loves you, check your birth certificate. And did I know about birth certificates. Mom never married. She didn't even know my biological father's name. "He was a big, tall guy I just met," she told me when I was six years old after first confessing that she had "popped my cherry" at a Grateful Dead concert. I had no idea what she meant, and Leo had to explain it to me later.

Mom hated her last name, Strano. Went by Alice Sunshine. She was a world-class doper. And lousy at filling out forms. On the birth certificate where she was supposed to name me, she filled in her own name. Thank God Leo officially fixed my name when he adopted me, but I had been going by Alex Strange before then.

Why Alex? Because that's what Mom had always called me. Why Strange? I was good with Strano, but Mom had warned me I'd regret it and that I should make up my own last name. Turns out in some quarters a strano is a painful enlargementof the anus caused by homosexual sex. Imagine being six years old and having that explained to you.

When Leo had asked me why I chose Strange as a last name I told him the partial truth—that strano is Italian for strange, and that as a kid I thought Strange sounded a lot cooler. I've never mentioned the real reason. I figure that's a need-to-know issue, and he didn't need to know.

What if I had picked Jones instead? What would I be doing now? Would I be writing about weird news? Perhaps that decision altered the course of my destiny.

Karma.

Or kismet.

Whatever.

I looked at my watch. Mickey's hands were on twelve and two. Too early for a drink, but I was tempted. In an hour, Leo and I were to have met with someone who might help clarify what all this commotion was about. I should head over to his house and see who showed up. But I also wanted to check on him at the hospital. There wasn't time for both. I picked up the phone to call Sarah, then realized I didn't have her mobile number. The only times I'd spoken to her on the phone had been on their landline. I phoned Good Sam and navigated my way to the nurse's station outside Leo's room. He was still sedated and having his jaw immobilized with bandages. No point heading over to the hospital right away.

I had a few minutes before I had to leave, so I scanned my desktop to see if anything urgent had shown up.

There was a bundle of letters bound in a rubber band. I snapped it off and wrapped it around the growing ball I kept by my keyboard. The envelopes all contained press releases. I dumped them in the circular file. I fired up my desktop computer, navigated to Google Docs, and opened the Outlook folder, the place where we list all the stories we have in the works for upcoming editions:

THE STRANGE FILES. Naked photographer snapping pictures of startled women after exposing himself met his match thanks to our photographer and Alex's column.

FREEWAY SHOOTER. More than 13 vehicles have been struck by bullets from a sniper along the Black Canyon Freeway. Story updates efforts to find the "Black Canyon Bandito."

DOGS GONE WILD. Dozens of wild dogs and coyotes roaming together in packs have been seen in the Camelback Mountain area. Residents report pets missing, children frightened.

OFF TO UGANDA. Arizona reservists are headed to Africa in support of the War on Terrorism near the border of the Congo. We talk to two of them before they head out.

NURSES SHORTAGE. Arizona State University says it cannot keep up with demand in face of nationwide nursing shortage. Hospitals are recruiting overseas, especially from Australia.

CAMEL NOT. The Arab-American League asks the governor to change the name of Camelback Mountain, saying it is demeaning. With Squaw Peak renamed, can Indian Bend be far behind?

TONTO FIRE: Monitoring the fire in the Tonto National Forest. Latest reports have it approaching the Mogollon Rim. Need to get aerial photos for Monday's paper.

Leo had a cabin on the Rim. I wondered if the fire would endanger it, but that was the least of my worries at the moment.

Next, I punched up my office email, which I kept separate from the personal email on my phone. Most were press releases. There also were offers to expand my breasts, grow my penis, make her moan all night long, get rich through multi-level-marketing, and three different writers from Nigeria trying to unload $15 million because they trusted me, and I just needed to send them some checking account information. The newspaper's spam filters sucked. There were also a handful of letters from readers, which I forwarded to the editorial page staff.

One letter was from a local Catholic bishop unhappy about a column I wrote on pederasty in the priesthood. "Whenever your parents would like to get married," he wrote, "I would be happy to perform the ceremony." Little did he know.

Next was a directive from our fearless publisher, Francis Van Wormer, announcing that the company's match in the 401K retirement plan was being discontinued. Great. Maybe I *should* join the Guild. It was followed by Abigail Conwest's weekly critique in which she pointed out all the violations of AP style in the paper, noting that on six occasions in the past week alone, staff writers had failed to capitalize fanciful appellations. I made a mental note to track down all of my fanciful appellations and put capital letters on each and every one of those suckers.

The last message was from Dr. Omar Franken. Franken had been pestering me about a column I had written that had trashed his new invention, Stealth Car Wax, which, when applied to a vehicle's surface rendered it undetectable to police radar. Or so Franken claimed. A nearly empty can of the stuff sat on my desk, a yellow Post-it note with Franken's phone number stuck to the lid. Franken's invention came to my attention through a civil lawsuit filed in Leo's court by investors claiming they had been defrauded. Hawker tipped me off to the suit and helped with a little experiment I conducted with the assistance of Brett Barfield of the Scottsdale P.D. I smeared most of the can's greasy contents over the body of my Sebring, and Hawker drove it up and down Scottsdale Road while Barfield and I clocked the car on his hand-held radar gun. Put simply, the gunk didn't work.

"Alexander Strange, this is Dr. Omar Franken. I insist that you get in touch with me or you will be hearing from my attorneys."

I had talked to Franken at length after the column was published and he insisted that I test his product again, this time with him present. I checked with Edwina and she had checked with the newspaper's lawyer. Their collective wisdom was to refrain from all communication with Franken lest it be used as evidence in a libel action against the newspaper.

A tall, skinny college-aged kid fashionably attired in baggy jeans, barely clinging to his butt, materialized in my doorway.

"Hey, why'd you hang up on me?" he asked.

"Hi, Eduardo. Nothing personal. The notion of talking to Conwest gave me a case of the vapors."

Eduardo chuckled. "You don't get along, do you?"

"Eduardo, your powers of observation will take you far. And on your way, how about taking this stack of papers with you."

I grabbed the pile of newspapers that had accumulated on my desk and handed them to him. Every member of the staff got free copies of each of the *Sun*'s editions and the stack on my desk had been building up for weeks. I'd missed one at the bottom of the pile. The headline read:

Homeland Security Chief Tours New Detention Center

The story recounted how a planeload of Washington officials flew down on the vice president's plane to get a first-hand look at the new Gitmo on the Rez. I wondered if they got lessons in waterboarding while they were there. Something about the accompanying photograph gave me pause. I looked at it again and realized what had caught my eye. Descending from the jet with all the Defense Department officials was none other than Francis Van Wormer.

(Note to self: Investigate newspaper publisher's ties to the DOD and for being a general douche bag.)

"Here, I'll swap you," Eduardo said, grabbing the old papers and handing me a copy of that day's edition.

"Hey, I like your latest," he said, nodding toward my collection of tabloid front pages I had pinned to the bulletin board by the door. "Phone Psychic's Head Explodes," it read. It was next to a *Weekly World News* headlined "Priest Bursts Into Flames at Exorcism." Neither compared, in my mind, to the front page I had framed behind my desk: "Elvis Seen in Biplane Circling Mars."

I glanced at the paper Eduardo had delivered. A one-column mug shot of Uncle Leo accompanied the story, which was stripped across the top of the page. The photograph was out of date. Uncle Leo had a few more wrinkles these days.

By Elmore James
Phoenix Daily Sun

SCOTTSDALE—Superior Court Judge Leonard D. Strano was evacuated by helicopter to Good Samaritan Medical Center today from his home here after shots were fired at his house. The judge's injuries were not known at press time.

Police cordoned off streets leading to Strano's neighborhood bordering Paradise Valley and would not discuss details of the shooting with reporters. Neighbors, however, said a car was heard leaving the area at high speed after the Strano's alarm system went off.

Neighbors interviewed at the scene did not report hearing any gunshots, which could indicate that whoever shot at the Strano house may have used a silencer.

Strano, nicknamed the "Rocket Docket" by courthouse insiders due to the judge's penchant for moving cases speedily through his court, made national headlines with a ruling that the U.S.A. Patriot Act cannot be enforced in Arizona because it conflicts with the state's constitution.

Strano also was recently named the chairman of a special Blue Ribbon commission appointed by the governor to review concerns from the Phoenix African American and Hispanic communities about alleged instances of police abuse.

A confidential source told the newspaper that the judge received a "disturbing" phone call on Friday, but whether there was any connection with that and the shooting was unknown. Other members of the commission could not be reached for comment...

"What the hell?" That "disturbing" phone call had to be what Leo was trying to tell me about in the voicemail he left for me, the message that was cut short. How would Elmore James know about that?

I dug into my pocket for the scrap of paper on which James had written his cell phone number and snatched the receiver off my desktop. After three rings it rolled over into voice mail.

I slammed the receiver back into its cradle.

"Damn." Where did that business of the race relations commission and the phone call come from?

Maybe James was still in the building. I bounded out of my chair and made a quick sweep of the newsroom, sticking my head into several cubicles, wandering up to the Photo, Sports and Features departments on the next floor. He was nowhere to be found. I weaved my way back down to my own office. The message light on the desk phone was blinking. I hadn't noticed that earlier.

I punched in the four-digit code to retrieve the voice mail.

There were several messages. Most were reactions to recent columns. One was an incoherent diatribe from a guy who called often but never left his name, ranting about the homosexual agenda and how I was a Nazi for trying to brainwash the masses. (Memo to Trilateral Commission: Track this dude down and grease him. He knows too much.) The last call was from Hawker:

"Hey. Just read a copy of your rag. James says the judge was threatened. Don't know who he talked to. Wasn't me. No fuckin' idea." He left his number.

The way James' story was constructed, it implied that there was a connection between the phone call Leo received and his involvement with the governor's race-relations commission. But it didn't say the call was threatening, just "disturbing." Where did Hawker get that? Even if there were a connection, how would James know about that? And why speculate without any confirmation? And why hadn't Edwina mentioned it? I looked over to her office, but her door was closed and the lights were out. Damn. The paper had been sitting on her desk when I had been in her office. Why hadn't I looked at the story? I must really be off my game.

My pocket began vibrating and I fished out my iPhone.

"Mr. Strange, this is Special Agent Collins. Agent Volker and I would like to speak with you."

"Volker and Collins. What a coincidence. I was just thinking about having a drink. Where are you?"

"We're at the airport," the agent replied, "but let's meet at the hospital—say in an hour?"

"Make it two," I said, then couldn't resist asking: "What's happening at Sky Harbor?"

"For a reporter, you don't seem to keep up with the news, Mr. Strange." He hung up.

I flipped on the television by my desk and tuned into CNN. The Department of Homeland Security had just raised the terrorist threat alert level to Red. It was in response to "non-specific threats to United States airline traffic." After that it was all gabble, no real information, although "sources" were telling CNN the threat was related to "American adventurism" in Africa.

I called Edwina on her cell phone but got a recording. I left her a message just in case she hadn't heard the news. I also asked what the hell Elmore James was talking about. Then I sent a message to the City Desk. It would be another night at the airport for the staff, but not for me.

I decided to surrender the cartridge Bevin had given me when I met Volker and Collins at Good Sam, and I'd try to flimflam them with some sort of story that would keep me out of hot water.

As for Sarah, the best plan would be to get her back on a plane to Salt Lake. I didn't need the complication of babysitting her. I turned to my computer and Googled my way to the Southwest Airlines website. They had twelve flights scheduled from Phoenix to Salt Lake, the latest leaving at 11:30 p.m. Maybe I could talk Sarah into taking one of them.

Finally, I shot an email to Ponitz asking him to pull any clips we had on recent court cases Leo presided over. I asked him to check the Bar journal and the legal reference service LexisNexis, as well. I'd get Hawker to help me check out Leo's docket, too. Somebody either wanted Leo dead or intimidated. I hoped Leo would shed some light on that when we talked, but, in the meantime, I could do some prowling on my own. Cops would be doing the same, I knew, but another set of eyes couldn't hurt, right?

I stuffed the newspaper into my backpack, shut the door to my office, and walked over to the City Desk. Eduardo had a phone cradled under his chin. "No, ma'am, we don't throw the newspaper into your sprinklers on purpose," he was telling the caller. "Yes, ma'am, we'll be happy to send another one over…"

I reached into the desk drawer where we keep the keys to our fleet of staff cars and retrieved the set for Car Number Eight. The men's room is next to the exit, and it occurred to me I might be in the car for a while, so I stepped in. A veteran reporter once told me that the first thing you do when covering a plane crash is make a pit stop. You never knew when you'd have another chance. Ever since, I always stopped before heading out the door, plane crash or not. Inside, the restroom smelled like an ashtray, and the two urinals were filled with cigarette butts. So much for the no-smoking policy. I zipped back up and decided I'd just have to hold it.

I took the stairs down to the rear exit and scanned the parking lot for the staff car. All of the *Sun's* vehicles were navy blue with small white numerals stenciled on their rear quarter-panels to identify them. When I opened the door to Car Number Eight, a Chevy, the superheated fumes from greasy leftovers swept over me sending my stomach lurching. It smelled like someone had deep-fried a corpse.

I held my breath, cranked the ignition, and turned the AC up to full blast. One summer, when the mercury hit 119 degrees downtown, *Sun* staffers placed a thermometer in a sedan with the windows rolled up tight for a story on the dangers of leaving pets and children in cars. It hit 160 degrees, the temperature at which you smoke a turkey. This car didn't feel much cooler and smelled like a sewer. I opened the crumpled sack on the passenger seat. No turkey. Just the greasy remnants of a cheeseburger.

"Animals. I work with fucking animals."

A notebook lay under the sack. You might think reporters would guard their notebooks with their lives, but they were always misplacing them. I flipped it open. The handwriting looked curiously familiar. I paged through the notes hoping to find something that would reveal its owner. Several pages in, a sheet was torn in half. And then it hit me: This was Elmore James' notebook; this was the page he tore out after writing down his cell phone number and handing it to me. On the next page was another phone number. I dialed it. After two rings it rolled over to voice mail and I hung up. But I recognized that clipped whisper. I heard it on my answering machine. Now why would James be calling Hawker? And how had he gotten his phone number?

Maybe he was a better reporter than I gave him credit for.

Maybe he was just doing his job.

And maybe Elvis flies biplanes.

CHAPTER 14

IT WAS MY first stakeout. Should have had coffee and doughnuts like a real detective. Instead, I was sipping a bottle of Arizona Iced Tea (bottled in Brooklyn) and munching a protein bar.

Jackrabbit Court is a U-shaped street running off Cactus Wren Lane in western Scottsdale. Drive onto Jackrabbit from the southernmost entrance off Cactus Wren and the home of Superior Court Judge Leonard D. Strano is the third on the left. Two more homes followed Leo's before Jackrabbit bends and re-emerges back on Cactus Wren. Altogether, twenty-two homes lined both sides of the small street.

Across Cactus Wren, sprawls a massive asphalt parking lot of the neighborhood Mormon church where the helicopter landed to airlift Leo to Good Sam earlier that morning. A scattering of queen palms in a small planting area near the entrance offered a skittering of shade. I waited in the smelly staff car, hoping that before the fumes overcame me I would spot the guy Leo had invited to our meeting.

A few minutes earlier, I had driven by Leo's house. Yellow police tape wrapped the wrought-iron gate enclosing the front patio. An empty Scottsdale PD cruiser was parked out front. The uniforms were either inside the house or they had positioned a ghost car there to discourage curiosity seekers. Either way, it seemed unlikely that our mystery guest would stick around once he saw that. So I planted myself in the church parking lot with an unobstructed view of both entrances to Jackrabbit Court, notebook and pen ready to scribble down the license plates of anyone driving by the house. I figured a fifteen-minute window either side of 3 o'clock would cover it. If someone pulled up to Leo's house, I would zip across the street to intercept him.

While I waited, I punched in Brett Barfield's number on my iPhone. He answered on the first ring.

"Hey, Brett, Strange."

"How's the judge?"

"You don't know?"

"Nah. They treat us like mushrooms. Feed us bullshit and keep us in the dark."

"Well, at the moment, Leo's getting his jaw bandaged. Broke it in the fall. No bullet holes. That's the good news."

"Broken jaw, huh. That explains why he sounded so incoherent."

"Yeah. Hey, I need a favor."

"And I should do you a favor, why?"

"How about because you owe me money."

"I do?"

"Last week. Poker. Your marker?"

"Oh, yeah. You saying this will erase the marker?"

"Of course not. That would be bribery. Listen up. In a few minutes, I'm expecting that I'll need to run some plates. You can do that, right?"

"Sure. All us crime fighters can run plates. And there's nothing we like better than taking a break from writing jaywalking tickets to help out needy newspapermen."

"Look, I wouldn't ask if it wasn't important. And there are other ways to get this—illegal, of course—but time is of the essence." I grimaced at the cliché.

"This have to do with the judge?"

"Yeah."

"You going to tell me what?"

"Yeah. As soon as I can make sense of things. Will you help me out?"

"About the marker?"

"Fine. But tell me, you guys getting anywhere with this?"

"By you guys, you mean the FBI?"

"What are you talking about?"

"The feebs have assumed jurisdiction of the case."

"No shit? How can they do that?"

"Don't have all the details, but there was some mumbo-jumbo about a connection between the shooting and some stolen federal property. I heard they presented the judge with a summons."

"Sarah, actually," I said. "Leo was unconscious when they showed up at the hospital."

"That so? Care to fill in your friends at the Scottsdale PD?"

"If I could, I would," I said. "They treat me like a mushroom, too."

I paused for a moment. "So, does that mean you guys are out of it?"

"No. They've got us running errands for them. We're trying to get a make on the shooter's ride. Neighbors heard a car peel out, but nobody eyeballed it. We've been checking security cameras nearby—at the church, the ATM down the corner, the Circle K, stuff like that. I haven't heard, but my guess is it was too dark."

"Figure the car was stolen?"

"Maybe. The feebs are combing stolen vehicle reports from around the state. They asked us, Phoenix PD, and the sheriff to look for abandoned vehicles. Nothing to talk about, so far."

I hung up and waited. Took a sip of tea. Important to stay hydrated.

A white Ford F150 pickup truck slowed at the intersection of Cactus Wren and Jackrabbit then continued on. I jotted down the number.

A late-model sedan drove by. The driver, a middle-aged woman on a cell phone, didn't even glance toward Leo's place.

During the half hour I monitored the traffic around Leo's house, there were a total of 39 vehicles that traversed Cactus Wren. Three slowed at the entrance of Jackrabbit, and I wrote down their numbers. Five turned onto the street. All but one pulled into a driveway and parked or pulled into a garage. The fifth car cruised by Leo's, but continued down the street and left the neighborhood.

I called Barfield and read him the plates.

"Hey, I just saw your column about the flasher," he said. "Funny stuff."

I hadn't noticed it was in that day's paper. I pulled it out of my backpack.

"You know," Barfield said, "you did what the Phoenix PD couldn't. You caught that dickhead."

Over Exposed and Behind Bars

By Alexander Strange

Phoenix Daily Sun

The Flashing Photographer has been exposed, and it isn't a pretty picture.

For the past several weeks, a man in a trench coat—yes, a trench coat in Phoenix in August—has been exposing himself to women then photographing their startled reactions.

Recently, he mailed a collection of his photos to an alternative weekly newspaper in which he defended his exhibitionist behavior as "an extreme art form."

Most of the incidents have occurred in Central Phoenix, and police have been on the lookout for him. But for weeks he has eluded capture by using a succession of stolen bicycles to flee the scene. That's right, a guy on a bike wearing a trench coat has gone undetected.

That all ended when he got caught at his own game. As he threw open his trench coat to flash a young woman just outside the *Phoenix Daily Sun* building, she raised her own camera and got a clear picture of the man in his birthday suit.

The woman was a photographer for this newspaper.

She provided me with a carefully cropped image of the flasher, and as loyal readers of this column will recall, his image was published in this space with an invitation to contact police if anyone recognized him.

Yesterday, police received an anonymous tip based on that photograph and arrested a 37-year-old Tempe accountant with the eponymous name Seymour Bodman—I am not making that up. Bodman was booked into the Fourth Avenue Jail on charges of indecent exposure. The first order of business at the jail, of course, was to take his mug shot.

Turnabout is fair play.

STRANGE FACT: Statistically, half the men convicted of indecent exposure go on to commit the crime again.

Weirdness knows no boundaries. Keep up at www.TheStrangeFiles.com. Contact Alexander Strange at Alex@TheStrangeFiles.com.

CHAPTER 15

UNCLE LEO WAS awake. He had regained little of his ruddy complexion, a spectral pallor still gripping his features. He was staring blankly at the TV suspended from the ceiling. Not all that unnatural a thing for a patient to do, I suppose, except the TV was off. I cleared my throat, and he slowly turned in my direction. He motioned me over to the chair by his bed. His hands shook, and his eyes were glassy.

"How's it hangin'?" I asked.

He squinted.

"Oh, hey, I wasn't stretching for any double meaning, there."

"Right," he hissed through clenched teeth. White bandages crisscrossed his head and jawline holding his mouth shut.

"Good God, you look like The Mummy."

"Broken jaw," he hissed. His teeth were clenched but his lips moved in exaggerated fashion to ensure the words came out intelligibly. "Gonna be wired shut for a few weeks. Doing surgery tomorrow."

"You sound like Thurston Howell the Third on Gilligan's Island," I said. "Lovey, where's my martini?" It was one of my better impressions.

"Fuck you," Leo replied, in a perfect impression of an annoyed Superior Court judge hospitalized with a broken jaw and a scorpion sting on his dick.

"Leo, I'm chagrined. I'm just here to cheer you up. After all, the phrase 'Needle Dick the Bug Fucker' has not once crossed my lips, now has it? But do you think, strictly speaking, that you may have engaged in sexual intercourse with an insect? This could give new meaning to the word buggery."

"Don't make me laugh," Leo hissed. "Besides, you don't know the worst of it. Damn thing's given me a permanent erection."

I was certain I hadn't heard correctly. "Say what?"

"It's true," Leo said, working the words out slowly through his clenched incisors. "Doc says he's never seen anything like this before. No idea what scorpion venom might do to it." Leo motioned for me to pull off the blanket covering his midsection. I did so cautiously, revealing a little tent poking up in the sheet.

"Damned thing may never go down. I could spend the rest of my life in the locked and upright position."

I didn't know what was worse: seeing it or my trying to calculate its size. It occurred to me that not all of Leo's marital difficulties might be so difficult to explain.

"You know, Leo, this could be bigger than Viagra."

"I don't think you'd get a lot of repeat customers," he said, wincing at a sudden stab of pain.

I reached over, picked up the blanket, and covered his little tepee. Then I sat down on the edge of the bed and gave his arm a squeeze.

"Leo, your weird medical condition aside, we need to talk. This has scared the living shit out of me. I was afraid I lost you this morning. What the hell is going on?"

Leo didn't say anything for a moment. He closed his eyes, and I was afraid he might be drifting back to sleep. Great. What was with all the jokes, Strange? Why didn't you get down to business sooner?

Leo's eyes opened, then, and he curled his finger, signaling me closer.

"Have you seen Sarah?"

"Not since this morning. She's still here at the hospital, right?"

He nodded. "She was here just before you came in. She said you found Fred."

I nodded.

"Take good care of that puppy. He's important…"

"…to Sarah, yeah, I understand. Speaking of which, she said she's afraid to go home, wants to spend the night with me in Tempe."

"I told her go on and go to Utah. It will be safer. And she has things she needs to do."

Safer? Why would Sarah be in danger? And what things to do?

"Tell me what happened this morning."

He took a breath. "I was leaving a message for you when I went outside to collect the paper. Did you get it?"

"Yes, but it was cut off."

"The patio, it was covered with leaves and shit from the storm. A real mess. Next thing I knew it felt like I'd stepped on a nail or got bit by a rattler or something. Never felt anything that painful. I fell flat on my face and that pretty much cleaned my clock. Then, I remember the sound of glass breaking, Sarah screaming, the cops, the helicopter ride and, oh, Jesus, that damned thing crawling up my leg. Worst case of the willies ever. I kept trying to grab it or smack it—stop it from crawling up my pants. It was relentless…"

"Leo, about the gunshots. Did you hear anything, see anything?"

"No. But there was one more thing. Kinda silly. But I recall the sound of little bells from outside the gate. Weird, huh?

I nodded in agreement. It did sound odd. But, then, what wasn't?

"Other than that, I can't remember a thing," he continued. "Memory's in bits and pieces… big gaps in between. Doc says that's normal after the fall. Got a concussion. Memory could get worse. Didn't know about any shots until the cops asked. Still don't. You prob'ly got more details than me."

He was starting to slur his words.

"Leo, does this have anything to do with this race relations commission you're on?"

He gave me a puzzled look. "Huh?"

I had my answer. James got it wrong.

"OK, Leo, that call you got at Kelso's. Tell me about…"

At that moment, Leo's eyes rolled back in his head, and he sunk into his pillow, his features collapsing like a deflated balloon.

"Leo! Leo!" I reached over, instinctively, and grabbed his chin and shook his head. His eyes sprang open.

"Aghhhh," he gasped.

"Oh, Jesus, I'm sorry. I panicked there when you passed out. Oh, man, I hope that didn't hurt."

He blinked a couple of times, tears boiling out of his eyes. He rolled his head back and forth as if to clear the fog. "Only when I breathe." He nodded off again.

I punched the buzzer for the nurse.

"Leo. Talk to me." I was anxious now. The nurse would be there at any moment.

He opened his eyes and tried to smile.

"What about the meeting today?" I asked.

Before Leo could answer, the duty nurse swept into the hospital room followed by the uniform who had been guarding the door.

"Judge Strano, are you OK?" the nurse asked, a slight Australian accent in her voice. She turned to me, and scowled. "The doctor gave strictest instructions there were to be no visitors."

She appeared to be in her mid-20s, five-sixish, with an athletic build and a round, freckled face framed by auburn hair.

"Schwing!"

It was Leo. I tore my eyes from Florence Nightingale to see him dragging off his blanket like a drugged matador, exposing his little tepee.

The nurse turned, stared for a split second, then put her right hand to her mouth and stifled a laugh. "I heard that and don't think I don't know what that means—I've seen *Animal House,*" she said, stomping her foot in playful frustration. She actually stomped it. It was the cutest thing I'd ever seen a woman do.

With that, Leo snorted and passed out.

"Judge Strano?" She grabbed his wrist to feel his pulse.

A monitor on the wall over Leo's head began making beep-beep noises. The nurse hit a button on the wall, and all hell broke loose. An orderly pushed his way past me to Leo's bedside. A half step behind him, a resident rushed in. Followed by another nurse. Then Sarah.

"Oh, my Lord!" Sarah cried. "What's happening?"

I scooted around an orderly and rushed to the door to steady her. "Come on, Sarah," I said, "let's give these people some room."

The door was blocked by two men in dark suits. It was Volker and Collins.

"Christ."

Collins winced at that. "I believe we had an appointment, did we not?" he said. "We'd like to go over that statement you gave Lt. Warren earlier today."

"Swell. Let's just step back into the room and have a chat," I replied.

"No, you don't!" It was the nurse, shaking her head. "Out of here. All of you."

"What do you say we go get a cup of coffee," Volker said. "You appear to have worn out your welcome here. Hard to imagine, isn't it, Agent Collins?"

"Inconceivable," Collins replied.

Belatedly, it dawned on Volker that something was amiss in Uncle Leo's room. Maybe it was the milling doctors and orderlies, possibly the excited tone in their voices, perhaps the blinking light over the hospital room door. This guy was a detective? He couldn't detect his glans penis with a tweezer.

Volker tried to step into the hospital room but the nurse still blocked his path, a courageous stance on her part given the Incredible Bulk's girth.

"Judge Strano has had enough visitors," she said.

"What's going on in there, miss?"

"The judge is in good hands," she said, her voice firm. "We are treating him right now."

She turned to me. "He *is* going to be fine."

"He didn't look so fine a moment ago," I said.

"Here, take a quick look and then scoot along." She took my wrist and led me to Leo's bed. The resident was injecting something into his IV bag.

"Leo, you OK?" I asked.

His eyes opened and he raised his free hand and weakly waved me over to him.

I glanced at Florence Nightingale, and she nodded.

Leo tried to say something, but I couldn't make it out. I leaned down.

"Fred…"

"What?" I asked. But it was too late. His eyes were closed.

The nurse put her hand on my arm and steered me back out of the room. "Run along now," she said. "He needs his rest."

"If you say so."

"No worries," she smiled, reassuringly.

I noticed her nametag said "Sanderson." I also noticed how taut her hospital uniform was where the nametag was pinned.

"It was *Wayne's World*, by the way, nurse Sanderson," I said.

Her brow wrinkled and she gave me the what-the-heck-are-you-talking-about look.

"*Wayne's World,* not *Animal House.* Schwing. Just for the record."

She rolled her eyes, then turned on her heel and shut the door to Leo's room behind her.

Evidently, my encyclopedic knowledge of film didn't impress her. Sarah didn't seem overwhelmed, either, when I turned from the door to see her, hands on her hips, scowling.

"What did Leonard tell you?" she asked.

"I could barely hear him, but he said something about Fred."

"Come on, Mr. Strange," Collins said.

"I'll be back," I intoned in my deepest, most Austrian Schwarzenegger impression.

Sarah sat down in a chair across the hallway by the nurse's station and shook her head. "Do you always have to make jokes?"

Thurston Howell the Third, now Schwarzenegger. It had been a day filled with lousy impressions. Maybe if I kept trying I could impersonate a mature adult.

We all need stretch goals.

CHAPTER 16

VOLKER AND COLLINS seemed underwhelmed with my contribution to their investigation. They didn't say so, but I guessed they weren't fans of my impressions of famous actors either.

"So, Mr. Strange," Collins said, his voice, as usual, a touch too loud, "your newspaper said that the judge received a disturbing phone call. What can you tell us about that?"

"I'm afraid you're talking to the wrong guy. That was news to me when I read it. For what it's worth, I asked Leo about the reference in the story to the race relations commission. It didn't seem to register with him."

Volker jotted something in his notepad. Maybe that was helpful. Nice if I could give them something. But I had decided not to tell the agents about the meeting Leo had arranged. Not until I knew more about it.

They asked if I knew of anyone who might be out to get Leo. I told them it might be a long list, but I was wondering the same thing.

"You had a chance to talk to Leo, right?" I asked. "He passed out before I could get anything useful from him. What did he tell you?"

Collins shook his head. "We had hoped to interview Judge Strano earlier, but we were delayed at the airport. And even if we had spoken to the judge, you know perfectly well we wouldn't divulge that to you."

Exhaustion and frustration showed on his face. I was hoping that his starchiness might have wilted a bit under the weight of a tiring day, that he might feel like sharing.

My life is so full of disappointment.

"Can you at least tell me what that summons is about?" I asked.

"I think we're finished here."

"Uh, gentlemen, there *is* one more thing," I said, digging into my pocket. I pulled out the shell casing, but it slipped from my fingers and hit the hard tile floor making a tinkling sound, like a little bell, as it bounced.

That's what Leo heard!

I scooped up the cartridge and handed it to Collins. "A neighbor kid found this at the scene and gave it to me. I promised him I'd turn it over to the police. Here it is."

Volker and Collins peered at the shell, turned to one another, a look of disbelief crossing their faces, and then simultaneously turned toward me. They had their synchronization routine down cold.

"Just when did you get this?" Volker demanded.

"Like I said, this morning when I was out at Uncle Leo's house."

"And it took you this long to turn it over? Why didn't you give it up this morning?"

"Forgot I had it. Sorry."

"You forgot?" Volker was red-faced and his voice was rising. "I've got a good mind to cuff you right now. You've interfered with a criminal investigation."

"Guys," I said, holding my hands up in surrender. "I didn't discover this at the crime scene. I didn't steal it. A kid who found it gave it to me. He'd been playing with it. He'd still have it if I hadn't talked him into turning it over. I've done the right thing by ensuring that it's gotten into the capable hands of law enforcement."

"What was the kid's name," Collins asked.

"How should I know? Just some kid playing outside the police tape."

The agents badgered me for a few minutes more, but I knew I'd weathered the storm.

"I don't know about you, but I've had about all the fun here I can stand. We done?"

Collins nodded.

"Good. In that case, I'm going to get Sarah and vamoose."

They looked at one another in surprise, then Volker said, "Ain't gonna happen, pal. We're placing Mrs. Strano under protective custody."

"Does she know that?" I asked.

Collins cleared his throat. "Not yet. We're making arrangements with the Marshals."

"Marshals? Wait a minute. You're not talking about police protection, you're going to disappear her into WITSEC?"

"The Witness Protection Program doesn't *disappear* people," Volker said.

"Well, guys, you're going to have a fight on your hands."

Not just with Sarah, but with me, too. Not that I'm as neurotic about government overreach as Leo. Not that Sarah couldn't handle herself. But with Leo down for the count, I felt a responsibility for our little family, such as it was, and there was zero chance Sarah would evaporate into the maw of the WITSEC program. Not while I was still standing. And standing I was, right over Volker. My shoulders so tense I thought they would snap. The little fuck made half a gesture to his hip, where he holstered his piece. My lizard brain sprang to life. It wanted him to pull it. I would hit him so hard on the top of his pudgy head it would pop out his asshole. Somebody was snarling. I think it was me.

I felt a hand on my forearm and looked down. It was Collins.

"Easy, Mr. Strange," he said. Not in his usual, too-loud voice. Quiet. Consoling.

I took a breath and looked over to him. He was trying to defuse the situation. I nodded, took a deep breath, and walked away. Collins had just done me a turn. Maybe he wasn't such a prick after all. Or maybe he just didn't want to fill out all the paperwork if Volker had plugged me.

Sarah was still seated outside Uncle Leo's door when I returned, trailed by Collins and Volker. A new uniformed officer was guarding the entrance to Leo's room.

"He's asleep," she said. "That overstuffed nurse you seem to like so much gave him a shot and said no more visitors."

Overstuffed?

"Take me home."

Sarah was spent. It had been a hellish day for her. I felt like a heel for not having tended to her earlier, leaving her stuck at the hospital all day long. Some stepson I was.

"OK, Sarah. I'm sorry. I should have gotten back here sooner." I thought I'd try an end-around the feebs. "Let's go."

"Hold on," Collins said. "Mrs. Strano, we believe it may be in your best interest to allow us to provide you with police protection. We are making arrangements as we speak."

Sarah looked up at me in surprise. "They're not talking police protection, Sarah," I said. "They're talking the federal witness protection program."

"Absolutely not," Sarah said, her voice loud enough that the nurses at the station stopped what they were doing and looked over at us.

"Mrs. Strano…"

"It's bad enough that I can't return to my own house. I refuse to be a prisoner, locked up God-knows-where."

She turned to me, waiting for me to take up for her. I was on her side in this argument, but I also spotted an opening to get her out of town.

"Sarah, I don't know if the government can make you do this, but given all that's happened, it might be smart to leave town for a while. Maybe you ought to reconsider and catch that flight to Salt Lake."

A look of fury crossed her face as if she had just been betrayed. She took several deep breaths, then nodded, resigned to the inevitable. "All right," she said weakly. She rose out of the chair and turned toward the elevator.

"But promise me something," she said. "You'll stay close to Leo."

I turned to Collins. "I'll see to it she gets to the airport. She was heading to Salt Lake last night when her flight was delayed by the haboob."

"The what?"

"The sandstorm."

Collins started to protest, but we turned and walked away. The feds didn't chase after us. If they wanted to ensure Sarah was safe, they knew where she was heading.

"Let's get out of here." As the elevator door closed, I felt my chest tighten.

"Where is Freddie now?" she asked.

I took a deep breath. "Kid across the street. He's got him, so Fred's in good hands for the moment."

We traveled in silence for a few moments. Sarah gave me a curious look. "Are you all right?"

I ignored the question. I was long weary of talking about my claustrophobia.

"I'm sorry about all this, Sarah," I said, changing the subject. "They sprang that protective custody stuff on me just a few minutes ago."

She rubbed her hands over her eyes. "Maybe it's for the best. You've got more important things to do than babysit me, anyway, and I refuse to be locked away somewhere."

A gusher of stomach acid leapt up my esophagus. I felt flush with guilt. Was I doing this just to get her out of my hair, or was it the smart thing to do? I decided to go with smart for the time being.

"Sarah, I checked on flights earlier today. We've got some time, and we can discuss this some more if you want. Would you like to go someplace?"

She didn't say anything, just hunched her shoulders.

"I can book you on one of several flights leaving later today. We could run by the house, pick up your bags."

She nodded, expressionless.

"Say, I'll bet we could get Fred a ticket, too."

She turned to me and smiled. "That would be a comfort."

"We can talk about it over drinks," I said. It was a lame attempt at humor knowing full well that her religion forbade the consumption of alcohol.

She surprised me.

"Please."

CHAPTER 17

SARAH AND I were sitting at the scarred oaken bar inside Kelso's Saloon. She was sipping a Grey Goose martini straight up; I was nursing a Cuba Libre. It had been a hellish day and I needed a drink. Sarah, too, although it isn't every day one finds an upstanding Mormon woman saddled up to a bar knocking back cocktails, martinis no less.

She turned to me, brushing her feathery blond locks from her face, a move that involved both a toss of her head and a wave of her hand—a fluid, synchronous motion, no doubt acquired from years of tireless practice. Any other time and any other woman, it might have been flirtatious. But Sarah's face was lined with exhaustion and her eyes were rimmed in crimson.

She forced a crooked smile. "So what's a good Mormon girl doing in a bar drinking a martini, that's what you're wondering, right?"

Something about my reaction made her smile again.

"Oh, Sarah, what a mind reader you are," she mused. "Maybe I should become a psychic."

"Not a phone psychic, though, OK?"

"Why not?" Her voice had modulated. It had gone from scratchy and tired to, well, she wasn't purring, but it was a whisker away. Vodka will do that, I suppose.

"I wouldn't want that pretty head of yours to explode."

"Explode?"

"Happens to phone psychics more than you know. I have it on good authority. Made the front page of the *Weekly World News*."

Sarah tipped her martini glass toward me and tapped it with her perfectly manicured fingernail.

"Empty," she said.

"There's a cure for that." I turned to Stormy Sheetz who was filling in for Kelso behind the bar.

"Two more, madam, if you would be so kind."

Stormy nodded. She took no offense to the "madam" reference, although she cut me more slack than most. She was beaten up in the press when her massage parlor was busted. I was one of the few writers in the Valley who noted that all her employees—she preferred to call them entertainers—had health insurance and 401K plans. A copy of the article, headlined "Stormy End for the Oldest Profession," hung in a frame behind the bar. I was pleased to see it there, my mug shot peering out of the newspaper clipping, keeping a stern watch over the tavern's tipsy customers.

While she poured, I turned back to Sarah.

"I give in. Why is a good Mormon girl hanging out drinking martinis? And, for that matter, why are you so friendly? For as long as I've known you—which hasn't been that long—you haven't said two words to me until Fred disappeared."

She nodded and patted my hand. "Thanks again for that, for finding Fred." She took a deep breath, then began:

"I was raised a Mormon. But I'm not a good Mormon girl. I was. For a while. Until I found out what happens to good Mormon girls."

Before she could continue, Stormy showed up with our refills. She leaned down to set them on the bar revealing her prodigious cleavage. She paused, ignoring several customers awaiting refills.

"Alex, I've had the TV on all day trying to keep up with the news. What's the latest on the judge?"

I wrenched my eyes away from her blouse to meet her gaze. "When

I left Good Sam he was sleeping," I told her. "He broke his jaw in the fall…"

"Yeah, I saw that a little while ago on the tube," Stormy said.

Dani hadn't wasted any time with that. "He wasn't shot, that's the important thing," I continued, "but the tumble banged him up pretty good. They're going to keep him overnight."

"They know who did it?"

"Not yet."

She nodded. That seemed to satisfy her curiosity. Then she added, "I talked to the judge for a few minutes last night. You'd been here earlier, I guess. Now's not the time or place, but I want to tell you about a business venture I'm starting. Something right up your alley. Tell you about it later." She winked, turned to Sarah and offered her a faint smile, then began working her way down the bar filling orders.

I turned back to Sarah. "As you were saying…"

She was frowning. I'd seen that expression before—it was the same scowl she wore after I had flirted with nurse Sanderson. Sarah, it seemed, had little patience for the distractions of other women. Maybe she didn't like it that Stormy was chatting up Leo the other night, maybe wondering if she had leaned over and exposed her cleavage to him, too. Maybe I was overthinking it.

"What?" I asked.

"I need to powder my nose," she said. I assumed she intended to freshen up, not snort a line. But it had been a day full of surprises.

I looked around the bustling tavern. Kelso's was awash in red, tan and black, the Diamondbacks' latest colors. I missed the turquoise, copper and purple, but the marketers had determined that "Sedona red" would move merchandise faster. It's always about the money.

The boisterous crowd was getting its game face on. The Diamondbacks were playing the second of a three-game home stand against the Giants, having won the ballgame last night 6-0. The D-Backs were two games in first place and most of the pundits speculated it would come down to them and the Cincinnati Reds for the National League pennant.

Truth be told, I was partial to the Reds. Family loyalty. My mother grew up outside of Cincinnati and used to regale me with stories of watching the Reds with her dad when she was a little girl. Her father worked for the euphemistically named National Lead Company of Ohio, a Cold War factory that processed uranium to be used in atom bombs. Since uranium eventually decays into lead, it wasn't an altogether unclever name. Over the years, pits holding the radioactive sludge that was a byproduct of the bomb making began leaking, and people began looking elsewhere for work. Mr. and Mrs. Strano, the grandparents I never knew, headed to Phoenix with their two kids, Leo and Alice.

Leo went on to college and studied law. Alice spent her short adult life as a Deadhead, gaining extensive firsthand training in the consumption of the popular pharmaceuticals of the era.

My iPhone buzzed and I picked it off the bar. It was a text message from a number I didn't recognize.

This is Bevin's aunt. Found dog he was hiding. Told him to return it to you.

I tapped out a reply:

Be there soon. Bevin saved the day by finding Fred.

She replied:

Taking Bevin to movies. We'll put dog in Judge Strano's back yard with water bowl. Side gate open. Maybe that's how it got out. OK?

I typed back:

Sure. And thank you.

That Bevin was turning into a bigger sneak than I had imagined. He must have kept Fred hidden in his room all day. But at least he gave his aunt my card. I started to text something else, then Sarah returned.

"Sorry."

I turned to her. "Why sorry?"

"I've been bitchy."

She had slipped back onto the barstool and crossed her legs. She looked at me over her drink, placed her hand on mine for just a moment, and then withdrew it.

"There's something I need to tell you," she said then took a breath, corralling her thoughts. "Last night, I was supposed to fly back to Utah. You know that. My flight was canceled because of the storm, but Leonard and I hung out at the terminal bar for several hours and we both got a little tipsy. We ended up Ubering home. He didn't want to risk a DUI."

Leo getting hammered wasn't headline news, but I kept my mouth shut and let her talk.

"It's the reason I was leaving that I want to tell you about."

She reached up and cupped the side of my face, turning my head so we were making direct eye contact. Hers were burning. "Your uncle is my hero. He is the only man in the world I have ever trusted."

"Hero?" I couldn't help myself.

Sarah took another sip of her martini and repositioned herself on the barstool.

"Have you heard about the Rev. John Jacoby? He was the bishop of that Mormon splinter group near the Utah border, the Original Order of the Church of Jesus Christ of Latter-day Saints. The polygamists."

"Didn't he just get out of prison?"

She nodded.

"He was convicted for rape, right?" I said. "The girl he molested, she stabbed him or something. I remember Leo telling me about that, although it's been years ago."

"Right." She took a deep breath. "Well, I was that girl he raped. I'm the girl who stabbed him."

For once, I had no snappy repartee. Her breathing had quickened and I was afraid she was going to hyperventilate, but she pressed on.

"Leonard wanted to tell you, but I begged him not to. I didn't want anyone to know."

"But I'm family."

Her eyes grew wide. "Alex, you have no idea how ashamed I am of what happened. It has taken me years to get healthy. Emotionally. I'm only now at a place I can talk about it."

"Sarah, you have nothing to be ashamed of. You were defending yourself."

"Not that," she hissed, then gulped some air. "I wish I killed the bastard. I was just a girl. He ruined my life." She was weeping. "You have no idea what that man did to me... forced me to do..."

She was turning pale.

"OK, Sarah, take it easy."

Suddenly, her eyes rolled back into her head. Before she tumbled off the barstool, I grabbed her and lowered her head, hoping that would help.

Just then, Abigail Conwest strolled by, glanced down at Sarah's blond hair splayed over my lap.

"Get a room."

Stormy Sheets rounded the bar and put an arm on Sarah's shoulders. "Let me handle this," she said, helping her upright, then steadying her as they left for the ladies' room.

I hadn't paid a lot of attention to the story about Jacoby's release from prison, but I recalled that Leo had an important role in the case. I grabbed my cell phone and found a story about it on the *Sun's* website.

A 16-year-old, identified as Jane Doe because she was a minor, had been forced into marriage with Jacoby against her will. During a stay in Phoenix, where Jacoby had been subpoenaed to testify during an inquiry into the polygamous practices of his sect, Jane Doe stabbed him in their downtown hotel room. Jane was arrested for assault. Jacoby was held on charges of child molestation. Jane Doe's mother, a member of the sect, testified during his trial that she had given permission for her daughter to marry the leader of her church. But while Arizona law allowed 16-year-olds to wed with parental consent,

Jacoby could not provide a valid marriage license. He was sentenced to the maximum twenty-four years in prison for child molestation.

Nonetheless, the county prosecutor decided to press assault charges against the girl. The public outcry was horrific. The local media went nuts. In a juvenile court hearing that lasted 32 minutes, she was acquitted. Her pro bono legal counsel was Leonard D. Strano.

Soon thereafter, Leo was appointed by the governor to fill a vacancy on the Maricopa County Superior Court, according to the story on the newspaper's website. In Arizona, Superior Court judges don't run for re-election. Voters simply vote to retain them or not. Even though he was widely viewed as the most liberal and iconoclastic jurist in Maricopa County, "voters have never forgotten that he was the attorney who saved Jane Doe," the story concluded.

What would the voters think about his relationship with her now?

CHAPTER 18

WE WERE DRIVING to Scottsdale. Our plan was to stop by the house and pick up Sarah's luggage, still unpacked from the night before. We'd grab Fred, then head to the airport. We had plenty of time before her flight, and I had a lot of questions that needed answers.

"Sarah, this whole business about your past. Does that have something to do with why you need to go to Utah?"

She nodded. "Leonard did more than get me off the assault charge. He also got me into foster care so I wouldn't have to return to my mother, the whore."

"Whore?"

"Yes. Whore. She's had five children. None of us know who our real fathers are. They don't just practice polygamy up there. It's communal sex, wife swapping. It's deplorable. Anyway, I was lucky. I had wonderful foster parents. They saw to it I finished high school. They didn't have the money to help me with college and I wasn't inclined. I left Arizona the day after my high school graduation and moved to Las Vegas."

I had decided to avoid the freeway and take city streets to give us time. Traffic was light. There were a few lightning flashes to the east.

"I never saw my sister—she's two years younger than me—or my brothers again. Not until recently. My sister, Rebecca, tracked me down in Phoenix even though I had changed my name after my second marriage."

"Second marriage?"

"I told you I wasn't a good Mormon girl. I was married twice before now. Neither marriage lasted more than a year. I've not been very…stable, you know?"

"So, how did Rebecca find you?"

"She's the smart one in the family. She's a lawyer in Ogden. She looked up the Jane Doe files, discovered that Leonard had been my attorney, and contacted him. The reason she was trying to find me is that I—we—have yet another sister, Ruth, whose daughter is just turning sixteen. Her name is Mary."

"So what's up with Mary?"

"What do you think? It's *déjà vu* all over again. My idiot sister, Ruth, wants to give her up to the church. Rebecca found out, got a court order stopping it—I don't know all the legal details—but there's a problem."

She paused for a moment, going internal, so I prompted her. "Problem?"

"Yes." She was sniffling and I saw tears streaming down her cheeks in the dim light from the dashboard.

"Mary *wants* to do it! She's been brainwashed."

"So you and your sister Rebecca are double-teaming her, trying to talk some sense into her?"

She nodded. "That, and my sister's trying to find other legal ways to block it."

"And that's why you're flying to Utah," I said, stating the obvious.

Again she nodded, pulled a tissue out of her purse, and dabbed her eyes.

"Sarah, do you think there's any connection between all this and the shooting this morning?"

"I don't know. I don't think so."

"But you told the cops, didn't you?"

She nodded. "I had to."

"So that's why you're telling me now. Cat's out of the bag."

"Yes, that's true, although when Leonard and I were talking last night at the bar, he persuaded me that you deserved to know."

She twisted in her seat to face me. "It was my doing, keeping this from you. But you have to know, Leonard, he was fearful you would disapprove."

"Of you?"

"No. Of him. I mean, let's face it. He rescued me from an older man who took advantage of me. Now here he's the old man in my life. You have to admit it's kind of weird."

Pathological.

"Since I seem to be telling all my secrets, did Leonard tell you how we reconnected after all these years?"

"Lay it on me."

Sarah cleared her throat. "Well, it's kind of a funny story."

"I could use a good laugh."

"Well, we didn't just get married in Las Vegas. That's where we met again after all these years. It was at a strip joint. Your uncle offered me a hundred bucks for a lap dance."

She paused, but I managed to keep my mouth shut. At that point, I was prepared to believe anything.

"Thing is, while I worked at this club as the bookkeeper, I wasn't one of the performers. I just happened to be walking through the lounge while Leonard was sitting there with a friend of his from Florida, another judge. I remember his name. Goodfellow. I thought it ironic, you know, that someone named Goodfellow would be in a strip joint."

"Sure."

"Anyway, Leonard, he grabbed my hand and tried to shove me some money. I suppose I should have been offended, but he was so cute with that string tie and white hair. He kind of reminded me of a western Colonel Sanders, you know? I didn't recognize him, not right away.

"Anyway, to make a long story short, I straightened him out and he apologized. But then he offered to buy me a drink. I don't know why I agreed, but I did. He can be a charmer, your uncle. So we started drinking. He took me to dinner and, well, we put the pieces together. You can't imagine how shocked we both were."

We drove in silence for a few minutes. I didn't know what to say about that. My head was reeling. A car flew past me on the right, and I realized I was driving slow in the fast lane. Plates on the car that had sped by me read SMOP. I knew that one: Slow Moving Old Person. How embarrassing.

I checked my mirror, switched lanes, and turned to Sarah.

"So, then he hired you?"

She nodded again. "I wanted to get out of Vegas, and he mentioned he had a vacancy in his office. I'm very good at office work. I had to go through all the county process, of course, but, yeah, I got the job."

And then some.

"Let me change the subject," I said. "What can you tell me about what happened this morning?"

"Oh, God. Let's see. Leonard was up as usual at dawn thirty. No idea how he does that. We were drinking until midnight. I've had a headache all day. I remember him leaving the bed. Next thing I knew, I heard glass breaking and then the alarm went off. Scared the pee out of me. I ran downstairs and there he was, on the patio, face down and twitching, like, well, we know why now."

"You didn't say anything about hearing gunshots," I said.

"I didn't."

"Leo, he say anything to you about a meeting he had arranged for this afternoon?"

"No, the first I heard of that was when you mentioned it to that Scottsdale detective, Lt. Warren."

"Was I imagining things, or did that bother you, that you didn't know?" I asked.

She cocked her head and shook it. "No. It didn't bother me. But I was surprised. He never said anything to me about any meeting. But I was supposed to be in Salt Lake, so it might not have occurred to him to say anything."

If she was happy with that explanation, so was I.

"Alex?"

"Yeah?"

"You know what we have in common, don't you?"

"Leo?"

"Not just that. We both have suffered because of our mothers. Yours was a druggie. Mine is a whore. And Leonard intervened in both of our lives to save us."

I nodded.

"Leonard didn't just adopt you. He's your real father. Maybe not biologically, but in every way that matters."

I nodded again. "And that's how you got to be my stepmother."

"All right, I give in. You can call me Mom."

"That's OK, I just did that to needle you. Now look at what you've done. You've taken all the fun out of it."

She laughed. That was good to hear.

"Well, stepmother dearest, we're almost there."

"Just one thing, stepson."

This was getting silly, but I played along.

"Yeah?"

"I've changed my mind."

"About what?"

I turned the corner. We were just a few blocks from the house.

"I'm not flying to Salt Lake with Leo in the hospital. I will not run out on him. I owe him that much."

"What about your sister?"

"Rebecca can handle things for a few days. I can't leave now. I won't."

"So, what do you want to do?"

"Can I stay with you, just for the night, until I get things figured out?"

"Sure. I guess I can sleep on the floor." I thought, maybe, that would give her cause to reconsider. But no.

"One more thing."

"Whatever you want, Sarah."

"Freddie. He can spend the night at your place, too, can't he?"

That was my out. My apartment complex didn't allow pets.

What I said was: "Sure."

CHAPTER 19

THE STAFF CAR still reeked of stale food, but Sarah hadn't remarked on it during our drive from downtown Phoenix. Maybe Grey Goose martinis dimmed her sense of smell. A couple of those and you'd be lucky to even feel your nose. But the vodka had loosened her tongue. That, and getting her disturbing history off her chest seemed to relax her. Now I knew why she always had her shields raised around me.

I'd already rescheduled Sarah's flight from the night before, so I would need to call the airline again and cancel. She'd given me her flight folder with her e-ticket receipt and I'd shoved it in one of my bulging pockets. When I'd called earlier to reschedule, the reservationist warned that the departure might be delayed because of the Red Alert and the ratcheted up security at Sky Harbor. Maybe staying put in Phoenix for the night made sense for that reason alone.

It occurred to me that maybe once I got her to the house I could talk her into staying there. I could sleep in my old room. Maybe she'd feel safe with someone staying over with her. That would certainly be a better plan than sleeping on the floor of my apartment.

It was nine and dark by the time we pulled into Leo's neighborhood, but the temperature still hovered near 100. Lightning flashes exploded over the Superstition Mountains to the east. The wind was gusting, blowing leaves and dust down the dampened street.

"Looks like this part of town's already had some rain," I said, turning onto Jackrabbit Court. A Scottsdale police cruiser was still parked in front of the house. Someone had covered the shattered front window of Leo and Sarah's house with plywood. Yellow police tape was remained tacked across the front gate and door, but it would be easy to step around. It was dark inside the house, but then, again, all the windows in the neighborhood were dark.

"Must be a power outage," I said. It was not an uncommon occurrence during Monsoon Season. Sarah reached into her purse and pulled out her garage door opener and pressed the button. Nothing happened.

"Definitely a power outage," I said. "You always carry that around in your purse?"

"It's a spare. My car has a built-in opener."

"May I?" I took it from her. It was tiny, no bigger than a pack of gum. Amazing how things are becoming miniaturized. I pushed the pea-sized button on it again. Nothing happened, of course.

I tossed it on the dash and stepped out of the car. She waited for me—a gentleman's role is to open the door for a lady. So I did. "Alex," she said, "you want to turn the headlights back on so I can see my way to the front door?"

"Wait. Let me get the flashlight from my Sebring." The convertible was a block away, where I'd parked it that morning. I sprinted over and unlocked the trunk. It was overflowing with junk—gym bag, extra running shoes, tools, jumper cables, backpack, a gallon plastic jug of water, short wave radio, blanket and, finally, the lantern I was looking for.

"What's that?" Sarah asked when I returned.

"It's a three-way light for highway emergencies," I told her. "Has a flasher, a regular flashlight and a fluorescent light, although I have a black light in there now."

"What's the black light for?" she asked.

"I used it for a story I did in Mesa on a scorpion hunter."

"Scorpion hunter?"

"There's this old guy over there, runs around the desert with his ultraviolet light to capture scorpions. They glow in the dark under a black light. I helped him search for them one night while working on a column about him. Still got the UV bulb in my lantern. Might come in handy. Come on, let's get out of this wind and we'll check out your house."

We walked to the entrance and I turned the handle on the patio gate. It was unlocked. When Sarah and Lt. Warren had left the house earlier, Sarah had taken the gate keys with her, so when the crime scene investigators had left, they had no way of relocking the gate. I raised the police tape, and we stepped in. The blanket of leafy debris from the morning still littered the red-brick patio floor.

"Sarah, let me show you how we scorpion hunters do this." I turned off the flashlight then flicked on the fluorescent ultraviolet bulb. The patio turned bright purple in the glow of the lamp. I began foraging around the patio, swinging the light across the walls and into corners.

"Ha! Look here."

In the amethyst glow of the lamp, a scorpion, glowing lime green, was crawling across the leaves, its menacing, spiked tail curled upward over its eight-legged body.

"Oh no," Sarah said, jumping back. "Is that what I think it is?"

"Yeah. Here, watch this." I turned off the black light and illuminated the same spot with the flashlight. "See him now?" I asked.

"Barely. That is so eerie."

I turned on the fluorescent bulb again and the scorpion reappeared, glowing iridescently in the dark. It was about an inch long, typical for bark scorpions.

"It's not that big, is it?" Sarah said.

"Nope. This is one of those rare times when size doesn't matter."

She shivered and wrapped her arms around her body. "Alex, are these creatures all over my house?"

I stomped it. "Could be. You ever have any problems with scorpions before?"

"No. Never. Why do they glow like that, it's like they're aliens or something? This is the creepiest thing I've ever seen."

"Pretty creepy," I agreed.

"What were you saying about some guy hunting them?"

I told her how scorpion antivenin was made at a lab at Arizona State University, how the toxin from the scorpions is injected into goats, how the goats' blood was extracted to capture the antibodies they develop, and how the plasma from the goats' blood was used as antivenin.

"And that's what they shot into Leonard? Goat's blood?"

"That's right. Goat's blood for an old goat."

"And you say they let these awful things sting goats to make antivenin?"

"No. They use electrodes to extract the venom from the scorpions, collect it, then inject the goats."

"Oh, that is so gross. Those poor animals!"

"Uncle Leo might not be alive right now if they didn't. Come on, let's go inside."

Sarah hesitated. "Alex, I want you to check the inside of my house with this lantern thing. I want to know if there are more of these, these *monsters* wandering around. I am freaked out by this. There is no way, no way in the world, that I'm ever sleeping here again. Never."

So much for staying here tonight.

"All right," I said. "Let's finish sweeping the porch then we'll go inside." I played the black light along the edge of the house, past the front door and back toward the wrought iron fence that separated the patio from the circular driveway. Suddenly, a mass of squirming green came into view.

"Check this out, Sarah. Babies."

Beneath the black light a momma scorpion was crawling toward the corner of the patio with a half dozen smaller versions of herself squirming on her back.

"Oh my God!" Sarah screamed. "They're breeding!" She stepped forward and smashed down with her shoe. She missed and momma scorpion scurried off in one direction and the babies scattered every which way.

"Looks like you've got a nest of them."

She did a little dance, trying to get her feet off the ground and away from the fleeing arachnids. "Let's get out of here!"

I unlocked the front door. We stepped into the darkened foyer and I swung the lamp in front of us to illuminate the room. The purple glow from the ultraviolet light was strong and we could see all around the living room at the left of the entrance, up the stairway to the right, and straight ahead toward the dining room and kitchen.

"This is weird," Sarah said. "I feel like I'm breaking into my own house."

A seashell pattern on the living room sofa and chairs glowed bright orange under the glow of the black light. Stitching on a throw pillow on the floor radiated electric white against the dark fabric. Labels on the DVDs of Leo's movie collection—those that hadn't been shot to pieces—glowed iridescently. I strolled around the room, playing the light downward and sweeping back and forth searching for unwelcome arachnids.

"Don't see anything in here, Sarah," I said. "But I'll go through the other rooms to be sure."

I squatted down to shine the light underneath the couch and was startled when a bright iridescent dot about the size of a nickel flashed to life underneath the adjacent end table. I jumped back, slipped, and landed on my butt.

"Is it a scorpion?" Sarah demanded.

"No. It's just some round thing that glows under UV. It's right here, under the end table." It was a silvery metallic disk with a fine wire several inches long running from its circular edge. I grabbed it and it pulled it free of the table where it appeared to have been held in place by rubber cement.

"What is it?"

I wasn't sure, but I guessed we had gone looking for one kind of bug and found a very different species.

I stood up to show it to Sarah when there was the sound of scratching at the back door.

"Oh my God!" Sarah shouted. "Freddie!"

It was a few steps to the French doors leading to the patio, and through the panes we could see the puppy.

"Freddie!" Sarah yelped again and flung the door open and scooped Fred into her arms and nuzzled him. In return, Fred gave Sarah a big lick on her nose.

"Where on Earth have you been? You naughty puppy. I have been so worried about you."

I set the bug on the coffee table and walked over to Sarah and Fred. He looked up at me and I gave him a pat on the head. Then he turned, peered out the open patio door, and growled:

"Gerruff."

I stepped outside and began to sweep the purple light around. From the corner of my eye I saw a blur of motion and then felt an incredible shock as something smashed into my face.

A flash of lightning.

Falling.

Oblivion.

CHAPTER 20

I LAY STILL in the darkness, disoriented, dizzy, and immobilized by nausea. A bongo drum was banging inside my skull. I moved my right hand to my forehead, drawn to a spot above the bridge of my nose, the epicenter of the throbbing. It was sticky. The hum and crunch of tires on pavement outside and the muffled rumble of an engine disturbed the silence. I rolled my head toward the direction of the sound and instantly regretted it as the movement sent my stomach lurching. I could see nothing; everything was black. Why was it so dark? I pondered that for a moment then slipped back into unconsciousness.

When I next opened my eyes there was light. But the sun wasn't up. The patio lamps were on. Power must have been restored. I was lying half in the living room and half on the patio, my legs stretched out through the doorway. Whoever hit me had left me where I'd fallen. My head, what was left of it, was pounding, but the world was no longer spinning, not like the first time I came to, which I dimly remembered. I leaned up. The bongo drum in my head started banging again. I pushed through the pain and slowly sat upright. The thudding continued, but the incapacitating nausea had subsided. I got on my hands and knees and crawled toward the kitchen, raised up, and flicked on the light. It was blinding, and I jerked reflexively setting off the bongos in my skull once again. I paused for a moment to let the pain subside. Slowly, I surveyed my surroundings. I appeared to be alone. A jolt of adrenaline shot through me.

Sarah!

I called out for her, but there was no reply. I staggered through the dining room and into the living room where earlier I had found the bug. Nobody there. I paused for a moment and looked around. The bug I had dropped on the coffee table was missing. Guess the slugger took it.

"Sarah!" I shouted. Still nothing.

I willed myself to the stairway leading to the second floor bedrooms and began climbing as fast as my wobbly legs would carry me. My pulse was pounding. "Sarah!" I shouted again at the top of the stairs. I flung open the doors to each of the two guest rooms and my old bedroom and peered inside. They were empty. I was breathing heavily.

My God, where is she?

I turned into the master bedroom. It, too, was unoccupied. I flicked on the light inside the bathroom. The face greeting me in the mirror was ashen and streaked with drying blood. A semicircular gash, centered on my forehead, appeared to be the source of the bleeding. My eyes were puffy. I touched my nose. It didn't feel broken. Yep, my forehead took the brunt of it. He must have used brass knuckles. I turned away from the mirror and stepped back into the bedroom. The king-size bed was unmade and rumpled, untouched since Saturday morning when all hell broke loose at the house. I stared at the room for a moment, sensing something out of place, but couldn't bring the image into focus. I walked back down the stairs and crossed the foyer to Leo's study. I turned the handle, but the door wouldn't budge. Right. Cops couldn't budge it either.

I turned back toward the open patio door. I was steadier now and the throbbing inside my head had diminished, down to a Bourbon Street hangover: Not enough to kill you, just enough to give you religion. I glanced around and realized my lantern was missing. My ball cap was lying on the rug, though. I scooped it up and gently fit it on my aching head.

I stepped onto the patio and called out to Fred, but he, apparently, was missing, too.

I needed to call the cops. Whatever was going on, I was in way over my pay grade. I glanced at my wristwatch. Mickey's hands were pointing to three and nine, 3:45 a.m. I must have been out cold for hours. I lurched into the kitchen and grabbed the receiver to the wall phone. No dial tone.

"Damn."

I was staring down the short hallway that led to the garage. It was the same doorway I had entered earlier when I had coaxed the Scottsdale cop into letting me into the house after the shooting. I walked the short distance and opened the door. Leo's black Buick Regal was still on the far side of the two-car enclosure. I stepped down into the garage and tried the passenger side door. Locked. It looked empty inside. Sarah's car was missing, and I paused over that for a moment, then recalled she said they'd left it at Sky Harbor Friday night when they cabbed it home.

I stepped back into the kitchen, fished my iPhone from my pocket ready to punch 911, when it began vibrating in my hand. It startled me and I almost dropped it. I glanced down at the screen, which showed I had voice mail.

"You have something we want and we have someone you want." The recording sounded mechanical, robotic. Must have been using some sort of voice modifier. "Call this number when you wake up." Then the robot voice spoke a seven-digit number.

I punched it into the phone. The same voice answered after one ring.

"Took you long enough to call. How's your head?"

"Is this Jacoby? You touch one hair on Sarah's head and I will hunt you down and disembowel you."

"Calm down. She's fine. I think she's growing kind of fond of me. But what's a Jacoby?"

There was music in the background. I couldn't quite make out the song. Radio? TV? Impossible to tell. There were no other voices.

"So you're not Jacoby. Fine. Who the fuck are you?"

"You kiss your mother with that mouth?"

"No. Your mom."

There was a pause on the line, then he came back: "Here's the program. The judge has something we want. Unfortunately, he's not in a position to deliver it. Your assignment, if you choose to accept, is to get it—*discretely*—then turn it over to us. Play nice, and the judge's wife goes free and you won't hear from us again."

"I've no idea what you're talking about," I said.

"Of course you don't. But the judge does and you have access to him. You have twenty-four hours. Oh, and by the way, if you want to see this lovely lady alive again—and her ugly mutt—don't even think about calling the cops. Not even your buddies at the FBI. We'll be watching you. We *have* been watching you. Don't fuck this up."

"Wait!"

"Don't bother calling this number. It's a disposable phone. We'll call you."

The line went dead.

"Jesus, Mary, and Joseph."

I stared at the iPhone for a moment in dumb silence, unsure how to react, what to do next.

Calm down. Think.

Leo told me his home office had been broken into sometime Thursday afternoon, after Sarah had left and before he got home. If the bad guys had already searched the place, what were they doing here again? Were they coming back to search some more, and it was our bad luck to be here when they arrived? Somehow that seemed implausible. Not after they'd already tried to kill Leo. Besides, they'd need light to look around and that could attract attention in the middle of the night. Cops might be cruising the neighborhood or come back for the dummy cruiser they left out front. No, that couldn't be it.

The bug I'd found was missing. Were they back here to clean up? A quick in and out? That seemed at least possible. Assuming they were the ones who bugged the place.

Was it just bad luck we showed up when they were here? What were the odds of that? Or could they have tailed us here? Was it an ambush? Grab the judge's wife and use her for leverage?

They. Who were they? The FBI believed Leo had come into possession of stolen federal property. Was that what they wanted, the same thing, whatever it was the feebs were after? Assuming this wasn't all an FBI op in the first place. But it seemed too thuggish for that.

But planting bugs and wiretaps, now that was right in the FBI's wheelhouse. Maybe that was an FBI bug I had found. Maybe that's why Leo's house phone was dead now. I thought about that for a moment, then recalled that Leo's phone service was tied into his cable TV and Internet service. When the power failed, it might have knocked out his modem.

Think some more.

I nervously checked my watch again. 4:05 a.m. Sunday morning. Should I call the cops? The FBI? Or should I first talk to Leo, assuming he wasn't still dorked on painkillers or whatever it was that zonked him yesterday?

Then I thought some more about Leo's study. Whatever it was the douche bag on the phone wanted, he thought it might have been hidden there, hence the break-in. I walked to the door and, for a moment, thought about kicking it open. Then my brain re-engaged. Didn't Leo hide a key to this room? I ran my hand over the doorframe, and for once got lucky: the key tumbled onto the carpet.

I unlocked the door and flicked on the light switch. The room was in shambles. The shelves along the back wall of the room had been stripped, books lying on the floor in piles across from Leo's wide, cherry desk. Whoever did this was thorough: The seat cushions to the leather couch along the side wall had been sliced open along the seams revealing the padding inside. Files from Leo's two legal-sized cabinets littered the floor. The emptied drawers of his desk were piled on the carpet. The carpet had been peeled back from the edges of the room. His favorite oil painting, an impressionist Grand Canyon landscape by Kassandra Clarke, was ripped from its frame. The case on his desktop computer had been removed. The glass enclosure from the overhead light was missing, exposing bare bulbs. Even the light bulb in Leo's Tiffany desk lamp had been unscrewed.

I mulled the scene for a moment and concluded nothing would be gained by poking around and contributing to the chaos. Why, I wondered, had this room been torn up, but not the rest of the house? Maybe they started with Leo's office and ran out of time, knowing his schedule, when he would return home from work. Or maybe they were just neater elsewhere. But if it were so crucial to retrieve whatever it was Leo possessed, then why try to ice him? It made no sense, unless they figured with Leo dead his secret would die with him.

One thing was obvious: Whatever it was they wanted, they didn't find it. Why else snatch Sarah? Which added credence to the idea that they tailed us here. Then I remembered the sound of a car leaving when I first came to. I felt in my pocket for my car keys, and they were there. So they didn't rip off the company Chevy. There had been no other car parked nearby when we arrived. So, they followed us. Had to be.

I locked the study door behind me and replaced the key atop the door frame, then climbed back up the stairs to check the bedrooms again. I figured if there were anything to be learned it would be in the master bedroom, so I searched the two guest rooms and my old bedroom first, just to get them out of the way, being thorough.

Each of the small guestrooms held a queen bed and a chest of drawers with a television resting on top. No curtains over the windows, no decorations, a solitary landscape painting over each of the beds. I turned one of the TVs on and, sure enough, there was no signal. The cable modem was down. Both guest room closets were empty with armies of hangers ready to do their duty. One room had a plastic palm tree in the corner, the other a small telescope aimed out the front window, perhaps for visitors with voyeuristic tendencies.

I'd already moved most of my stuff from my old room to my efficiency apartment. Where my cardboard cutout of Mr. Spock once stood guard between my old bed and desk was empty space. My superhero coffee mug collection, once gracing the windowsill, was in my tiny apartment kitchen. But the bookcase full of science fiction and detective novels was still there, protected by Philip Marlowe and John Carter, the warlord of Mars.

In the master bedroom, I opened the first of two walk-in closets. It was Leo's. His shirts were grouped by colors, although most were white. On an adjoining rack, his pants hung neatly, again, color coordinated. His suits, all in his trademark off-white, were grouped on a lower rack. Nothing revealing other than the statement the closest made about Leo's anal retentiveness. Sarah's closet was a disaster, clothes balled up on the floor, belts and necklaces hanging from hooks one atop the other, no discernable order to how her dresses, shirts and blouses were hung. She had either been in a rush to pack or she was a slob.

Next, I turned my attention to Leo's dresser. It was a six-drawer upright. The top drawer held watches, handkerchiefs and the ordinary bric-a-brac one would find in any man's dresser. Socks, neatly arranged by color in drawer two. Boxer shorts, assorted colors, in drawer three. Next came Bermuda shorts and polo shirts. Nothing useful.

I approached Sarah's dresser with a twinge of unease. It felt funny poking around in her private things. Hers was a six-drawer horizontal dresser of pale oak matching Leo's with three drawers on each side. The first drawer I opened, top right, was a jumble of panties. Subsequent drawers were filled with bras, shirts, shorts, and an entire drawer with jewelry boxes of various sizes—filled with earrings, necklaces, watches and rings scattered about. They offered no clues other than Sarah was in desperate need of an organizational consultant.

A wide mirror hung on the wall over her dresser, and once again I assessed the damage. My forehead was swollen and pulpy, blood oozing from the point of impact above the bridge of my nose, a mess of torn skin and bruises. I looked like Mike Tyson had bitten my forehead.

Their bathroom was my next stop. It was a two-sink, two medicine-cabinet affair. His and Hers. Leo was an Old Spice, Crest, Head & Shoulders, and Gillette Trac 2 kind of guy, everything organized, arranged on three shelves, tallest bottles to the left, descending to the shortest on the right with toothbrushes, hairbrushes and fingernail clippers on the middle shelf, medicine on the bottom. I retrieved the medicine bottles and examined them. Motrin, Tums, Claritin. There was a bottle of Lipitor for cholesterol. The last was a prescription bottle filled with pills for high blood pressure. Was Leo having heart problems?

Sarah's cabinet held Jessica McClintock, Colgate, Lady Schick, and Suave shampoo. I reached into the medicine cabinet and picked up the bottle of Jessica McClintock. I sprayed a small burst into the air and sniffed. It evoked memories of Sarah: Sarah at Kelso's, Sarah in the car earlier in the evening. I read once that everyone has a dominant sense, that people whose foremost sense was hearing, for instance, would prefer blindness to becoming deaf. Inconceivable to me, but there you have it. At that moment, though, I understood the power of scent, the emotions it could evoke. Jessica McClintock was Sarah Strano.

I put the bottle of cologne back on the shelf and stepped out of the bathroom, concerned about the medications I had found in Leo's cabinet. But I also had to admit the voyeur in me was let down that there was nothing more exotic—No Viagra? No birth control pills? No edible underwear? —to be discovered in this plundering of Leo and Sarah's most private place.

Or was it Leo's most private place?

If Leo had something to hide, why would he leave it here? Why not at the courthouse, in the safe in his chambers? Or in a tin can in the backyard? Or...

...or in the mail?

The letter Leo had dropped into the mail chute as we were leaving the courthouse Friday afternoon, could that be it? Could this thing, whatever it was that the kidnappers were looking for, could it be something Leo mailed, maybe for safekeeping? I knew I had no more time for speculation. Leo held the key to this mystery and to Sarah's safety. I needed to see him right away and find out what he was caught up in.

I left the house via the front door, turning the lock on the door handle as I did so. I fished around my pockets for the key Sarah handed me when we had arrived, but I couldn't find it. Maybe I'd given it back to her. Couldn't remember. My wallet, car keys, and everything else in my pockets were still there, though. But why not? Her kidnappers needed me to be mobile.

The blue Chevy staff car was sitting in the driveway. My Sebring was still parked curbside down the street. I eased into the Chevy and drove it over to the Mormon church nearby, parking it under a lamppost in the sprawling parking lot. I didn't want the Chevy to be discovered sitting in Leo's driveway when the sun came up. I trotted back to my car in the pre-dawn darkness, the jog reviving the banging in my skull. On an impulse, I lowered the Sebring's visor, popped open the mirror, and checked the damage again. I couldn't wander around the hospital looking like that. They'd snatch me and send me down to ER straightaway. I needed a shower, a change of clothes and...

... change of clothes.

That's what was missing in the master bedroom: Sarah's luggage. There were no suitcases, not in the bedroom, nor in the closets. I was sure of it. I started to leave the car to go back and double check, but I had locked the door to the house.

Damn.

No, wait. The garage door opener. I'd left it in the staff car on the dash. For a moment, I considered retrieving it and reentering the house, but then discarded the notion. I knew there were no bags in there. It would be pointless to retrace my steps. So what did it mean that Sarah's luggage was missing? Very considerate of a kidnapper.

I needed to get cleaned up and head to the hospital. But I hesitated about driving to my apartment. If I were being watched, I'd just lead them to my place. They might not know where I lived. Why risk giving that up? Were they tailing me right now? I peered out the car's windows. The early morning darkness surrendered little. If one of their goals was to make me paranoid, it was working.

Calm down, I told myself. Be sensible. If Robbie the Robot wanted me, he already could have had me. For whatever reason, they needed me to deliver this thing, whatever it was.

It had been just twenty-four hours since shots were first fired at Leo's house triggering this chain of events. During that time, I had been banging about like a blind man in a maze, clueless where any of this was leading. I needed to talk to Leo.

But first, I needed to recruit some reinforcements.

CHAPTER 21

MORRISON HAWKER'S HULKING silhouette filled the emergency room entrance of Good Samaritan Medical Center, his polished charcoal scalp almost brushing the top of the doorframe where he stood glowering as I approached in the pre-dawn gloom.

"What the hell you done?" he demanded. Hawker was dressed in his trademark chinos and a white t-shirt that struggled to contain his massive pectorals. Bench-pressing 400 pounds three times a week and a regular diet of steroids will do that for a fellow.

"What took you so long?" I asked.

I had called Hawker on his cell phone as I left Leo's neighborhood a half-hour earlier. He sounded wide awake when I called and here he was clean-shaven, alert, wearing his bling—gold chain, matching ear stud, Rolex, big-ass gold ring on his right hand.

"Strange, get your white ass in here," he hissed, leading me out of the ER entryway. I was struck once again, as I often was, at the dichotomy between his intimidating physical presence and his whispery high-pitched voice.

"Restroom down there," he pointed toward the hallway. He was holding a yellow Izod golf shirt. "Hurry up now. Here's a clean shirt. Like you asked."

I checked the tag for the size of the shirt he had handed me as

I walked to the bathroom. Large. My size, but much too small for Hawker, even if he were going for the tight-shirt, gosh my shirt, it must have shrunk, weight-lifter-on-steroids look. I decided not to ask where he got it.

In the hospital restroom, I stripped off my rumpled and bloodstained denim shirt and tossed it in the overflowing trashcan. Start of a new day and the janitor hadn't cleaned the restrooms yet. I cupped my hands under the faucet and water began pouring out, activated by a motion sensor. No need to touch the handles. Can't be too careful about germs. Especially in hospitals.

"You a real mess," Hawker said, pacing the floor behind me impatiently while I splashed tepid water on my face trying to dissolve the dried blood. "We fiddle-farting here," he belly-ached. "We should talk to the judge."

I got Hawker's anxiety, but he was being pushy.

I yanked a paper towel free from the wall dispenser and gently dabbed my face. "Take a chill pill Mohawk," I said. "That's why we're here; to talk to Leo. But we can't just go barreling up there with our hair on fire. Gotta keep our cool."

I appreciated Mohawk showing up on a moment's notice. The guy was somebody you could count on when the going got weird. But I was struggling with the kidnappers' admonition not to call the cops. If I ignored them, would I put Sarah in greater jeopardy? If I didn't, would I forsake an opportunity to save her?

The feds were expecting Sarah to arrive in Salt Lake. By now, they'd know something had gone sideways. If I didn't alert the FBI, they'd be coming after me. Was that a bad thing? Or was that an opportunity? Or was I clueless?

The gash in the center of my forehead was still oozing and I dabbed it with a damp paper towel.

"While I'm standing here bleeding to death, I got a question for you," I said.

"Huh?"

"You been talking to that puke Elmore James?"

"James?" Hawker shook his head. His eyes were wide in surprise. If he were faking, he was good at it. "Haven't told that douche bag nothin'."

I decided to ignore his double negative. And I hadn't asked him if he had *told* James anything. "Then why is your phone number in his notebook?"

"Fuck I know?" his voice rising, though still raspy, irritated with my line of questioning. "Go ask *him*."

"Our story yesterday said Leo got a phone threat. You know about that?"

"No. But the judge gets threats all the time. We don't pay no mind."

"James didn't get that from you?"

"No. I called *you* about that, remember, when I saw his story."

Oh, yeah.

"Right," I said. I wanted to catch him in a lie. Hadn't worked. He was either genuine or a very good liar; either way, I was feeling like a jerk. Besides, I needed an ally, so it was time to make amends. "I believe you," I said.

I turned back to the mirror and blotted the center of my forehead with the damp paper towel again.

"You bring Band-Aids?"

"Here you go," he said. His voice was back to normal—if you can ever call it normal—so my apology must have mollified his feelings.

Hawker removed a strip of dark brown tape from a box marked Rainbow Aids.

"What the hell is that? It looks like electrical tape."

"It's for African Americans. Matches our skin. Not that pink stuff you call 'flesh.' Flesh comes in all colors."

"Whatever."

Hawker placed the brown bandage on my forehead, and I turned to inspect it in the mirror. I had grown a third eyebrow—albeit a wide, flat one—in the center of my forehead. I looked ridiculous, but no worse than a pink Band-Aid on a black person. Turnabout's fair play.

I dampened some paper towels and washed off my upper body. No deodorant, but it would have to do. Then I slipped on the polo shirt Hawker had brought. It fit tighter than I expected.

"You been workin' out?" Hawker asked.

"Twelve ounce curls, every afternoon."

We left the restroom and walked toward the elevator bank at the far end of the hallway. Seeing the elevators reminded me of how Leo had dropped that envelope in the mail slot at the courthouse, and I mentioned it to Hawker. He shot me an appraising glance, but before he could say anything I threw him a curve.

"Mohawk, does it seem odd to you the kidnappers would bring Sarah's luggage with them?"

"Why not?" He had an unusual expression on his face, not the Shar-pei thing, something else.

"It just doesn't seem to fit. I mean, how the hell would her abductor know she already had bags packed, and why would he care?"

"You said they tossed the place?"

"On Thursday afternoon."

"But they were going through it again? Looking for…planting… taking out bugs?"

"Or looking for something else…"

"Right. Maybe looking for something else. Maybe the bugs have nothing to do with you gettin' slugged. Maybe they found her suitcases before you got there. Just took them along."

I nodded. "Hell, for all we know, maybe the cops grabbed them for some reason. Or maybe someone else was in the house."

"Right," Hawker said. We stepped into the elevator, and he pushed the "up" button. "Back up. What you said earlier. You thinkin' about the letter? The one the judge mailed at the courthouse?"

I nodded. The elevator doors closed and I felt the walls closing in. Soon they would crush us. There was no way out…

"Are you listening to me?"

"Sure. What was it?"

"You think it might be what the kidnapper's looking for?"

"It what?"

"The letter, fool."

"Oh, yeah. Could be. Or maybe it was in Sarah's luggage. Sarah was leaving town. Maybe Leo gave it to her for safekeeping."

"Nuh-uh," he said.

"Why not?"

He shot me a disgusted look, like I was a scorpion that needed squashing. "Think about it. The package or whatever they want in the suitcase, they got the suitcase, why call you?"

Duh.

"You know," I said, "if the feds find out about the kidnapping, first thing they're gonna do is grill Leo about what the kidnappers are after." Talking this out helped with the claustrophobia.

"Yeah," Hawker agreed. "You thinkin' the summons the judge got, that about what the kidnappers want?"

"I assume so."

The elevator doors slid open to a crowd scene. Nurse Sanderson and an orderly were at the foot of a gurney, which was flanked by two uniformed police officers. Volker and Collins, looking rumpled and exhausted, were at the tail end of the processional. It was Uncle Leo on the gurney, his face unshaven and grim.

"Move to the rear, please, gentlemen," ordered the uniforms.

Hawker and I did a double take then each moved to our respective corners at the back of the elevator car. The orderly rolled the gurney in just as the FBI agents made us. "Wait a minute," Volker blurted. But by then the doors were closing.

"Nephew." It was Leo, his voice weak and raspy, peering up from the gurney.

"Leo, we were just on our way to see you," I said. "What's going on?"

"It's none of your concern," Agent Volker interrupted.

I whirled on him: "Shut up, you fat fuck!"

The uniform pushed me back, but not with a lot of enthusiasm. From his facial expression, it was clear Volker had worked his charms on him, too.

"We're moving the judge to a more secure location in the hospital, Mr. Strange," said Agent Collins. "He'll also have better care there."

Nurse Sanderson nodded. "The judge had a rough night. We're moving him to ICU."

"Intensive care?" I felt a jolt of panic.

"No worries. We'll take good care of him. He's had a bad go of it, though. We want to make sure we keep an eye on him."

"Find... Sarah..." It was Leo, his voice thin, his face anguished. "Find Fred..."

Fred again?

"Talk to...talk to... Jake..."

Before he could say any more, the doors reopened and Leo was whisked out of the elevator. The two FBI agents led the gurney down the hallway while the orderly pushed from behind, nurse Sanderson trailing.

The uniformed officers blocked us as we attempted to follow.

"We have orders to restrict visitors to this floor," the cop on the right said.

"You don't understand, I have to talk to Judge Strano," I protested. "I'm his nephew. We need to talk to those FBI agents, too."

The cop shook his head, pushed the button for the lobby, stepped out and the door closed.

"What the hell was that about?" Hawker asked.

"The kidnappers must have gotten to Leo somehow."

But how? I punched the button for the fourth floor. As soon as the door opened I jogged to the nurse's station outside Leo's old room. The cop outside the door was gone. The nurse behind the desk was a middle-aged Hispanic woman with graying hair. She was adjusting a monitor at her workstation.

"Ma'am," I interrupted. "My name is Alex Strange and I am Judge Strano's nephew."

She looked up and frowned. "I'm sorry, sir, but Judge Strano is no longer here."

"Yes, I know that. I was just wondering. Do you know if he received any telephone calls while he was here?"

"I doubt it. Not during my shift. We were told not to release his room number to anyone."

"Could we check with the other nurses?" I asked.

"Well, I could leave a note if this is important."

I thanked her and gave her my card.

"You think it was that simple?" Hawker asked. "They just called him?"

"Maybe. How else?"

He shrugged.

We were walking back to the elevator when an idea pulled me up short. I turned around and walked back to the nurse's station.

"Do you mind if I take a peek in his room, make sure they got all his stuff?"

She was on the phone and waved me on.

I swung open the door to Room 402 and walked over to the bed. No bag. I glanced around the room. Nothing. There was a small closet by the bathroom. Inside was a bathrobe, a change of clothes, a pair of hospital booties on the floor—and the powder-blue overnight bag, empty. There was nothing of interest in the bathroom.

Oh, well, it was worth a try. Then I noticed the nightstand by his bed. It had a small drawer. I walked over and opened it.

Pay dirt.

Leo's wallet, wristwatch, wedding ring—*and his cell phone*—were inside the drawer. It was an older model flip phone. I opened it and pushed the button for recent calls. The last call Leo had received—less than an hour ago—was from a familiar number. I fished out my iPhone and looked at my recent calls just to confirm. They were a match. It was the kidnapper's number. If it were a disposable phone, they had used it to call Leo before ditching it.

So Robbie the Robot had managed to reach Leo. Maybe that call put him over the edge. How very clever of them to call him on his cell phone. Never would have occurred to me. Then again, there was just one person who knew the phone was here: Sarah.

I shivered at the mental image of what they might have done to get that information from her, to get his number.

I shoved Leo's phone, wallet and other things into my bulging pockets.

"What now?" Hawker asked as we re-entered the elevator.

I took a deep breath. "You ever play post office?"

CHAPTER 22

HAWKER AND I parked our cars by the Orpheum Theater on Adams Street, crossed Cesar Chavez Plaza, and approached the entrance to the Superior Court Complex, set back from Jefferson Street by a broad plaza. To the right, a statue of a riderless horse standing atop the Book of Justice honored fallen law enforcement officers. To the left and nearer the double glass doors leading to the courthouse entrance were a quartet of naked green people—a man holding a child on his shoulders flanked by his wife and another child. Looked like they were running. I'm not sure what those statues were supposed to symbolize. Maybe they'd had their day in court and were fleeing without so much as the shirts on their backs.

The courthouse was closed to the public on Saturdays, but Hawker used his magnetic key card to slip into the building through an unguarded employee entrance. It was hidden from the street behind a circular auditorium that fronted the courthouse off the plaza. By taking this route, we bypassed the main lobby with its guard station and metal detector.

"Some security system you got here," I said.

"What?"

"If somebody wanted to blow up this place, all they'd have to do is conk somebody like you on the head, swipe their keycard and do what we're doing on a weekend when nobody's around. Saunter in, plant a bomb, and wait for the place to fill up on Monday morning. Then boom."

"Some of us are easier to conk on the head than others."

"Nobody as big and tough as you, of course, but you get the point."

"Don't forget the cameras."

"Where?"

"Up there." Hawker nodded toward a small ceiling mounted video camera. "Over there, too."

"So we're on Candid Camera."

"Check."

"I didn't see anyone at the guard post when we passed by the front door," I said. "Do you think the place will be empty?"

"No. There'll be security monitoring the cameras."

"Which means we might stumble across a guard while we're up to no good."

"No sweat," Hawker said. "You with me. I got twenty-four-hour access to the building. Besides, I know most these guys." With that, Hawker looked up at the nearest camera, smiled and gave it a brief wave.

"Show off."

"We on a mission from God. Relax."

"Last time I heard, knocking off a post office box was a federal offense, ungodly to the max."

"Check," Hawker said. "But we ain't gonna to do that. Just goin' to the mailroom—not the post office. First, we go upstairs."

The mail drop for the courthouse was off the main elevator bank behind the lobby. Hawker led us to a service elevator at the far side of the building and pushed the "up" button.

"Can't we take the stairs?" I asked.

"Cameras will record us going to three," he said. "Get questioned, I needed some paperwork. Or something in my desk. We go up, then take the stairs down. Behind the lobby elevators."

"Devious."

"I've been devious for a long time. Besides, I really do need something in the office."

We stepped out of the elevator on the third floor to a dimly lit hallway. Someone had forgotten to turn down the air conditioning, too.

"Saving electricity, I see."

"You're welcome."

Uncle Leo's chambers were down the corridor. Hawker slipped his electronic key card into a receptacle by an unmarked door just beyond the main entrance to the courtroom.

"I like using the back door," he said. He gave me a sideways glance to see if I got it.

I rolled my eyes. "Whatcha need in here?" I asked, but Hawker was already through the entryway and heading toward the receptionist's desk. He fished around her center drawer for a moment and pulled out a ring-full of keys.

"Ah-hah!" he said, pleased with his chicanery. "Mailroom key."

We exited Leo's chambers through the same unmarked door and strode to the reception area where during the week lawyers and plaintiffs and defendants and witnesses commingled outside the courtrooms on that floor. There were no cameras here in the interior hallways. They were reserved for the main lobby and the entrances and exits. We opened a gunmetal gray door and descended two flights to the first floor. Hawker led us down the carpeted interior hallway to another door.

"We're right behind the elevator bank," Hawker said in his hushed voice. "Mail chute dumps into here."

A sign on the door said USPS ONLY. My heart sank. Underneath were printed the pickup hours: Monday-Friday 11 a.m. and 5 p.m. Leo had dropped the letter as we were leaving the building, precisely at 5 p.m.

While Hawker was fumbling through the keys trying to find the right one, I reached over and turned the door handle. It was unlocked.

"Security in this building is staggering."

We stepped inside and Hawker flipped the light switch.

"Oh, crap," I moaned.

The mailroom was empty.

Either nobody in the courthouse tried to mail anything after 5 p.m. and the post office had already picked everything up, or someone else had beaten us to the punch earlier in the day.

"What do you think, Mohawk?" I asked. "Who did this? The bad guys or the mailman?"

"It's postal worker."

"Whatever."

Hawker tapped his foot several times and stared at the ceiling. "No way of knowing. But they called the judge. So they didn't find what they were looking for. If they were here at all."

I considered that for a moment and let out a deep breath. "Right. So, either they don't have the letter or they do and it's not important. But if it is what we're looking for, then it will show up in somebody's mailbox soon."

"Either way, the kidnappers still need Sarah," he said.

"So where else should we look? Back up in chambers, right?"

"Uh huh."

We slipped out of the mailroom, turning the light off behind us, and headed back to the stairs. Suddenly Hawker froze in mid-stride. "Just thought of something. Prints. We need to go back and wipe down the room."

"No, we can't do that," I said. "Our prints will be on the door handle and light switch, sure, but if we go back in there and wipe the room we might be destroying evidence, evidence that might lead to the kidnappers."

Hawker squinted at me, his face tightening. It was clear he didn't like that idea at all.

"In fact, Mohawk, we need to *tell* the FBI. The sooner they can get here the sooner we may find out who is behind this."

"Hold on. Hold on." Hawker was shaking his head. "You sure you wanna do that? Kidnappers said no cops. Better think about that."

What might happen is we might catch the sons-of-bitches. But I didn't need to debate it with him. First, we needed to search Leo's offices. At least I'd talked him out of wiping the room.

We re-entered Leo's chambers and flipped on the lights.

"Hmm, if you were a mysterious whatever, where would you be?" I asked.

"There's the safe," Hawker said. "The filing cabinets. Computer files."

"Hell, it could be taped under his toilet seat," I said. "We look everywhere."

And then my phone began vibrating.

"Mr. Strange?" a familiar voice answered.

"Collins, what the hell is going on with my uncle? He looked awful."

He ignored that. "Mr. Strange. we need to speak to you. Right away."

"Good. I have a few things I have to tell you." I looked up to see Hawker glaring at me.

"Where are you now?" Collins asked.

"Uh, well, not far. Where do you want to meet?"

"FBI headquarters. Thirty minutes."

"No good."

"What do you mean, no good? I'm not asking, I'm telling you."

"That ain't going to cut it, Collins. Not that I don't trust you, but I don't trust you. I can't have my freedom of movement restricted right now."

"How about I arrest you? That restricted enough?"

"How about I run over to the newspaper first and let the world know Sarah Strano's been kidnapped," I said. I had no intention of doing anything of the sort, but he didn't know that. I glimpsed

Hawker out of the corner of my eye and could see him wince. He *really* didn't want me bringing in the feds.

"How do you know about that?" Collins demanded. He was shouting.

"I know because I was there when she was snatched."

"What!"

"Yes. I was there. That's why I was on my way back to the hospital…"

"You should have called us the instant this happened…"

"The instant it happened I was knocked cold."

"Mr. Strange, you need to come in right away."

"Look, Collins, the kidnapper is planning on contacting me again. He expects me to get something from my uncle. Got no clue what that is, but I can't do Sarah any good if I'm Guantanamoed, now can I?"

"Mr. Strange, you're interfering with a kidnapping investigation."

"Look, there's one more thing. He warned me not to go to the cops. He said not to go to—and I quote—'your buddies at the FBI.' He said he was watching me, has been watching me. If I show up at your doorstep, I could jeopardize Sarah."

"Mr. Strange, you're a newspaper writer, not a law enforcement officer. This is no time to be playing games. You're putting Mrs. Strano's life at greater risk by not cooperating. Now, will you voluntarily meet with me or do I have to get a warrant for your arrest?"

I wouldn't do Sarah, or Leo, any good behind bars. I'd pushed back as hard as I could.

"OK, Collins. As the Italians like to say, I give up. FBI headquarters it is. Be there soon."

I turned to Hawker feeling defeated and exhausted. "I'm sorry, Mohawk, there's no way to avoid this."

He nodded. "You're cornered. But I'm not. I'm going to go through this office. Every inch. I'll call if I find anything."

"But look, I'm going to have to tell them we were here. They could storm over here, so you may not have a lot of time."

"Hey, I work here. They wanna make somethin' out of that, let 'em."

I nodded. "Call me."

"Yeah, I'll call. But careful what we say. Big Brother has big ears."

I nodded, ready to leave, but I paused for a moment to scan Leo's office one last time. Earlier, it had seemed like such a good idea to search the place. Now, somehow, I had a sense of foreboding, like it had been a big mistake and, maybe, an even bigger one to leave Hawker to snoop around without me. What that was about, I don't know, but he caught the uneasy look on my face and rested one of his gigantic paws on my shoulder.

"Game ain't over till we win," he said.

Nice line. Supposed to be reassuring. But it wasn't.

CHAPTER 23

THE FBI PHOENIX Division is housed in a gleaming, new five-story building in the northern part of the city. When seen from a drone, the rock garden outside the entrance is designed to resemble a fingerprint. The narrow windows evoke a DNA pattern. All these extra touches went into the $155 million price tag   or about the cost of five F 15E Strike Eagle fighter jets.

Hey, freedom isn't free.

Ordinarily, it would take me just a few minutes to get there, but this was not ordinary. I drove east on Adams, top down, looking around for tails. At the first light, I turned right, then right again onto Washington heading west to the state Capitol complex—past the memorial to the USS Arizona, the battleship sunk at Pearl Harbor. There were a handful of cars and pickup trucks behind me. I pulled over at a parking meter and let them pass.

A large man with a deep tan approached the car on foot. He was wearing work slacks, a checkered shirt, and what appeared to be expensive hiking boots. He was about my height, but built like a lumberjack. He leaned into the car. "Looking for a ride to Flag," he said. "Any chance you're heading that way?"

I'm an easy mark for the homeless. Figure I could be in their shoes someday. I grabbed my wallet. The man smiled, exposing a set of perfect, white teeth, not what you'd expect on the streets.

"Not looking for a handout, friend," he said. "Just a ride." I told him I was going just a few blocks. I offered a twenty, but he waved it off and walked on.

The encounter left me a little rattled. I waited a few minutes at the curb. Who was that guy? Could he have been a tail? That was a reach. *Don't be a child. Man up.*

I cranked the Sebring and circled the Capitol, glancing around, checking my mirrors, feeling ridiculous and paranoid. The empty streets yawned at me. I drove to Van Buren and entered I-17 northbound and punched it to Deer Valley where I exited and pulled into a service station to see if any of the cars exiting the freeway behind me looked familiar. They didn't.

If I were being tailed, they had something on their cars a hell of a lot more powerful than Stealth Car Wax—a cloaking device, maybe.

KTAR was taking a break from some Dittohead's ravings for a spot of actual news. The death toll from the Ebola outbreak in Chicago was escalating, fourteen victims now. The overnight storms had reignited the dry timber of the Tonto National Forest near Payson. Another driver on the Black Canyon Freeway had reported hearing gunshots. Police were investigating if the Black Canyon Bandito had taken aim at passing motorists again. More reports of wild dogs in Scottsdale. A Tucson family had burned to death in their home—a damaged natural gas line was suspected.

I turned the Sebring into the parking lot and stepped out of the convertible. The mid-morning sun felt hot on my back. Shimmering heat waves percolated up from the pavement. A faint breeze rustled the fronds of a line of queen palms. I felt the tingle of anxiety shoot through me; my stomach was doing flip-flops again. Wasn't I too young to have an ulcer?

"Once more into the breach," I whispered to myself as I approached the broad concrete steps leading to the entrance. I pulled the handle on the glass door. It didn't budge. I stuck my face against the glass and peered inward, but the reflective surface and dim interior surrendered nothing to my straining eyes.

"Marvelous."

I fished the business card Collins had handed me the day before and punched the number into my cell phone. After three rings, it rolled over into voice mail.

"Now what?"

Then a disembodied, tinny voice asked, "May we help you, sir?"

I spun around toward the source of the sound and realized it had come from a speaker above the doorway.

"Uh, yeah, I'm here to see Special Agent Collins. He was supposed to meet me."

"Special Agent Collins. Well, sir, I'm sorry, but we show that he's not in the building at this time."

"I tried to call him a minute ago and got no answer."

"We'll be glad to try to reach him for you. What is your name?"

"Strange. Alex Strange."

"Oh, Mr. Strange, got a note here. You're expected."

There was a loud buzzing, as if someone had poked a stick into an angry nest of hornets. I yanked at the door handle. This time it yielded with a metallic click as the magnetic lock disengaged, and I stepped into the lobby. It was chilly, the AC working full force in a deserted building on a Sunday morning. These would be federal tax dollars at work. No need to pinch pennies. Ah, the miracle of deficit spending.

The guard motioned me to take a seat on the public side of the security desk, opposite the metal detectors that have become *de rigueur* in most government facilities nowadays. "We'll reach Agent Collins for you," he said.

I sauntered over to a grouping of comfortable chairs and sat down on the one nearest the FBI seal mounted on the wall. I suddenly had the urge for a cigarette, which was bizarre since I didn't smoke; never had. I was nervous with time to kill. That's what people did in circumstances like this—light up a coffin nail. Or fire up a nice California blunt. But I didn't do weed, either.

Impatient and irritated with wasting time, I pulled the iPhone from my back pocket and began dictating brief notes to myself.

TO DO:

Call Edwina. (What does she know?)

Call Mohawk. (Has he found anything?)

Charge cell phone.

Track down that swine Elmore James.

Call Dani Vaquero. (Can she help? How?)

Get tickets to D-Backs for Bevin.

I clicked off my notes and noticed I had a text message. It was from Brett Barfield. He had the IDs on the plates I he'd given him. I jotted down the names and addresses in my notebook. Two were women from Phoenix. One, a man from Goodyear. The final was a federal government plate—no specific name attached. The government plate was the most intriguing. Could Barfield find out who had been driving that car? Before I could call him back, my phone vibrated.

I looked at the home screen. It was two o'clock and the caller ID said it was Collins.

"Mr. Strange?" His voice was quavering.

"Where are you?"

"Hospital. Listen. Something's happened. Your uncle seems to have suffered a heart attack or a stroke or something. He's unconscious. They're putting him on a respirator."

"What?"

"Yes, it's serious. You better get over here right away."

"You're not fucking with me?"

"No. I'm sorry."

"OK, I'm coming."

"Mr. Strange?"

"Yeah?"

"You might want to say a prayer on the way over."

CHAPTER 24

THE SCENE IN the ICU was chaotic. I stood paralyzed in the doorway, panic-stricken at the possibility of Leo's dying. Nurse Sanderson grabbed me by the hand and escorted me to a chair in the hallway. She tried to be comforting, saying the things nurses say to people like me in situations like that. But when she told me that if Leo died he would "go to a better place," I snapped.

"Maui is a better place. The south of France is a better place. Fucking dead is not a better place."

I jumped out of my chair. "And another thing…" But as I looked down at her and saw the stricken look on her face, I shut up and skulked away feeling like a jerk. But, still, I didn't want her's—or anyone's—sympathy.

The FBI agents had been giving me some space, letting me come to grips, but with that outburst Collins intervened. "Come on, Mr. Strange, let's go get a cup of coffee."

Out of the corner of my eye I saw a flash of movement by the elevator. The door opened and a man scurried in. I recognized him. A TV puke from Fox News.

The uniformed cop who had escorted me turned and bolted toward the elevator, but he was too late. Any notion that Leo's change of condition might be kept under wraps had evaporated.

We took the stairs to the hospital's coffee shop and I gave the feds a statement, telling them everything I could recall about the night before. I suppose I should have held back some things, like discovering the bug under the table, but I didn't. I still harbored deep concerns about who the kidnappers might be, and the fact that the weapon used to shoot at Leo was a favorite of the FBI added to that anxiety. Why should I trust these guys? But with Sarah's life on the line, what choice did I have? I waited until the very end of the conversation to tell them about Hawker and me searching the courthouse mailroom. I wanted to give him as much time as possible to go through Leo's chambers.

"Jesus Christ," Volker grumbled. "You fucking amateurs."

Collins squinted at the profanity. Maybe he *was* Born Again. Right about now, I wouldn't mind starting over myself.

"Tell me something, Volker," I said. "Were you the guys who ransacked Leo's study?"

He sneered at me.

"You had a warrant to search the place, right?"

Neither agent said anything.

"Come on, guys. Search warrants are public records."

"It wasn't us," Collins said. "But if you knew the judge's office had been ransacked, why didn't you say something about it earlier? In fact, Lt. Warren said you warned her not to enter the study. Did you know about the burglary then?"

I thought about being cute. Telling them I could neither confirm nor deny, give them a taste of their own medicine. But this wasn't the time for foolishness.

"Leo told me about it the night before," I admitted.

"And you kept this secret, why?"

I took a deep breath. "I promised him I wouldn't say anything about it. But it's pretty clear now that he has—or had—something somebody, including you guys, want really fucking bad. I don't know what that is. And for all I know, it was you guys who trashed his office…"

"Come on!" Collins said. "You know better."

I shook my head no. "Before all this, I would have agreed with you. But something is sideways here and I'm not in a trusting mood." I pulled out my notebook and pen.

"You bug Leo's house, was that you? You have a warrant to do that?"

"We're done here."

The agents insisted that I accompany them to the courthouse, but I dug in my heels. "You know what I know. As soon as I hear from the kidnappers, I'll call you."

"You ain't callin' the shots here, pal," Volker said. "You're either coming with us or you're going to jail."

"Try hard not to be stupid, Volker," I said. "If I'm in jail, it will be all over the news. I can promise you that. Then what? You think that will help get Sarah back?"

"You need to accompany us to the courthouse, Mr. Strange," Collins said. "Agent Volker is correct."

"No. I am not leaving this hospital. I am going back down to the ICU."

Volker's face turned red, and he rose from his chair. Maybe he was going to cuff me. But Collins intervened.

"All right, Mr. Strange. All right. These are unusual circumstances. But keep your cell phone on and do not leave. We are not finished yet."

The coffee shop TV was tuned to Fox News. Just as we were leaving, the station broke in with the story of Leo's lapsing into a coma. That didn't take long.

I left the cafeteria and returned to the ICU to look in on Leo. It was an awful sight. A respirator had been taped to his mouth, pumping air into his lungs. I didn't want to think about the implications of having that tube jammed down his throat would have for his broken jaw, which the doctors had to unbandage. Good thing he was unconscious.

A middle-aged woman in a blue suit walked up from behind me and tapped me on my shoulder.

"Excuse me, sir," she said. "Are you a relative of Judge Strano's?"

I figured she was going to give me some grief for invading the ICU, but that wasn't it.

"Yes, I'm his nephew," I said.

"Would you happen to know if Mrs. Strano is in the hospital? We have some papers for her to sign."

Figured it was insurance, but that wasn't it, either. She showed me a document entitled: "Durable Power of Attorney."

"Mrs. Strano needs to sign these release forms so that we can void Judge Strano's living will," she said. "Or she can choose not to, of course."

"What's that mean?" I asked.

The woman cocked her head and paused. "Well, I should discuss this with Mrs. Strano. We have very strict privacy rules these days, you know." She was referring to a federal law that went by the acronym HIPPA, short for the Health Insurance Portability and Accountability Act, which, among other things, makes it very difficult to examine people's medical records. Reporters hate that law.

"Is this about his medical records?" I asked.

"Not exactly."

"Well, perhaps I can help. I'm not just his nephew, I'm his adopted son and, if it matters, I am in his will."

"Well, it's just a formality," she said. "But Mrs. Strano has the judge's power of attorney according to our records from when he was here two years ago."

I remembered that. Leo had cut his chin falling into his hot tub and required stitches. He was drunk as a skunk. But that would have been a previous Mrs. Strano.

"Is that up to date?" I asked, pointing to the document.

"It's what we have on file." Then she giggled. "The language is actually quite funny."

I guess I didn't get the joke. She pulled down her smile. "It states that his wife, a Mrs. Dorothy Evans Strano, has his durable power of attorney or..." she started to laugh again "...or her successor."

At that, I smiled, too.

"Yeah, that sounds like Leo. The current Mrs. Strano is named Sarah. What does she have to do?"

"She doesn't have to do anything," the woman said. "But unless she signs this form, the judge's end-of-life instructions are to be followed to the letter with no exceptions."

"Can you translate that for me?" I asked. "I'm a journalist. Small words help."

She placed a hand on my shoulder. "What it means is that unless his wife instructs us otherwise, after forty-eight hours the doctors are to discontinue life support."

Rocket Docket to you; Uncle to me

By Alexander Strange

Phoenix Daily Sun

He is renowned for his tireless work habits, his obsession with punctuality, his unvarnished bluntness and the off-color jokes that, on two occasions, have earned him censures from the Arizona Bar Association.

He has made headlines, most recently for trying to block the federal government from building what he called a "torture chamber" in Arizona.

They call him the Rocket Docket because he moves more cases through his courtroom than any other judge in Maricopa County.

I just call him "Uncle." That was his title before he adopted me, and it has stuck.

Uncle Leo — Superior Court Judge Leonard D. Strano to you — would have found the commotion surrounding him Sunday morning at Good Sam richly ironic had he been conscious to witness it.

An unapologetic liberal, Uncle Leo is revered by plaintiffs' lawyers who practice before his bench. The Medical Association loathes him. He has handed down more malpractice judgments against physicians than any other judge in the state.

Imagine, then, his amusement—or perhaps bemusement—if he could have left his body to see the dozen or so doctors and nurses, surgeons and orderlies, the tangle of tubes and wires, the defibrillator, the desperation on their faces, their ferocious determination to restart his failing heart and their heartbreak when he slipped into a coma.

"Fools," he would have told them. "Do you have any idea how

much saving me will cost you? Spare yourselves and let nature take its course."

He had been admitted the day before after cracking his head on the red brick of his front patio. Again, irony. The fall, a tumble he took after being stung on the foot by a scorpion, may have saved his life. A hail of bullets flew harmlessly overhead as he hit the deck.

Who fired those shots and why remains a mystery.

The initial diagnosis after Uncle Leo was airlifted to the hospital was a broken jaw. When I last visited him, his mouth had been bandaged shut. But he had also been in shock when admitted to the hospital, and Emergency Room doctors discovered that he had been stung not once, but twice, by a bark scorpion whose toxic venom, while rarely fatal to an adult, can nonetheless cause intense pain and may lead to other medical complications, such as convulsions.

It appears that Uncle Leo, barefoot in the early morning, no doubt retrieving his newspaper, was stung on the bottom of his right foot when he and a member of the genus *Centruoides* had an encounter of the worst kind. He told me that as he lay on the patio, stunned from the impact of the fall, it attacked him again.

To counteract the scorpion venom, doctors administered antivenin and tetanus vaccine and antibiotics and antihistamines. To combat the agony of the scorpion's stings, they gave him painkillers. To restore his heartbeat, they gave him their all.

It may have been all for naught.

He now lies comatose in the hospital on a respirator. The medical staff will wait forty-eight hours before pulling the tubes, a stipulation of Uncle Leo's living will.

What caused this? It could be that the combined stress of being shot at, breaking his jaw, the blow to his head and the cocktail of pharmaceuticals injected into him was too much to endure, doctors surmise. Or it could be some subset of that. Were the convulsions he was experiencing a reaction to the scorpion's venom, sheer agony from the stings themselves, or something else—perhaps something related to the fall? Or was something else broken in his aging body?

While doctors attempt to answer those questions, it will be up to others to solve the mystery of how Uncle Leo's life became so tragically unraveled in the course of a few hours.

Who wants him dead? Is it revenge for some previous decision from the bench? Or is it an attempt at intimidation? If so, they don't know my uncle very well.

I never knew my father. My mother drowned when I was a child. Since then, Leonard Strano, my mom's older brother, is the only family I've had.

It was Uncle Leo who saw to it that I finished high school and got a college education. When there was no one else, he saw to it that I had a roof over my head, food in my belly and, more important than anything else, that I wasn't alone in this world.

Now it looks like I might be.

Uncle Leo has never been a religious man. If it comes to it, I hope his doubts about the afterlife prove misplaced.

So, too, his skepticism regarding the competency of our criminal justice establishment, of which he was an important, if cynical, cog. I hope the police prove him wrong on that count, too

Contact Alexander Strange at Alex@TheStrangeFiles.com or at www. TheStrangeFiles.com.

CHAPTER 25

I pushed the send button. In seconds the column would appear in Edwina Mahoney's email queue. It also would be routed automatically to the online production staff, which would post it on our website. Another version of the column would be transmitted to the newspaper's Copy Desk for publication in the Monday edition of the newspaper. Tens of thousands of readers who logged on to the *Sun's* website would see the article before the paper hit the streets Monday afternoon. Still more who subscribed to the *Sun's* daily e-newsletter would have the column sent to their in-boxes via email. A tease off my Facebook page would alert readers to find it on the website. A Twitter notice would direct traffic to the column.

I punched up Microsoft Outlook and typed in Dani's address. I attached a copy of the column in an enclosure with a note telling her it was about to be posted on our website. If the TV station wanted, I said, I'd come by to do an on-camera commentary.

Journalism wasn't my motivation for all of this. I wanted to send the kidnappers a message. That I had been there at the hospital with my uncle. Leo might be comatose, but they couldn't know what he might have told me beforehand. I was terrified that if they believed Leo was taking their secret to his grave, they would have no motivation to keep Sarah alive. They had given me a deadline, but I hadn't gotten to Leo in time to learn what the kidnappers—and the FBI—wanted.

It wouldn't take long for people to become suspicious about Sarah's whereabouts. Why wasn't she at the judge's side? What's this about a Do Not Resuscitate order? Is she just going to let him die? I could imagine all the questions that might be raised.

It was imperative that news of Sarah's kidnapping not leak out. If it did, there would be a media shit storm. The attempted assassination of a judge was big news in and of itself. Couple that with the kidnapping of his young wife and it would be a national sensation. That kind of attention would not be good for Sarah's chances of survival.

I glanced at my watch. Less than forty-six hours remaining until Leo's DNR instructions were to be obeyed. And Leo, damn him, would have it no other way. He wrote it in his living will, and he would expect his wishes to be followed to the letter. But those letters included a safety-valve. I had to find Sarah, get her to the hospital, and stop the countdown.

Me. Like I would know how to do that.

The red light on my desktop phone was glowing. I punched in my passcode. "You have twenty-three unheard messages, twenty-three messages total," the sugary computerized voice said. Most were from news organizations looking for reaction to the shooting. Several of those asked if I could help them contact the judge's wife. Little did they know.

This was the first local news story in a while to eclipse the unrelenting coverage of the fighting in Uganda and the rising death count in Chicago. I knew it would dominate the evening newscasts and would be the lead story in the Arizona Republic tomorrow morning. There would be no dodging my colleagues in the news media. I was, after all, Leo's blood relative. They would be looking for some comment from me.

I called back the reporter from the Arizona Republic and gave her a few quotes, the sort of thing you would expect from a concerned relative. I denied having any idea who would want to shoot my uncle—which was easy since I was clueless. I also tipped her to my column on the Sun's website, suggesting she might want to pull some quotes from there. I told her Sarah was unreachable, which wasn't a lie. I declined her invitation to meet in person with a photographer. I returned a call from KTAR and chattered on-air for a few minutes. Again, I denied having any knowledge of who would want to harm Leo.

My cell phone rang—it was Dani. She was at the TV station and had just received my email. She said all the right things: she was so sorry about Leo; she was concerned about how I was doing. She sounded sincere, and I believed her and appreciated the call. Eventually, though, she cut to the chase: would I do a stand-up outside the newspaper. I said sure. We agreed on a time.

I returned calls to two other television stations and in both cases ended up in voicemail, which suited me. I left a few quotes and referred them to my column on the newspaper's website. The desk phone rang and it was a reporter from the Associated Press. I gave him the same quotes I gave the Republic reporter.

The next message was from Dr. Omar Franken, his third call in as many days.

"Please, Mr. Strange, I have been trying to reach you. I am disappointed you have not responded to my emails. I must speak to you about your article. You have my number."

Click.

I deleted the message. Even though I'd been instructed by the newspaper's lawyers not to discuss my column with Dr. Franken, I had an unsettled feeling. He was being unusually persistent. Had I somehow screwed that up? Forget it, I told myself. Don't borrow trouble. The radar tests were conclusive. There's no time for that right now. Stealth Car Wax was a fraud.

The next two callers were subscribers upset that their Sunday newspaper hadn't arrived. I took calls like this with regularity ever since the Daily Sun dropped its Sunday edition in favor of a beefed-up weekend paper on Saturday. I didn't bother to forward the calls to the Circulation Department. After a while, what's the point? And I was weary of smart-assed comments from readers to the effect of "how can you be a daily paper when you're only six days a week?" And, "You call yourselves the Sun and you don't publish on Sundays?" It didn't help that I agreed with them.

The fourth call was from Sherry Ann Knight, formerly Henry Forester Knight, who claimed to have been kidnapped by aliens as a child and selected to deliver a warning to Earth about an upcoming plague from outer space. Sherry Ann had worked for Stormy Sheetz for a while before she was run out of business. Stormy was an equal opportunity employer.

The phone rang and it was Edwina Mahoney. She was calling on her cell phone en route to the office. She'd heard a radio report of Leo's condition while driving to Sunday brunch after church and had detoured to the newspaper.

Now, waiting for Edwina to arrive, I was second-guessing myself about the column I had just filed. The first obligation of every journalist is to tell the truth. Or to at least try. I was holding back things I knew. That may not be lying, but that's not the absolute truth, either. What would my journalism professors have to say about me writing a column and not mentioning Sarah's kidnapping or my own involvement?

On the other hand, I rationalized, the truth doesn't always appear like a flash of lightning. It's most often built, like a wall, a brick at a time. At any given moment, in any given story, the truth may be only partially revealed, a piece of a larger puzzle awaiting final assembly. The hope is that over time, with enough reporting, you can eventually get it right, stack enough bricks to make something that stands up, like that wall. Just because this wasn't the whole truth didn't mean it was wrong, just unfinished. Even if leaving out Sarah's kidnapping might be criticized as a break of faith with my readers, that was small stuff compared to someone's life, I told myself. Journalism isn't theology, after all.

I checked my cell phone to make sure it was charged. I switched it from vibrate to ring. How long would it be before the kidnappers called?

Something about that question tickled a synapse. What was it?

Then it struck me: My cell phone. Just a handful of people had that number. The staff never gives out personal numbers to callers. I had gotten dozens of calls today from people trying to reach me, all of them at my office phone, my only published number. The person who called me on my cell was Dani, with whom I had traded numbers. How the hell did the kidnappers get my cell phone number to call me? Not even Sarah had my number. We never talked. I started running down the list of people who shared my number, people outside the office, that is. It wasn't a long list.

CHAPTER 26

EDWINA MAHONEY STEPPED into my cluttered office, swept a magazine off the chair across from my desk, and sat down. She pulled her glasses off and rubbed her eyes.

"What a nightmare," she said.

She was wringing her hands in her lap, shaking her head side to side. A tear leaked from her left eye and coursed down her cheek.

I hate it when women cry. Not knowing what else to do, I said, "Look, Ed. He's not dead. Leo's tough. He'll pull out of this. I'm certain."

She nodded.

"And I'm fine, too."

She cocked an eyebrow. "How nice for you."

She dabbed at a tear with a finger. I grabbed a box of Kleenex and shoved it over to her. "Here. You're going to get my upholstery wet."

She pulled out a tissue and touched the corners of her eyes.

"Ed, I have to ask you something," I said.

Edwina dabbed her eyes some more, then nodded. "Shoot."

"Did Leo call you on Friday and tell you about a threatening phone call he received?"

She shook her head. "No. Not a call. I talked to him a bit at Kelso's after you left. And he didn't say he felt threatened. Just that it bothered him. But I don't think he would have brought it up if he weren't concerned."

"So why the hell didn't he tell *me* about it?" I blurted.

"You were gone."

"Huh?"

"He got the call on his cell phone. Right after you left. I saw him talking on the phone. He had a troubled look on his face. I wandered over and that's when he mentioned it."

"He took the threat seriously? He tell you what it was?"

"He didn't say. And I didn't take it too seriously. He was being a little melodramatic." She paused, pinched her nose, then shook her head. "But you know, Alex, now that I think about it, who would have his cell number?"

Great question. But I had another.

"Is that how James got that detail for his story in Saturday's editions?" I asked. "Did you tell him?"

"Not exactly. I called and left him a message. Told him to try to confirm it with Morrison Hawker. But I never heard back and we were on deadline, so I edited it in myself."

"Why?" I was surprised, but at least that cleared up how James had Hawker's phone number.

"Why not? Leonard never said it was confidential?" Edwina had straightened in the chair and was looking me in the eye. "You saying I screwed up? That I betrayed a confidence?"

"It caught me by surprise, is all, reading that in the story."

"You wouldn't have used it." It was a statement, not a question.

"No, I wouldn't have. Not without knowing more about it. But what's done is done."

Edwina leaned forward and gripped the edge of my desk. She held eye contact for a 10-count then let go. I swear, for at least a moment, there were dents on the desktop. Her hands were shaking as she folded her arms across her chest. She was beginning to tear up again.

"Look, Ed, I'm sorry. This is a tough time. But I had a reason for asking. We need to talk about this. And I don't like it when you have that look in your eyes."

"What look?" Her voice was barely audible.

"The 'I-think-I'll-fire-this-insubordinate-asshole' look."

"No, I'm going to leave now," she said. She rose and turned to the door.

"Hang on, Edwina," I said. She turned, scowled at me, and turned again to leave.

I slammed my fist down on my desk so hard the computer mouse jumped off the surface and landed bottoms up, like an overturned beetle, its glowing red underbelly exposed and vulnerable.

"Sit down!"

"Are you talking to me?"

"Right now. Sit. This isn't over."

If editors had heat vision, I would have been a puddle of Alex. But she sat.

"There's more to this than you know. You're gonna have to make a decision. What gets said here stays here. You agree?"

"Agree to what? And I don't like your tone."

"Ed, I hate trusting anyone, but I've got to trust you," I said. "But what I'm about to tell you cannot see print. You can't use this. You have to promise."

For a moment she said nothing, composing herself. She smoothed her dress and leaned back in the chair.

"Alex, I will promise you that I will not disclose anything you tell me. After all, I told you earlier your most important job right now is to help Leonard. But I will not promise that it will not see print. I've got four reporters working this story right now and there is no telling what they'll turn up. But whatever you tell me will stay between us. That I can promise."

"I understand," I said. "But this could put you in an awkward spot dealing with the reporters on the story."

"I'll put on my big girl panties."

"OK. This is going to take a little while."

She nodded. "But before you get started, you've got to tell me something," she said. "I've been dying to ask ever since I came in here."

"Shoot."

"What's with the electrical tape on your forehead?"

CHAPTER 27

"MY GOD, WHAT a fucking mess."

Edwina was in a dark mood by the time I filled her in. Midway through my recounting of the past twenty-four hours, she rose from her chair and began pacing the small space between my desk and the office door. Now she stood facing me, shaking her head and nervously twisting the ruby ring on her right hand. The bright red stone matched her fingernails and lipstick. She stopped her hand wringing for a moment and slipped her glasses off and pinched the bridge of her nose. She had more twitches than a pitcher down on the count.

"Yes, it's a mess and the clock is ticking," I said.

"You're saying only Leonard's wife can countermand his DNR instructions?" *Wife* not Sarah.

"That's what I was told."

"We could try to intervene, legally. Get our lawyer to file something."

"Can you do that?" I asked. "I've read the directive. It's very precise. Leo wrote it, after all."

"We can try. Actually, you can try. You're family. You're the one with legal standing to intervene, I'd guess."

I liked that idea. "Good call," I said.

Edwina stopped pacing and sat down. "Besides that, what's the plan?"

"Plan A is the feds find Sarah."

"Nice," she said. "In the meantime, I trust you won't be sitting around with your dick in your hand."

"Edwina, such language!"

"Stop it." Then she cracked a small smile. "That was a little crude, wasn't it?"

"But on point. No. I won't just be sitting around. Hawker's tossing Leo's chamber. Might be a clue in there."

"And?"

"And, what?"

"That's it, that's all you got?"

"I'm working on it."

She scowled. Some people scowl and it's a sign of disapproval. When Edwina scowled, it was a sign of the coming Apocalypse.

"And I have an unformed idea about using my column."

"Meaning what?"

"I want the kidnappers to know I was with Leo at the hospital. That's why I mentioned it in my column, to send a signal that there is at least a chance I know what he knows, that they can't count on him being comatose or dead to end their problems. I also left out Sarah's kidnapping, which I hope tells them that I'm playing ball."

I paused to make sure she was keeping up. She gave me bring-it-on with her hands.

"I might have to do something more explicit, use my column to communicate with them. I'm at their mercy right now, don't have their number. It's just a thought at this point, so don't get all Journalism with a Capital J on me."

"I'm cool with that," she said.

"You are?"

"You look surprised."

"I am. I figured we would have to fight about it. I was even prepared to offer you complete deniability."

She snorted. "Like a Watergate plumber."

That was embarrassing.

"Look, the column I wrote is accurate…"

"Please…"

"…as far as it goes. Just because I don't tell everything doesn't mean what I do tell isn't factual."

"No. It just means it isn't the whole truth." She ran her hands through her hair. "Look, I already told you I was chill with it. You're not lying. You're self-censoring. And for a good reason. But don't try to gussy it up. We aren't being completely honest with our readers, but let's at least be honest with one another."

"Whatever."

"Exactly. Whatever. We print all we know, somebody may die. We wait, who knows, maybe we save a life and live to write another day. This isn't even a close call as far as I'm concerned."

"They don't teach that in journalism school," I said.

"Welcome to the school of life."

Edwina looked at her watch. "It's six o'clock. I'm leaving. Try to stay out of jail. Let's regroup here at nine o'clock tomorrow."

"Roger."

"Meanwhile, has Hawker checked in?"

I shook my head and held up my cell phone. "He doesn't call, he doesn't text. I don't know what to think."

"Do you always have to be funny?"

She was strumming my desktop with her claws.

"How do you type with those nails?'

She ignored that. "You trust him?"

"As much as I trust anyone, which isn't a lot—you excepted, boss—but there's something sketchy about him that I can't put my finger on."

"He has an unusual background," Edwina said, "but Leonard always spoke well of him."

"When was that?" I asked.

"Oh, now and again."

Edwina let out a deep breath and paused, resting her rubied hand on the doorframe. She looked down at her feet, then turned to meet my gaze, reading my mind.

"You're wondering about me and Leonard. Well, don't worry. He's crazy in love with…" She couldn't spit out her name.

"Sarah," I offered.

She nodded. "Look, it's like this. Have you ever had a best friend? Someone with whom you are utterly simpatico? Somebody who, when she's not around, your day is empty?"

I considered that for a moment. She was being sincere. Offering a window into her soul. She deserved a sincere and honest answer.

I replied: "No."

CHAPTER 28

I LEANED BACK in my chair and stared at the ceiling for a moment. I wondered why Hawker hadn't called. I wondered why the kidnappers hadn't called. I wondered why I was sitting there wondering instead of doing something.

I considered driving home, changing clothes, grabbing a bite. I could use a shower. Instead, I turned to my computer and pulled up the AP budget to see what else was going on in the world:

* The war was raging in Uganda. Special Operations forces had reached the uranium mines on the border with the Congo, and operatives from Ravenous Unlimited Global Holdings were securing the area. Meanwhile, the House Minority Whip was raising questions about the Administration's close connections to the energy industry and American involvement in the conflict.

* Scientists, employing stem cells, had discovered a way to repair severed spinal cords in rats—no doubt a great relief to paraplegic rodents everywhere. Right-to-life activists were protesting the use of fetal cells in the research.

* An outfit in Chicago had invented a way to take the ashes from cremated remains and compress them into diamonds. The gift for the man who has everything. With the Ebola epidemic raging in the Windy City, there might be plenty of business for that.

* The birth rate in Singapore was dropping and to counteract that the government was outlawing the use of condoms, unperturbed by the consequential rise in sexually transmitted diseases that was certain to spawn.

* Three DeLoreans, the same classic automobiles featured in the movie "Back to the Future," had disappeared from a showroom in Naples, Florida. No sign of a break-in. No tire tracks leading outside the building. No residue from flux capacitors. They just vanished.

* A confessed cannibal in Germany was sentenced to eight years in prison for meeting another man on the Internet and eating him. The presiding judge refused prosecutors' argument for a life sentence, ruling that the defendant's motives had been misunderstood.

* And scientists announced that the blood-thinning properties of vampire bat saliva might prove an effective treatment for stroke victims. Maybe vampire bats were misunderstood, too.

My cell phone rang. It was Hawker.

"Mohawk, where you been?" I asked.

"Tied up." There was something odd in his voice. I had a hard time making out his words over the din in the background—people chattering, the indistinct sound of a television set, the clinking of glasses.

"I've been trying to reach you all afternoon," I said. "You heard about Leo?"

"Collins told me."

"You under arrest?"

"We gotta talk, but not on the phone. Where you?"

"At the paper."

"I'm at Kelso's. Meet me."

I turned off my computer, checked the desk phone one last time for messages, and took the stairs to the back lot. I steered the Sebring east on Adams, passed the Orpheum Theater, and found a parking spot near Renaissance Square right behind a red Ford F150 pickup truck. I checked the license plate: W8LFTR. Parking was congested and the sidewalks were crowded. The Diamondbacks had played a 2 p.m. rubber match with the Giants. The ballgame was over, but the bars and restaurants would be doing a brisk business with fans lingering downtown. Two steroid-eaters in wife beaters and ball caps staggered out Kelso's door. Instinctively, I braced for a confrontation as they marched toward me. Two against one. It wasn't fair, but I could always hold back. But they wove around me, laughing, belching. They piled into the pickup truck.

The chilly air washed over me as I stepped into the saloon. It was packed, just like the night before when I had been there with Sarah. Kelso and Stormy were both behind the bar, peddling drinks and raking in tips. The room was loud with laughter and the tinkling glassware. The Diamondbacks must have won.

I spotted Hawker across the room at a table near the exit, but he had company.

"Agent Collins," I said as I approached the table. "We can't go on meeting like this." Collins stared back blankly offering no acknowledgment. He looked like he hadn't changed clothes in the past two days. I wasn't quite sure, but I was willing to bet that he hadn't used a manly man's deodorant in a while either. Collins was on a course to single-handedly wreck the FBI's button-down image. Me, I had no image to wreck.

"So nice to see you, too, Mohawk," I said. "I hope I'm not interrupting anything."

"Sit down, Mr. Strange," Collins said. "We've got a few things to discuss, the three of us."

I lowered myself into an oak armchair between the two men.

"Sorry," Hawker said, staring out across the bar, avoiding my gaze.

"What happened?" I asked.

The question was for Hawker, but Collins interjected: "What happened, Mr. Strange, is that we found your friend rifling the files in Judge Strano's office."

"He works in Uncle Leo's office," I replied, all innocent. "What's the big deal?"

Before he could answer, Kelso waddled over to the table, his enormous beer belly jiggling as he walked. He placed a fleshy paw on my shoulder.

"Alex. I heard the news about the judge. I just want you to know how very sorry I am."

I looked up at the barkeep. He looked like he might cry.

"Thanks, Kelso, I appreciate that."

"Can I get you fellas something?"

"No," I said, "we just need a place to sit and talk for a minute, that alright?"

"Sure." With that, Kelso turned and wobbled away. I watched his retreat and, looking up at the television set above the bar, saw Dani Vaquero doing a live talk-back to the news anchor in the studio. I couldn't hear what she was saying, but I had a pretty good notion since she was standing underneath the covered entrance to Good Sam's Emergency Room.

Collins leaned back in his chair and as he did so his suit coat flopped open revealing a holstered automatic on his hip.

"I am very sorry about your uncle, too, Mr. Strange," he said. "Not just on a personal level but because with him comatose we may never get to the bottom of all this."

"*All this* meaning why you guys wanted to serve him in the hospital, I presume."

"That, too."

"And why you bugged his house."

He squinted at me, but said nothing.

"You wanna tell me about that?"

He rolled his eyes. "The only reason you aren't in jail right now is that we need you in case the kidnapper calls. The only reason your sidekick here isn't in jail is because it seems possible that with his intimate knowledge of the judge's office, he might come in handy.

Although that has yet to be demonstrated." He gave Hawker a look of sneering contempt.

As usual, Collins was talking several decibels louder than necessary. It's a wonder everyone in the joint hadn't heard our conversation. How does one politely tell a guy with a gun to get his hearing aid fixed?

"Collins, nobody wants to get to the bottom of this more than me," I said, "but so far, you've turned up squat."

I looked around to make sure we weren't being overheard, half expecting Collins to interrupt, but he was giving me the stone face.

"The thing we can do to help Sarah and Leo is to find what the kidnappers want. I don't know if it is a letter Leo might have mailed. Or a computer file. Or a dossier. Or a tattoo on Mohawk's ass."

I swept the room, then continued:

"Or could it be what you guys were looking for in the first place?"

Collins didn't blink.

"I got news for you, Collins: Sarah's kidnapping isn't going to stay under wraps too long. People will start wondering about her whereabouts. I've already gotten calls. It's unfashionable to disappear when your husband is in the hospital. So we don't have time for circle jerks. We've got to figure out what the kidnapper is after. If you know, you need to tell me."

If he heard me, it wasn't evident. He might as well have been tuned into a broadcast from another planet. Maybe he'd turned his hearing aid off.

"And I'm scared shitless," I continued, "because it's been a full day and I haven't heard back from the kidnappers. The clock's ticking. Only Sarah can save Leo."

Hawker reached over and grabbed my forearm. Hard. "What?"

"You don't know?"

Hawker shook his head. I told him about the DNR. "We don't find Sarah, Leo's toast."

His face crinkled up and his eyes filled with blood. I've never seen anything like that. He turned to Collins, with a look of intense hatred.

"Easy does it, Mr. Hawker."

Imagine sitting at a table with Bruce Banner when he gets pissed off. Hawker could crush Collins, and maybe me, too, if he lost control. What was that about?

"Mohawk," I said, regaining his attention. "Game's not over until we win, right? We'll figure this out."

I eyeballed the room again, but nobody was looking our way. The jukebox was playing John Volpe's remake of "The Duke of Earl." *Wheel of Fortune* had replaced the news on the television behind the bar and Stormy was fiddling with the remote. She switched it to something that elicited a round of boos. I looked up and it was the Knitting Channel. She switched to ESPN.

I turned back to Collins. He had a wry smile on his face.

"What?" I asked.

"We don't get along, do we?"

I rolled my eyes.

"Let me ask you something. I've been wondering about this all afternoon, ever since we talked at the hospital." Collins paused, waiting for some sort of acknowledgment.

"Yeah?"

"What's with the electrical tape on your forehead?"

Hawker jumped in: "It's not electrical tape, asshole. It's a Band-Aid."

"Black Band-Aids?" Collins asked. "What for?"

"It's skin colored, you racist," I replied, touching my forehead.

"Maybe for him, not for you."

"Yeah, well, I borrowed it from him. And, anyway, it's not black, it's chocolate."

"If you say so."

"Christ."

He winced. "Must you?"

"Must I what?"

"Must you use the Lord's name in vain so often?"

At that, Hawker snorted. "What? You like Born Again?"

"Yes, as matter of fact, I am," Collins said, straightening his posture, squaring his shoulders, chin up.

Bingo.

"Me, too, baby," Hawker said. "I found Jesus the day I discovered he was gay."

Collins's face reddened. "What did you say?"

"You didn't know? Jesus was queer. Had to be. He was unmarried, right? All unmarried dudes back then were gay. I read it somewhere. Made a believer out of me."

I was afraid Collins might pull his gun and shoot him. Instead, he started fiddling with the volume control of his hearing aid.

"Look, Collins, this is getting us nowhere. You wanted me here for a reason. What's up?

"What?"

"Can you hear me now?" I mouthed.

"Very funny. OK, Mr. Strange, I'm weary of this as well." He shot Hawker another withering glance. "I'm overdue for a hot shower and some sleep. And I don't relish hanging around this dive with the likes of you and Tonto here." I thought Hawker might come out of his chair and break his neck, but he just shook his head.

"Here's the deal," Collins continued. "We need to get you wired."

"Wired? How?"

"Got your phone?"

"Sure."

He handed me a slip of paper. "Log onto this site."

I opened my Safari browser and typed in the web address. "Now what?"

"Click on that link at the bottom," Collins said.

I looked at him. "Why should I?"

He gave me the dead-eye cop stare for a few moments then said, "They pull the plug in forty-eight hours."

No time to screw around. I clicked on the link and my phone went blank. I turned it to Collins. "Now what? You killed my phone."

"Give it a minute."

It was more like five, but eventually the little white apple with the bight in its side appeared and the phone relaunched.

"Now what?"

"Now," Collins said, "we will pick up any conversation—ingoing and outgoing—on your phone and be able to record it. And we will know your location at all times through your GPS coordinates."

"Big Brother lives."

That elicited a smile, but his eyes were hard. Collins had all the warmth of an undertaker's assistant.

"May I assume it is also picking up this conversation?" I asked.

"No. Good idea, but the program doesn't work that way."

"Marvelous."

"Isn't it, though?"

"Like those ankle bracelets parolees have to wear when under house arrest," I said.

Collins formed a pistol with his thumb and forefinger and gave me a shot.

"I'm not sure I like this, Collins."

"That possibility occurred to us," he said dryly. "That's why we arranged this little rendezvous. We anticipated you might not be flush with enthusiasm. But since you've been kind enough to meet us here"—he turned to smile at Hawker—"I've got agents inside and outside tagged on you. They'll track you wherever you go. The kidnapper calls, we'll be right there with you."

"I don't get it," I said, shoving the phone into my pocket. "This seems so complicated. I'm not suggesting this, but why not just Guantanamo me?"

Hawker turned to me and cautioned: "Careful what you ask for."

Collins sighed. "Locking you up, although an attractive option, might hinder our chances at catching the kidnappers. Said another way, we have reason to believe it may be useful to let you wander around. For a while."

"And that would be why?"

Collins's lips curled into a sardonic smile. "Let's just say we're going fishing and we're putting you on the hook."

CHAPTER 29

"So, you bait," Hawker smirked. He was trying to make light of the situation, downplaying his culpability in luring me into Collins' little trap. But I didn't blame him. Hawker had been caught red-handed in Leo's office. He was lucky not to be in the slam.

"Bait? I'm fine with that. If it works."

Until I came up with a better idea, what did I have to complain about?

Collins had left us seated in Kelso's and had strolled out of the tavern with perfect nonchalance, never looking back, never acknowledging who among the throng still hanging about the saloon might be his agents.

Out of the corner of my eye, I spied Kelso squeezing from behind the bar carrying a bottle and three tumblers. He waddled over and sat down at our table, uninvited but not unwelcome. "Gentlemen," he said brandishing the bottle of Bushmills, "a toast to our friend and a wish for a speedy recovery." With that he poured two fingers of whisky into each of the glasses.

We tinked our glasses and downed the golden liquor in one quick gulp. Kelso refilled the tumblers.

I hadn't ever seen an actual bottle of booze at a table in a bar before—outside of Westerns—much less a bartender drinking on the job. But this was the West and Jake Kelso wasn't just a bartender, he was the owner. I guess he could do as he damn well pleased.

"To Uncle Leo," I said. If they noticed the catch in my throat, they were too polite to show it. We downed the second round of shots. I felt the whisky burn its way down my throat and into my stomach. I liked the physical sensation, that fire in the belly. It matched the way I was feeling: inflammatory. I was ready to kill somebody. Or cry. Or both.

"I'll leave the bottle," Kelso said.

I stood up, self-conscious about keeping my balance after a couple of shots on an empty stomach. I took Kelso's fleshy hand in mine. I started to say something and couldn't. Just looked at him. I had one living relative in a coma and not that many friends. I knew I could count Kelso among the latter.

"You need anything, I mean anything at all, don't hesitate, all right?" he said.

"You bet. Thanks." There actually was something I wanted from him. I wanted to know what Uncle Leo meant when he uttered "talk to Jake" from his gurney in the hospital elevator. I needed to get him alone for a moment. Then he made it easy:

"Say, I don't mean to pry," he said, peering at my forehead, "but whatcha got there, that tape? What's that about?"

"Oh, I ran into a fist."

Kelso started to ask what I meant when I interrupted: "Say, you wouldn't have a Band-Aid here laying around somewhere, would you. Need to change this one." I reached up and felt the bandage. It was loose and peeling off my forehead. I pulled it the rest of the way off.

Kelso grimaced. "Man that's an ugly looking gash. Shaped like a horseshoe, ain't it?"

"What?" I was glad for the distraction. I stepped away from the table and walked over to the bar and peered at my image reflected in the mirror. Hawker and Kelso joined me.

"No, it's not a horseshoe," I said, "it's the letter C."

Kelso peered over my shoulder and I saw him examining my

battered image in the mirror. "Sure enough, it's a C in the mirror, but that's because it's the reverse image. Looking straight at your face, it's a backward C," he said.

"Backwards?" I asked, not quite getting where he was going with that.

"Yeah, like hot type."

"Like what type?" Hawker asked.

"Hot type," Kelso said, nodding toward a case filled with blocks of foundry type hanging behind the bar, part of the tavern's newspaper motif. "Back when dinosaurs roamed the earth and I was a young reporter working for the *Republic*, that's how newspapers were printed. You melted lead and molded it into raised type; you inked the letters; then rolled them onto paper. It was called letterpress. Because you pressed the inked letters onto the paper. The trick was, the raised letters were backwards and the words read right to left so that when they inked the paper they came out correctly."

"So, the asshole who hit me might have had a ring on with the letter 'C' on it?" I mused.

"Like they letterpressed your head," Kelso said with a sympathetic tone in his voice.

"Could be a clue to who popped me."

"Let's take a closer look," Hawker said, turning my face toward his and peering intently at my damaged forehead. He pulled on the skin to examine it and suddenly I could feel the wound start to bleed again.

"Ouch," I yelped. "Whatcha doing?"

He jumped back. "Sorry. Just lookin'."

I inspected the damaged skin again in the mirror, grabbing a bar napkin to dab at the blood that had begun seeping from the wound again.

"Man, that's nasty," Hawker said. "Might need a stitch."

"I got a first aid kit back in my office," Kelso said. "We need to get a new bandage on that. Come on back and we'll get you fixed up."

This was the opening I was hoping for, and I followed Kelso to his office. It wasn't much bigger than a walk-in closet, with a small metal desk, a clutter of papers, an adding machine, computer, and a photograph of a plump young woman flanked by a little boy and girl.

"New picture?" I asked.

He nodded while rummaging through his desk drawer in search of a Band-Aid. "Took it earlier this summer. Up at Leo's cabin on the Rim. He lent it to me for the weekend."

The woman in the photograph was Kelso's daughter. I'd seen her once or twice when she had dropped by the bar. She and her two kids had moved to Phoenix from North Carolina after her husband, a Marine, was killed during a suicide attack at a roadblock outside Baghdad.

I felt my stomach tighten. Her kids would never see their father again. Would I ever see Leo again? I recalled Friday evenings watching old movies, digging into his vast collection of pirated DVDs. And our occasional weekends up at his cabin on the Mogollon Rim and our annual fishing trip to Naples, Florida, where we never fished but watched sunsets from the deck of his converted trawler while we drank. Was that all over?

I shook it off. "I've seen her once or twice," I said. "Nice looking. Must have gotten it from her mother, huh?"

Kelso nodded, said nothing.

He handed me a business card.

"I've known your uncle for a long time, since before he was a judge, when he was practicing," he said. "When I was a reporter, he did some favors for me. Me for him, too. He asked me to give this to you. Handed it to me after you left the bar the other night."

It was Leo's official business card. I turned it over and on the back were the numbers 727 in his signature green ink.

What the hell did 727 mean?

I felt Kelso staring at me as I studied the card. I looked up and he gave me an inquiring look.

"Thanks, I appreciate your holding this for me." I slipped the card into my pocket.

"I was looking for an excuse to get you alone, to give that to you," Kelso said, having the good manners not to pry. When I didn't volunteer anything, he continued: "We do need to do something about that forehead of yours."

He fished out a Band-Aid from another drawer in his desk. "Seriously, now, you need to see a doctor and have that looked at," he said while gently applying the bandage across the gash on my forehead. "But the least we can do is cover it up in the meantime."

As I strode back into the bar, Stormy Sheetz intercepted me. "Oh, Alex, I'm so sorry," she said, embracing me. "The judge is such a sweetheart." She released her grip and held me at arms' length, grasping my triceps. Her eyes were misty. It was a new look for her. I hadn't seen this softer side before.

"Thanks, Stormy," I said.

The softness in her expression hardened. "You're a reporter. You *are* going to find out who did this, right?" Her eyes bored into mine, challenging me, offering strength, assurance, insistence—all at the same time.

"Working on it," I said.

"Good," she said, cocking her head, giving me a different look, an appraisal, and a nod. "I believe you will."

Was she psychic or did she just want to give me a boost? Either way, her earnestness was palpable. And her confidence was contagious. She held me like that for a moment. I didn't object.

Then, breaking the spell, she asked: "I know you don't have time for this right now, but when this is over, I have a proposition for you?"

"Proposition?"

She smiled. "Not that kind, silly." She allowed her eyes to stray across my face and I felt self-consciously aware how overdue I was for a shave. "Well, not this time, anyway." She winked.

I think one of Leo's scorpions must have been hiding out in my pants because I was instantly tumescent.

"My partners and I, some girls I used to work with, are starting our own Internet news service," she said. "I'm very excited."

She slipped her hand into the back pocket of her skin-tight slacks and fished out a business card. It read:

The Nightie News

Michelle 'Stormy' Sheetz

Anchor

Seeing the dumbfounded look on my face, she laughed. "You've seen the Naked News, that program in Canada, haven't you?" she asked.

"Yeah."

"Well, this is a spin-off, kind of. But instead of strutting around in front of the cameras disrobing, we're going to wear sexy lingerie. And we're going to wear it the whole time, not strip, like they do. And we'll specialize in local news; that will be our niche."

"Niche?" There was a niche market for women reading the news in their underwear?

"Right. That's where you come in. We want to talk to the *Phoenix Sun* about a partnership. You think the newspaper might be interested?"

I could only imagine Edwina's reaction, although that madman Van Wormer might go for it. "Tell you what, Stormy," I said, "I'll talk to my boss about it."

"Terrific." She gave me a 100-watt smile, patted me on my cheek and scampered back to the bar.

Hawker was sitting at the table, his eyes wide, as I walked back over. "What that about?" he asked.

"Things just keep getting weirder and weirder," I said, fishing Stormy's business card from my pocket. "Take a look at this."

Hawker looked at the card, turned it over. "What's 727 supposed to mean," he asked.

"What?" I'd handed him the wrong card.

"This from the judge? His green ink. Does it mean something?"

"Wrong card," I said. "This is what I meant to show you."

I handed him Stormy's business card. He glanced at it for a moment, but seemed uninspired by the proposition of a gaggle of former hookers doing a local TV show.

Different strokes.

"What's this mean?" he repeated, returning his attention to Leo's card.

Idiot!

"Sounds like an airplane to me," I replied, dismissively.

Hawker squinted at me for an instant. "Yeah. Seven-twenty-seven comin' out of the sky." He took another look at the card. "Only guy I know uses green ink. Has to have some meaning."

I just shrugged. "Your guess is as good as mine."

"Where'd you get it?"

This was getting tiresome. "Oh, found it in Kelso's office. No big deal."

"Maybe it is, though," he said. "Could it be an area code?"

I decided to play along. "Maybe it's a combination," I ventured.

"Maybe it's some kind of code," he said. "Like, what letters do seven two seven give you on a telephone? Could that mean something?"

I fished out my iPhone. "Seven is PRS. Two is ABC. I guess we could work through the combinations." I pulled my reporter's notebook and a Bic pen out of my back pocket and handed them to him. He began scribbling out the possible combinations.

"PAP, RAP, SAP, PAR." Hawker paused. "That do anything for you?"

"No." I grabbed the bottle on the table.

I noticed Hawker staring at me as I poured another round of shots. "You know alcohol won't solve your problems," he said.

"Neither will milk."

"Didn't you say the kidnapper gonna call you again in the next twenty-four hours?"

I glanced at my wristwatch. "Yeah. If he meant it literally, that would be around four in the morning. Most of the day's gone and I haven't got a damned thing to show for it." I threw the shot down.

"Fuck it." Hawker grabbed his glass and downed it.

I dug into my pocket. Out came a pocketknife, keys, a balled up handkerchief, several credit card receipts, two quarters, and, finally, my cell phone, now infected with a U.S. Government-made tracking virus.

"You know, Mohawk," I said, hoping to distract his attention from Leo's business card, "we live in interesting times. You realize it's been just over a hundred years since the Wright Brothers first flew? Since then we've landed on the moon, sent spacecraft to every planet in the solar system including Pluto, which isn't even a planet anymore. We got so many satellites orbiting the Earth it rivals rush hour in Dallas, and now, with this"—I held up my phone—"we can tap into the most confidential conversations between people no matter where they may be on the face of the Earth. It's a pity George Orwell didn't live to see this triumph of modern science."

As it turned out, Hawker's mind only operated on one track at a time. "Seven-twenty-seven. What the hell does that mean?"

"You mean the aircraft?" I was startled by the voice behind me. I looked up to see Garreth DePutron standing over the table. Christ, this was turning into a convention.

"Hey, Garreth," I said, alarmed at what he might have overheard. "You guys know each other?" I asked, nodding to Hawker. "Mohawk, meet Garreth DePutron. Garreth's our editorial page cartoonist. Mohawk, here, works for Uncle Leo."

While the men shook hands, I poured myself another drink. DePutron had reinvented himself again. He was wearing a baggy Hawaiian shirt, jeans and sandals. "Let me guess," I said. "Parrot head?" He winked at me. "Kelso, another glass," I shouted toward the bar. I was getting a little buzz. I liked it.

Hawker handed DePutron the business card with the numbers 727 on the back. "We trying to solve a puzzle," he said. "Any ideas?"

Damn. Why not broadcast it to the whole freaking planet? I reached over and snatched the card away from Garreth.

"It's nothing, Garreth," I said. "Come on and sit down and have a drink with us."

"What you mean nothing?" Hawker, the moron, blurted. "It could be a clue."

"Jesus, Mohawk, speaking of clues could you, like, get one?" I looked around the bar to see if this exchange had attracted any attention, but nobody was glancing our way

"So what's this about?" DePutron asked. "What kind of mystery we trying to solve? I love mysteries." He was grinning, excited, like this was going to be some fun.

"Mohawk and I were trying to guess what the hidden meaning might be in those numbers," I said. "Mohawk, if anyone can figure this out, it's Mr. DePutron, here. He's a walking encyclopedia of obscure facts and a master of Trivial Pursuit."

I slipped Leo's card into my bulging pants pocket. "OK, Garreth, pretend you're a detective and this is a clue. What would the numbers seven-twenty-seven mean to you?"

Kelso waddled over with another tumbler and I poured DePutron a shot. "You're behind," I said. DePutron, lost in thought, ignored the invitation.

He laced his fingers behind his mop of disheveled brown hair and leaned back in the wooden chair. "Well, I assume you've already run through the obvious possibilities: codes, alphabet sequences, combinations, dates and such. Have you thought about…"

"Wait a minute," Hawker interrupted. "What do you mean by that?"

"By what?"

"Well, I don't know, like dates?"

"Seven twenty-seven," DePutron replied. "That would be July twenty-seventh, right? Leo Durocher's birthday, Belarus Independence Day, the Korean War Armistice, and the annual Take Your Houseplants for a Walk Day."

"Bull…" Hawker blurted. His gaping jaw was wide enough to fly a 727 into.

"Oh you ain't seen nothin'," I said. I'd watched DePutron do this routine before. You could make some serious money in a bar betting on him. "Ask Garreth to run out pi to a hundred figures. No, on second thought, don't."

DePutron looked perplexed. "What? Did I say something?"

"No, Garreth, you did good," I said. "You are one of Mother Nature's wonders." I had encouraged this nonsense, but I knew I needed to stop it. What DePutron had said about dates reminded me of something: Leo's day planner. He put everything in there. But I hadn't seen it at his house when I looked around. Was it in his chambers at the courthouse? I needed to get Hawker alone to ask him. Creature of habit that he was, Leo not only lived by his schedule he also kept a running diary of his activities in the journal. It could have been seized as evidence by the police or filched by the kidnappers. But if not, it might hold some useful information.

I grabbed the arms on my chair and pushed myself up. "Garreth," I said, leaning over the table, "you've been a big help, thank you, but we've gotta split. Come on, Mohawk."

"Hey, this yours?" DePutron asked as we turned to leave. He was holding my iPhone. I was tempted to abandon it now that Collins had infected it with the tracking virus, but I took it from him.

I marched across the street toward my Sebring but stopped short of the curb, and I turned to Hawker who had followed me from the saloon. "We can't take my car," I said. "Nor yours. They may be bugged."

"You paranoid?

"Maybe. But there was a bug in Leo's house. For all I know the feds planted it."

Hawker's eyes got big. "So what's the play?"

"We'll walk back to my office," I said. "It's just a few blocks. We can Uber it from there, or maybe I can get the keys to another staff car if nobody's around to notice I've already got one checked out—it's parked over by Leo's house."

"Then what?"

We began hiking west on Adams. The newspaper was six blocks away. A slim young woman with coal black hair in a red miniskirt with matching high heels smiled in our direction from the corner. I returned the smile. Hawker seemed oblivious. I looked over my shoulder. If we were being followed by anyone, they were invisible.

Hawker and I had been through the mill the past twenty-four hours. He had risked a great deal breaking into the courthouse mailroom and Leo's files. And he'd gotten caught. All to help me out. Or to help Leo out, depending on how you wanted to slice it. But the next couple of moves I had to make without him. I had to try to find Leo's day planner. The place to start would be up in Scottsdale, at Leo's house. It seemed unlikely he would have left it at work; he lived by the damn thing. I had a notion of how to do it, how to get in, but it would be a one-man job.

"Hey," Hawker stopped walking, forcing me to stop and turn to face him. "I asked you a question: What the hell are we doing?"

"I've got to run an errand."

"Alone?"

"I'm afraid so."

"Bullshit," Hawker said, his husky voice rising. "We're in this together. What's this about?"

The girl in the miniskirt turned her attention to a couple of guys on her side of the street talking baseball. I turned my attention back to Hawker. This was no good. I had to keep him in my camp; I might need his help later on.

"I'm sorry, Mohawk," I said, working hard to sound sincere. "I've put you at too much risk already. I just don't feel right asking you to risk anything else. Hell, you could be in jail by now because of me."

Hawker's features softened and he put one of his gigantic paws on my shoulder.

"Not doing this just for you," he said. "The judge is more than a boss. He's my friend. I want to get to the bottom of this. Just like you."

I turned to resume our trek to the newspaper. "Here's the deal. Garreth gave me an idea when he mentioned 727 might be a date. I thought of Uncle Leo's planner. It might contain something about how he got himself, and Sarah, into this. He's religious about writing down all his activities and plans. We've got to find it, assuming the cops or somebody else hasn't already grabbed it."

Hawker nodded.

"When you were going through Leo's office at the courthouse, did you see it anywhere?"

"Now you mention it, no," Hawker said. "Wasn't looking for it. Judge probably took it with him. Never left without it."

"Any chance his new secretary would have it?" I asked.

"Nah. She was a temp. Her last day was Friday." He did his Shar Pei thing then added, "She hated me."

"Don't most people?"

He shot me the bird.

"So, she's gone now?"

"Yeah. Judge was interviewing for a new assistant before all this happened. He's had a few. Runs most of them off."

"Or marries them," I said.

"Judge said Sarah was the best," Hawker said. "Too bad he couldn't keep his fly zipped."

I paused and gently rubbed my forehead, grimacing as my hand brushed the Band-Aid. I used that as an excuse to look around again to see if we were being tailed. Hey, it works in the movies.

Two guys, young, yakking in Spanish, wearing backwards ball

caps and baggy pants were crossing the intersection behind us; a gay couple holding hands passed us on the sidewalk. Nobody was behaving conspicuously. Was that good or bad?

I turned back to Hawker. "You scoured his office and didn't notice his planner. No way we can get back in there anyway. That means it must be at the house, right?"

"You said you gave the place the once-over."

I nodded. "Did I see his planner or his briefcase anywhere around? No. I also didn't see Sarah's luggage from the night before. Which makes me wonder: are they both missing or might they still be there, maybe together?"

Hawker shook his head. "We had another theory—that the kidnappers snatched her *and* her bags."

"What if I was wrong? What if I just didn't look hard enough?" Where had I looked? I reran my mental tape of the frantic moments after I had come to after being slugged. I had searched every room, looked in the closets and bathrooms, what was left? I was groggy. Might I have missed something?

"That's lame," Hawker said. "You think we can toss the joint? Without gettin' caught?"

"Why not?" I asked, stalling.

"You kidding? We're being watched. Besides, the place will be locked up tight. Bound to have been searched, dusted for prints, taped off, under guard. Probably got a patrol car there."

Car?

The night of Sarah's kidnapping, I frantically tore through the house looking for her. At one point, right before I got the message from the kidnappers, I looked into the garage. Leo's car was there, but Sarah's wasn't, which made sense since Sarah said she and Leo got tanked at the airport bar waiting out the sandstorm then took a cab home. They must have taken her car to the airport.

Might Leo have left his planner in her car? Or had Leo, perhaps, left his briefcase in the trunk of his own car, which was still sitting in the garage, locked, the last time I saw it? I knew it wasn't in the passenger compartment of his car because I had glanced in there. I had to check out both possibilities.

The newspaper office was a block ahead, just this side of the aging New Windsor Hotel. We strolled past a huge armless saguaro flanked by a pair of squat Palo Verde. The phallic imagery was unmistakable. The author Bill Roorbach, who had stopped by the newspaper once for an interview during a book signing tour, called them the "cock and balls of Phoenix."

I stopped outside the newspaper entrance, where a golden metallic sunburst hung over the double glass doors, a design identical to the image of the sun embedded in the newspaper's masthead. A panhandler shuffled by without pestering us. A television news van pulled out of the FOX station down the street, heading east. First, Fast, Fascist.

"The night Sarah was kidnapped," I told Hawker, "I was panicked, but I don't recall seeing Leo's planner or his briefcase. Not sure it would have registered the first time I searched the place. Of course, they might have been in his study, what the kidnappers were looking for when they trashed it. But, here's the idea: what if Leo never had a chance to unpack his briefcase? It could still be in his car, in the trunk. I never looked there."

"So," Hawker said, "you're saying we break into the judge's garage? Check out his car."

"Yeah. Except I won't have to break in. I have Sarah's garage door opener." I'd left it atop the dashboard of the staff car still sitting in the Mormon church parking lot by Leo's house.

I led Hawker into the small lobby of the newspaper building and we approached the security desk to sign him in as a guest.

"Working Sundays, huh?" the guard asked. I hadn't seen him before, but there was a lot of turnover on the security staff. Most worked part-time. The guard from earlier in the day had clocked out. I showed him my ID badge, which also served as a magnetic keyless entry device, similar to the one used by Hawker earlier in the day to enter the courthouse.

"Twenty-four-seven," I replied. "The staff of the *Phoenix Daily Sun* never sleeps."

"What's the Fourth Estate?" Hawker asked. I followed his gaze to the plaque in the lobby:

> *"News is history shot on the wing. The huntsmen*
> *from the Fourth Estate seek to bag only the*
> *peacock or the eagle of the swifting day."*
> **—Gene Fowler**

"It's from French history," I told him. "The first three estates in French society and government were Kings, Lords and Commons. But the press, the Fourth Estate, watched over all the rest."

"That you?" he asked. "The Fourth Estate? You some kind of huntsman?"

Forty-eight hours ago I would have laughed at the question. But now I turned to Hawker:

"Like it or not, we're on a quest."

We took the stairs to the second floor of the newspaper and walked to my office. I had been formulating a plan as I returned to the newspaper. But I had made one small miscalculation that I needed to fix.

"I should have asked DePutron to come with us," I said. "I'm going to call back over to Kelso's and see if he's still there."

"Then what?"

"Then, the two of you are going to get in a staff car and hotfoot it out of here taking my iPhone with you."

"So you figure the feds will tail us…"

"While I head over to Leo's."

Hawker reached down and lifted the rubber band ball off my

desk and bounced it on the floor. He caught it and bounced it again. It was the size of a grapefruit and rebounded like a basketball off the threadbare carpet. He nodded at the ball then looked at me, a grin forming on his meaty face.

"How long it take you to collect these rubber bands?" he asked.

"Ages."

Hawker gave the ball one more bounce.

"So, make sure I understand. You were the bait, now I'm the bait along with your cartoonist pal. That about it?"

That pretty much cut to the chase.

"What the hell," Hawker said, tossing the ball into the air and catching it. "I been arrested once today. Make it a quinella."

CHAPTER 30

THE WHITE PANEL van with the colorful red, yellow and blue KPX-TV logo on the side pulled up to the front door of the newspaper. I bolted out of the double glass doors and plunged in, never daring to look around to see if I'd been spotted. Dani Vaquero began pulling away before I could close the door.

"Hey…"

"Hey, yourself," she said. "What's with you? We're partners—you remember? And you're—what? —out to lunch on the biggest story of the year. Where ya been, *amigo*?"

Where had I been? I'd been through hell. She was staring straight ahead, stiff, her body language as hostile as the tone in her voice. She was wearing big, black-rimmed glasses; gave her kind of a sultry librarian look. There was a familiar fragrance in the air.

"Well, I've been a little busy, you know, what with my uncle in the hospital and all," I said. "And what's with the glasses? You look like Elton John."

"They're my fucking driving glasses, asshole, for when my contacts are out," she shot back. "And Elton John is twice the man you are. And watch your fucking language. And what's with the fucking Hawaiian shirt? You going to a luau?"

The Hawaiian shirt was Garreth DePutron's, part of my brilliant plan to avoid detection by the FBI. I had talked Garreth into swapping shirts, the idea being that when he and Hawker left the newspaper together anyone watching would mistake DePutron for me. A shorter me and a skinnier me, but with the shirt I had been wearing. If the ruse worked, I would be free to check out Leo's house.

I also swapped cell phones with DePutron so they could lead the *federales* on a wild goose chase. The big risk was that the kidnappers might call while we were pulling this switcheroo, and I didn't want to miss that call. So, we set my cell phone to call-forward to DePutron's, which I was now carrying. If the kidnappers called, I didn't know if the feds would still be able to track their location with the call forwarded. But I had little confidence in their plan anyway. The kidnappers already told me they were using cheap disposable phones, and even an idiot would know to stay on the move. I was determined to find Leo's planner. My instincts screamed that it would hold the key to this mystery and maybe, just maybe, lead me to Sarah.

Dani was still giving me the evil eye, tough to do behind those Coke bottle lenses.

"Hey, Dani, could you cut back on the X-ray vision," I said, "considering the circumstances?"

"Yeah, well, my condolences, Strange. I mean, I'm sorry your uncle is in a coma. I really, truly am. But why'd you stand me up?"

So much for the sympathy play. "I'm late. I'm sorry. We were supposed to meet—what? —two hours ago. Something came up, OK?"

"What kind of bullshit is this, anyway? You only call me when you need something? A ride?"

"Look, there's still time for you to get something up for the ten o'clock newscast. Let's hustle over to Leo's house and we'll set up over there. Should still be a little light. Be a great backdrop. You'll have it exclusive."

She glared at me over the top of her ridiculous glasses. "Exclusive. Right." All venom and sarcasm.

"No, dude," I protested. "For real. I've dodged all the other stations. Returned their calls, but only left messages. You'll have the only interview."

She twisted her head around, her eyes squinty, her lips pursed. After a heartbeat she relented. "I'll take that as an apology. Deal."

Whew.

"Tell me what's going on," she said. "Why the sudden need for transportation?"

I liked the way she pronounced "transportation," making it "pour" instead of "per," the way a gringo would say it.

"Is that Jessica McClintock you're wearing?" I asked.

She turned to me again, her eyebrows arching. Was she surprised, maybe impressed, that I recognized her cologne? I recalled it from Sarah's bathroom, when I went snooping through her things the night she was kidnapped. I wasn't about to tell Dani, though, that I associated the fragrance with Sarah.

"You're stalling."

"Look, I don't think there's anything I can tell you that you don't already know. You seemed to have it all during your newscast." She *seemed* like she had it all, anyway, when I saw her on the television at Kelso's. Never mind that the volume was off.

"Who you kidding, Strange," she snapped. "It's your uncle we're talking about here. You telling me you got nothing?"

"Dani, I swear, I've got less from the cops than you. They haven't told me shit, less than shit." This was more or less true. Most of what I knew had nothing to do with the police. "It's been crazy. I spent some time in the office, knocked out that column I sent to you. I had to give a statement to the FBI."

"Yes?"

"Don't get excited. I wasn't much help to them."

That earned me a sneer.

"When I got done with the FBI—that's why I was late" (more or less the truth)—"I knew I needed to call you. I also need to get back over to Leo's to pick up a staff car I left over there. So…"

"So you figured you'd kill two stones with this one bird?"

"Uh, yeah, more or less."

"*Really.*" She drew it out to three elongated syllables trilling the Ls.

She drove in silence for a few minutes, the only sound in the van was the steady hiss of air conditioning blowing in my face. Dani exited the Red Mountain Freeway at McDowell, then turned north on Scottsdale Road. As she made the turn, her headlights splashed a dead animal at the road's edge, maybe a dog or coyote. I wondered if it had been part of that wild dog pack we'd been writing about. If so, one less canine to terrorize the neighborhoods. I leaned back in the seat, tried to relax for a moment, ease some of the tension, thinking about what was next.

"You're a terrible liar, you know," she said, breaking the silence.

"I know. It's one of my many failings."

"That's it? You know? You got nothing more to say?"

"I could tell you how much I love that perfume you're wearing."

"*Pendejo!*"

"Or how much I love your accent."

"*Pendejo!*"

"Where you from, anyway?"

"Vegas."

"Everybody talk like that in Vegas?"

"*Pendejo!*"

I pointed to the Mormon church parking lot where I'd left the car. "It's the blue Chevy under the lamp post."

Dani skidded to a halt a foot from the staff car and I hopped out. I held the door for a moment and turned back to her.

"By the way, Dani, what exactly does *pendejo* mean?"

A broad smile spread across her face. "Fuck you," she mouthed, shooting me the bird as she peeled out. It was all I could do to wrench my hand free of the door handle as she sped away toward Leo's house to set up for the shoot.

Well done, Strange. Haven't lost your touch with the fairer sex.

It took a few moments fumbling around in my pants pocket to find the keys. I unlocked the driver's side door and the rank odor of stale food swept over me again. All the leftovers from yesterday had spent another 24 hours cooking in the closed car. I snatched the garage door opener off the dash and closed the door, leaving it unlocked. It was 8:30 p.m. Dani would have to hustle to get this recorded in time for the 10 o'clock report. Then it would be time for me to burgle my uncle's house.

The swishing fronds of the queen palms overhead scratched the silence of the early evening. The palms stood as sturdy sentries along the grassy swath between the parking lot and the street. At the far end of Jackrabbit Court, a Scottsdale police cruiser was parked under the dim glow of a lonely sodium vapor streetlamp. Different location than the last time I was here. I took a quick glimpse but couldn't make out anyone inside.

Dani was set up at the curb in front of the house, hand-held, no tripod. "Come on," she shouted, "I got a deadline."

"Wow," I said, "you sound just like a real reporter."

"Bite me."

Pleasantries concluded, we began:

"You've written a column on your newspaper's website about Judge Strano, your uncle, and what he has meant to you in your life. How are you feeling right now?"

Jeez. That's your best shot?

I gave her the expected babble about Leo, how he was the father I never knew.

"You were at the hospital. Can you describe what you saw?"

Better.

It was painful, but I recounted what I had seen, the same stuff I had included in my column. If she was looking for some emotion, she got it.

"How is Sarah Strano, the judge's wife, handling this?"

That was a curveball.

"She's in seclusion right now," I told her.

"Your newspaper reported that the judge received a threat the day before the assassination attempt. What can you tell us about that?"

I could have kissed her for that.

"Yes, my uncle, Judge Strano, received a disturbing phone call on Friday. I am not at liberty to disclose details of the threat" (I didn't have a clue), "but I can tell you this: The shooters tried to silence my uncle. They tried to keep him from revealing something very damaging to them. But I have a message for them, and you can help me deliver it, Dani."

I looked straight into the unblinking eye of the camera.

"You tried to kill my uncle and you failed. And while he may be in a coma, he did not take his secret with him. I know what you want. And you won't get away with this."

Dani dimmed the video camera's lights. "Alex, that was terrific. We're even now." She extended her fist and we bumped.

"What was that about a secret?" she asked. "That sounded like you have something these people, these shooters, want."

"Dani, I can't say any more about it right now. You were right; I'm a lousy liar (although I was getting more practice of late). I was holding back earlier. I'll make you a promise, though: If and when this comes down, you will be the first to know."

She nodded. "So what's next?"

"I'm about to do my John Robie routine."

It went over her head. She was too young to have ever seen *To Catch a Thief*. So was I, for that matter. But I had an uncle with this fabulous movie collection.

"No, I mean, it sounds like you were baiting them."

Smart.

"Something like that."

Truthfully, it was a spontaneous remark. With Leo comatose, I was afraid the kidnappers might assume that whatever he had over them was safely locked in his unconscious mind, that Sarah was no longer needed as a bargaining chip. I had to make them believe they couldn't afford that assumption. I needed to buy some time.

I was surprised Dani's camera lights hadn't drawn a crowd from the neighborhood or the attention of the cops. Maybe TV trucks and camera crews were now old hat for the neighbors, no longer stimulating a trip outdoors to gawk. The cruiser down the street was still empty. They must be prowling the neighborhood on foot. Or they'd gone for doughnuts. Or it was a dummy car, like before.

I walked up the driveway to the side gate, opened it, and entered the graveled yard. I tried to lock the gate behind me, but it wouldn't latch at first, and I had to give it an extra tug. The lock was slightly out of alignment. This had to be how Fred got out, an unfortunate combination of an open garage door and an unlatched gate. Was this also the route the burglars used to sneak in? Seemed awfully convenient.

Plan A was to enter the garage through the door Sarah had accidentally left open. Maybe it was still unlocked. I tried it, but, no luck. I had a key to Leo's house, but not on me. It was back at my apartment in Tempe. So, it was time for Plan B.

I walked back to the driveway, re-latched the gate behind me, and pulled the garage door opener out of my pocket. I punched the button. The door began rising and the garage light blinked on. As I dove under the opening door, I slipped, cracking my knee on the concrete. I rolled clear, and pushed the opener button again. The door paused. I punched again, and it closed. It had taken only a moment. If the camera lights hadn't stirred the natives, maybe I could get away with this.

But landing on my knee hadn't been part of the plan. When I pushed off the concrete floor it buckled. I struggled upward and took a few tentative steps to shake off the pain—to no avail. It was throbbing.

There was a hook with spare keys inside the door leading to the kitchen. I shoved the garage door opener into my back pocket, hobbled to the kitchen door and the handle turned. I cracked the door and peeked in. It was dark. I reached around the corner, not daring to set foot inside, and played around the wall with my hand searching for the keys. I was beginning to sweat and could feel my heart racing. Any moment, there would be sirens, flashing lights, banging on the door, cops with guns drawn. My hand touched the tangle of keys on the hook. I snatched them and closed the kitchen door.

Hurry.

There were two separate sets of keys. I pushed a button on the first set, but nothing happened. Had to be Sarah's car. I shoved that set of keys into my pocket. There was a symbol of an unlocked padlock on the key fob of the remaining set. I pushed it once, then again, and the locks on the Buick's doors clicked. I opened the front passenger door just as the garage light timed out. Now I was able to see only by the car's interior light. I stuck my head in the car.

Where is it? Where is it?

Nothing in the front seat. Not so much as a gum wrapper. I was neat, but this was ridiculous. I stuck my head between the seats and peered into the back. It was empty as an editor's soul.

Damn.

I backed out of the car, mindful of my aching knee, and turned to the rear of the Buick. It took a few moments of fumbling about for the trunk release, but I finally found it above the license plate.

Empty space yawned at me. Nothing in the truck except the car's jack. I started to close the lid, then paused. Why would Leo, neat freak that he was, leave the jack sitting on the carpet of the trunk? Then it struck me. How stupid could a guy get? Collins had acknowledged they had searched the house. They would have checked out Leo's car, too. They must have pulled the jack out and not replaced it. I started to the slam the trunk lid, but froze when I heard muffled voices inside the house.

Holy shit!

It had to be the cops. That explained the empty patrol car at the end of the street.

As I lurched toward the side door, I felt the keys slip through my nervous fingers and they fell to the concrete floor. The garage erupted in a cacophony of sound, the Buick's headlights flashing on and off, the horn blaring. I dropped down to grab the keys, smacking my injured kneecap again. An arc of pain shot up to my hip.

Christ.

My heart was thudding like a Harley. Sweat poured into my eyes.

Forget the keys!

I whirled toward the side door as a bayonet of pain shot through my knee. I unlocked the door and flung it open. If I turned left, it would take me back to the gate by the driveway. But I didn't want to be caught out in the open. So I wheeled right and limped across the small graveled yard to the six-foot-high concrete block fence. I squirmed between the tangle of towering oleanders lining the fence and hauled myself up and over into the adjoining yard, landing in a crouch in the crushed granite.

Go! Go!

As I attempted to rise, my right knee buckled again and I toppled backwards, impaling myself on something sharp and painful.

"FUUUUCK!"

I jerked away and turned to see the four-foot tall prickly pear cactus that had just speared me. I felt my back. It was sticky with sweat, and now, I imagined, blood. Behind me, across the fence, I heard something. A hushed voice. A man's. I lurched upright and bolted through the neighbors' back yard. As I sprinted, pain arcing up my leg, I passed the sliding glass doors of the neighbors' living room. Inside, I could see an older couple watching a computer monitor, their backs to me and oblivious of my screams and the drama playing out in their yard. I caught a flash of a nude women on the screen reading from a sheaf of papers. It was the Naked News. Maybe Stormy was onto something.

I staggered around the side of their yard, flung open the gate, then limped across the street, looking back nervously, sure to see flashing lights. I hobbled to the staff car in the church parking lot, then fumbled in my pockets for my keys. As I dug them out I spilled receipts, change, and Sarah's airline flight folder onto the pavement. Where was Batman's Utility Belt when you needed it? I scooped the stuff up, tossed it on the passenger seat, and fell into the Chevy.

The car burned rubber pulling out of the parking lot. Didn't know it could do that. I turned left on Scottsdale Road and floored it. After a few blocks, I pulled into a side street and waited for sirens. One minute. Then another. Nothing. If those were cops inside the house, they would have given pursuit. If not cops, who?

I reached into my back pocket and retrieved the keys to Sarah's car that I'd liberated from the hook in the kitchen. A seed of an idea was germinating. I turned on the overhead light, then plucked Sarah's airline flight folder off the passenger seat and opened it. Inside was her expired airline ticket from the previous night. Wedged next to it in the folder was a ticket of some sort. I pulled it out of the folder and held it up to the light. It was from the airport parking garage. On the back of the ticket, in Leo's signature green ink, were the words: "Terminal 4, Level 6, G17."

I took Scottsdale Road south to the Red Mountain Freeway rather than the more circuitous, but faster, route along the Pima Freeway. Figured I'd have a better chance of spotting a tail that way. I ran the red light at Scottsdale and McDowell and turned right onto Belleview, a residential street, and circled about the neighborhood for a minute. Then I slipped back out into traffic keeping a constant watch in my rear-view mirror. Just like in the movies.

I pulled into a park-and-rob and bought a Coke and a couple of Snickers. When was the last time I'd eaten a real meal? The clerk gave me an anxious look as I approached the counter.

"What?" I asked.

Why would an unshaven, unwashed white guy in a bloodstained Hawaiian shirt with a big Band-Aid on his forehead make anyone nervous? Don't you just hate profiling? On impulse, I bought a lottery ticket, too. Who knew, maybe my luck would change.

None of the cars in the store's parking lot followed me when I pulled back out onto Scottsdale Road. Nobody entered the road ahead or behind me. If I was being tailed it was undetectable to me, but if they were pros I supposed it would be. Then again, maybe my little ruse with Hawker and DePutron was working.

Traffic was backed up at Sky Harbor. Cops were stopping all vehicles entering the airport, occasionally pulling one out of line to be searched. Welcome to Terror Alert Level Red. When it was my turn, the cop waved his flashlight around the interior of the car and raised his eyebrows at the bandage on my head.

"How'd you get that?" he asked.

"Ice hockey," I said.

That got an eyebrow raise, but he waved me through.

I took the ramp into the Terminal Four parking garage and circled upward to Level Six. The garage was packed at the lower levels, but began thinning out as I drove higher into the structure. Sarah's car, a white Ford Focus, was right where Leo's note said it would be in Row G. I pulled into an empty spot five spaces down, clambered out of the Chevy and jogged back to the Ford, ignoring my throbbing knee. I started for the trunk when headlights reflected off the concrete pillar beside her car. Someone was coming. Could I have been tailed? I ducked around the front of the Ford and peeked over the hood. The headlights passed by harmlessly, one aisle over, then aimed down the exit ramp. No time to dither. I grabbed the key to unlock the trunk, but couldn't find the lock.

Where the fuck is it?

Then I remembered: The key fob had a trunk release. This is what happens when you're used to driving a dino-mobile like my Sebring.

I heard an engine coming up the ramp behind me. A deep, throbbing diesel. The rumbling up the ramp was growing louder. I punched the key fob and the trunk unlocked. What would I find there? Oh God, I suddenly worried, what if Sarah's in there? I opened the trunk lid. Inside, nestled beside a gym bag and a sack of laundry was a brown alligator briefcase.

Excelsior!

I yanked the briefcase from the trunk, slammed the lid, and scuttled around the side of the car to avoid being seen as an extended-cab pickup lumbered up the ramp. It drove by harmlessly and turned up to the next level. I considered taking Sarah's car and leaving the staff car in the garage. If I had been tailed here, they would be looking for a blue Chevy, not a white Ford. But something told me no. It had the feel of tampering with evidence, as if I weren't in over my head already. It might make me a suspect in Sarah's disappearance, getting caught driving around in her car. They might have an APB out for her plates. Maybe it was that driving Sarah's car would creep me out. No, better stick with the plan.

I climbed back into the Chevy and headed down the parking lot ramp. There was no security gauntlet to pass through leaving the airport, suicide bombers being one-way kinds of dudes. I had to find someplace secluded to examine the briefcase. I drove north, back toward Scottsdale, and turned west off Scottsdale Road onto Jackrabbit until it dead-ended at Saguaro near the base of Camelback Mountain. Another right turn and I was weaving my way through the upscale mountainside neighborhood. I took a left on Palo Verde. Up ahead was a small stretch of undeveloped desert. I drove the sedan over the curb into the brush until I was certain I couldn't be seen from the street. I killed the engine and rolled the window down.

I leaned on the steering wheel for a minute to relieve the tension of the past hour. My knee throbbed and the puncture in my back burned like hell. I could tell it was still bleeding. DePutron would be annoyed I'd ruined his shirt. Edwina wouldn't be pleased, either, with bloodstains on the seat of the company's car.

It was quieter here than nearer the highway. But quiet is relative in the Sonoran Desert when you are in the heart of a metropolitan area. A passenger jet roared overhead en route to Sky Harbor. Nearby, children laughed, a door slammed shut, then it was still again. I stepped outside the Chevy to get a breath of fresh air. The interior lamp of the car cast a small pool of light at my feet through the open door. I saw something move next to a baseball-sized stone. I kicked at it and a brownish-yellow scorpion, about an inch in length, scurried away into the darkness. I shuddered. Little bastard was probably a cousin of the bug that stung Uncle Leo.

I plopped the briefcase onto the hood of the car and it landed with a thunk. The case was fastened by a single brass latch; the other was sprung open and, based on what Leo had said on Friday afternoon, was inoperable. I thumbed the button of the good latch and it popped open. Inside the briefcase were manila file folders stuffed with court documents, a pair of reading glasses in a brown vinyl case, a set of keys, and a prescription bottle filled with blue pills—something called Sildenafil, whatever that was.

There was also a black leather notebook with the initials L.D.S. engraved on a small brass plate in the lower right hand corner of the cover. My hands trembled as I reached for the notebook. I unzipped the binder and opened it. A row of slots lining the inside cover bulged with business cards. Seven chrome-plated rings were anchored in the spine of the book. There was a mild glare obscuring the first page, a clear plastic sheet holding a photograph. I turned it in the weak light leaking through the windshield and, as it revealed itself, I felt my throat close up. It was a color snapshot of Leo and me standing in front of a used Honda Civic, a high school graduation gift from Leo. My first set of wheels. This would have been how Leo started his day, with a picture of us.

I looked up into the night sky filled with the sparks of a million distant suns. They were spectacular in this small patch of desert, partially shielded from the light pollution of the city by Camelback Mountain. "Leo…," I whispered. I took a deep breath. "You fuckhead, you better not die."

I picked up the planner and leafed through it. Every page was filled with Leo's scribblings. There were lists of things "To Be Done" and "Appointments" on the left-hand pages. The facing pages contained extensive notes, Leo's diary of each day's activities, written in his unmistakable green scrawl. Paging through the book, I saw there were three months'-worth of calendar pages. He must have archived the rest, updating the planner from time to time with fresh pages. If there were a clue to be found in here, it would have to be something that happened recently.

I turned to July 27—727—expectantly. The "Appointment" column of the calendar page was filled with what appeared to be ordinary court entries: a hearing on a motion for summary judgment, jury selection in an upcoming trial, lunch at the Bar Association. The journal entries were equally unrevealing. July 27 would have been three weeks ago. But the phone call Leo received had occurred on August 18, the anniversary of my mother's death. That was a big gap. I continued leafing through the planner, jumping ahead to last Friday. The "Appointments" section, again, appeared to be routine. But there was an unusual entry in the journal:

"Deposited AF2 doc at WF."

I found myself holding my breath, realizing I was looking at the clue I had been searching for. "Deposited AF2 doc at WF." When I met Leo at the elevator he had been sweating; said he'd just run an errand and hadn't cooled off yet. I started dissecting his notation. "Doc" in another era might have referred to "doctor," but lowercase "doc" was a common postscript on computer documents written in Microsoft Word. Leo was barely computer literate. Still, I guessed it had to refer to a document, perhaps a letter.

"WF" might have stumped me, but the word "deposited" gave it away. You make deposits at a bank, and one of the biggest banks in downtown Phoenix was Wells Fargo. It was where I maintained my checking account. I had a safe deposit box there, too. Leo had a key to it.

I dug into my pants and pulled out my key ring. I had about half a dozen keys—to my office, my apartment, the Sebring, my mailbox and the safe deposit box. I leaned closer to the windshield to capture the light. The numbers 727 were engraved on the safe deposit key. That was the message Leo was trying to send me!

It was so obvious. Why hadn't I realized that right away? Then again, I didn't know my own license plate number either, so what did I expect?

What must have happened began taking shape. Leo took a document of some sort to the bank, to my safe deposit box, otherwise the "727" note would make no sense. But what was "AF2"? Had to be an abbreviation for something, the key, to whatever this was about. Its meaning eluded me.

For the most part, the safe deposit box contained important documents—things like my birth certificate, my legalized name change, my Social Security card, insurance paperwork, and so forth. Leo kept a copy of his Living Will and Last Will and Testament there, too. He'd always said that when he croaked he wanted to make sure I had a copy lest one of his exes tried to cut me out of my inheritance. Seemed funny at the time. There was nothing funny about that anymore.

Leo had gone to the bank and left something in the box. It would be a clever place to stash something. While he was a signatory on the box, the account was in my name. It would make tracing it back to Leo difficult.

I turned back to the planner and paged forward to August 19, the date Leo had arranged his mysterious meeting. In the Appointments column, at 3 p.m., was scrawled in green ink the initials: AS/MT I knew AS was me. Who was MT?

In the distance I could hear sirens, faint at first, but they were growing louder. In the direction of Scottsdale Road. Nothing to worry about, I knew, but I still had the jitters after my narrow escape at Leo's.

Then there here was a rustling sound off to my left, among the weeds and brush. Startled, I turned, but could see nothing. There was another slight movement, then a head poked out. Then another. Canine heads. Their eyes gleamed yellow in the dim light from the open car door.

"AHWOOOOOO!"

The howl sent a chill up my spine. "Jesus!" I shouted. "Get out of here! Beat it!"

It was the smell of food—those damned leftovers in the car! If I weren't mauled to death, I'd wring the neck of the asshole who left that crap in there. I tossed the planner in the briefcase, slammed it shut and whirled for the door. As I did so, the case popped open and papers, files and the planner, itself, were flung to the ground in a narrow arc between me and the approaching canines.

Oh, Christ.

There were three more of them now, including two coyotes. One of the coyotes howled again, slinking closer. They were mangy, fearless, and hungry. The dog on the right, a big one, part-shepherd, began snarling, baring its fangs, saliva dripping. I threw the emptied briefcase at him. "Scram!" I shouted. Another of the dogs began barking, and the snarling shepherd hunched down as if ready to leap. I lunged forward, scooped the planner off the dirt, and spun to the driver's side door. The dogs charged. The nearest coyote sprinted straight for the door, which I slammed in its face. The animal jumped up at the open window, snapping at me. The snarling shepherd leaped onto the hood of the car. I heard myself scream as I leaned away from the window and desperately rolled it up with my left hand while fumbling with the keys in my right.

I fought the key into the ignition, cranked it, and stepped on the gas. The big dog on the hood tumbled off, howling, as I peeled out leaving a cloud of brown dust behind me. I glanced back in the rear view mirror to see the dogs giving chase. I pressed the accelerator and the car flew over the curb and into the street, fishtailed, then straightened as I sped away. I looked back again and the dogs had receded into the darkness of the desert.

My heart was pounding, my knee was throbbing, and the piercing pain in my back had not subsided as I drove east on Jackrabbit. So much for the theory that you can't feel pain in more than one place at one time.

The sirens were louder now as I retraced my route back towards Scottsdale Road. I had to decide where to go next. Forget my apartment or the office. If the FBI had figured out our misdirection play, if they had tracked down DePutron and Hawker, they would be watching for me at those locations. Or so I feared.

I needed to buy some time, get some rest, before going to the bank. And I needed to think about that, too: How to get in and out of there without attracting unwelcome attention. I needed to call Mohawk. I needed to look through the planner some more and see if there was anything else to be learned from it. And I still needed to hear from Sarah's abductors.

I was a very needy fellow.

Flashing red lights were approaching from my right as I neared the intersection at Scottsdale Road. My heart skipped a beat.

The cops!

But no. It was a fire engine and it was turning off Scottsdale Road into the adjacent neighborhood. As it did, I could see it was a hook and ladder truck.

Now what?

Ahead, I could see blue and red lights reflected off houses and the tops of swaying palms. A spiral of flame shot up above the rooftops.

I drove past the Mormon Church where I had parked earlier and pulled the car into a side street two blocks away. I locked the car after hiding the planner in the trunk, then trudged toward Jackrabbit Court, still favoring my injured knee. The wind was picking up again.

Another storm on the way. In the distance, to the east, a flash of lightning was muted against the manmade light show at street level. The neighborhood was in chaos. Police and fire trucks were everywhere. People were milling about in their front yards. Black smoke filled the air and its acrid odor burned my nostrils. Flames licked the roof of the burning structure. The ladder on the fire truck I had seen moments ago was rising and a stream of high-pressure water erupted from its tip.

The plume of water was directed at Leo's house.

CHAPTER 31

I was sitting in a graveled yard about a block away from the smoldering ruins of Leo's home, dumfounded, with no more conscious thought than the trunk of the Palo Verde tree against which my aching back was propped. I was exhausted physically, emotionally, and mentally. My synapses were overloaded; the nerve center responsible for actual thinking had shut down, circuits blown, a cognitive flat line.

Maybe it was shock.

I had sat transfixed as the firefighters fought to bring the fury of the conflagration under control. Was it normal for a house to burn this furiously? I didn't think so.

I had been curiously unmoved when they brought the bodies out. There were gasps and cries from onlookers when they saw the blackened corpses with the smoking remnants of police uniforms still clinging to their charred remains. Several firefighters had risked their lives for that. The dead cops made a macabre sort of sense. Why else had I gotten away? It explained the empty police cruiser. The voices I'd heard, they weren't the cops, they were the assholes who set the fire, who wanted Leo's home and all it contained, destroyed. They weren't taking any chances. The cops were collateral damage, potential witnesses the arsonists-killers-kidnappers couldn't afford. It was a miracle I got out of the house alive. Had I lingered even a moment longer, mine would have been among the corpses hauled away by the meat wagon, no sirens needed, no need for haste.

Earlier, while firefighters were still struggling to bring the fire under control, a hand touched my shoulder and I looked up to see Bevin Darcy and his aunt, leaning over me.

"We saw you sitting here and we were worried," she said, kneeling down beside me. She held a small flashlight, and the light reflecting off the crushed granite of the yard illuminated her features. She was frowning. "You feeling all right?"

I nodded. "Yeah, thanks for asking." It wasn't true, but I had to say something.

"My name's Vicky," she said. "I'm Bevin's aunt."

"Younger sister, I gather."

She smiled. Small freckles spread across her cheekbones. Her large brown eyes seemed filled with concern. She was pretty.

"I don't think it's such a good idea you just sitting here like this," she said. "You look exhausted. Why don't you come inside, let me get you something to drink, maybe some coffee?" She had a hopeful, encouraging look. Her eyebrows formed those upside down smiles, just like Lt. Warren had when we first met.

"Thanks," I replied, "but I'm meeting some people here. A friend and a member of the staff. They called a little while ago."

"Then they can call you again when they get here. Come on."

She took my hand and began to pull me to my feet. Her hands were small but strong. I struggled upward, my knee reminding me of the abuse it had endured earlier that evening.

We stood facing one another for a moment. She was a foot shorter than me and slim, wearing a loose-fitting tank top and Bermuda shorts. Roughly my age, late twenties, I guessed. Or she could have been 18. Those freckles.

"How'd you spot me?" I asked. "I thought I was inconspicuous under this tree."

She smiled, a big, toothy, tomboy grin. "Bevin saw you on TV. I wouldn't let him go outside. Channel 12 was panning the neighborhood and they focused in on you under the tree. Bevin started yelling, 'Aunt Vicky, Aunt Vicky, it's Mr. Strange.'"

Wonderful. So much for keeping a low profile. Of course, I had brought it upon myself. I had made three phone calls when I arrived. First to the *Sun*, second to Dani Vaquero, and the third to Hawker's cell phone. Dani had been there within minutes, first on the scene. Second time in one night. She showed up any more often she'd have to start paying property taxes. Our balance sheet had been even. Now she owed me.

I avoided Dani and the reporters and photographers from the *Sun* who swept upon the neighborhood. I would have become part of the story if I had talked to them—only natural they'd want to interview the judge's nephew. The *Arizona Republic* photographer arrived much later, too late to get pictures in the newspaper for the first editions. Somebody's appendage would be in a wringer over that.

Bevin grabbed my other hand and began tugging. "Come on, Mr. Strange," he said. "I'll show you my room."

I'd been ignoring the boy, so I kneeled down and looked at him at eye level, ignoring the sharp pain that greeted the maneuver. "Hey, Bevin, thanks for keeping an eye out for me."

I thought he might appreciate that, but his eyes were filled with concern. His voice choked. "Is Freddie all right?"

Vicky intervened. She was showing concern, too. "We went to the movies before you returned. You found the dog, right? He isn't, he…" she faltered.

"No, Fred's not in there," I said.

He's with Sarah, wherever the hell she is.

Bevin and his aunt looked at one another, then he walked over and wrapped his arms around her legs.

She looked at me.

"We were terrified…" She paused. "No, I was terrified that by making Bevin take the dog back home, I might be responsible…" Her voice trailed off again.

"I rose from my knee and put a hand on Vicky's shoulder. They were slender and cool. "It's all good. No worries."

She nodded. "That's a relief."

I looked down at Bevin. "That was great work, finding Fred. Thanks for watching out for him."

"Tommy Veals said I should call the pound."

"Who's Tommy Veals?"

"He lives there." Bevin pointed to a house at the end of the street.

"So you told this Tommy kid you had Fred and not your aunt?"

"Yeah. I told him you and me are best friends, and if he told on me you'd beat him up."

"Bevin Darcy!" Aunt Vicky didn't like that.

He looked at his aunt, then me. "Am I in trouble, Mr. Strange?"

"Any chance you could just call me Alex?" I asked. It had become a ritual.

He looked up at his aunt, his eyes wide, pleading.

"Young man," she said, "you exhaust me."

I needed to say something about the little arrangement I had made with her nephew in exchange for him turning over the cartridge.

"Uh, Vicky, it dawns on me that I may owe you an apology. Or at least an explanation."

"What for?" she asked, her eyebrows curling upward. They were the color of copper, like her hair, which she wore in a ponytail.

"Well, yesterday, I told Bevin that if it was OK with you and his mother that maybe I would take him to a Diamondbacks game sometime…" I felt like a 12-year-old confessing to my mom. Except my mom never believed in apologizing for anything and didn't expect any.

"You promised!" Bevin interrupted.

"Well, yeah, I did," I acknowledged, looking down at Bevin then meeting his aunt's curious gaze.

"You see, we made this little deal…"

"I know all about your deal," she said. "Bevin told me. But you don't have to do that. I'm just glad you talked him into turning over that evidence from the shooting." She paused, shaking her head. "My God, what a horrible two days we've had. And your uncle. I'm so very sorry…"

"Aunt Vicky, he promised," Bevin blurted.

"I did, Bevin, you're right," I said. "And if your aunt says it's OK, that's just what we'll do."

Before she could respond, DePutron's cell phone began vibrating and I fished it out of my pocket. Could it be the kidnappers? No. The caller ID showed it was Hawker's phone. I answered and told him where I had parked the staff car and agreed to meet him and DePutron there.

"I'm afraid I have to go now," I told Bevin. "Can you show me your room some other time?"

"Sure, Alex," he said, stealing a quick look at his aunt to see if she noticed him calling me by my first name. "How about when we go to the game, I'll show you when you pick me up, all right?"

Vicky nodded.

"It's a deal, Bevin," I replied.

I turned to Vicky and took her hand. "Thanks for the offer. Coffee sounds pretty good right now. I hope you let me take a rain check."

"Well, that depends," she smiled.

"On what?"

"On whether you can come up with a third ticket to the game."

I was leaning against the car when DePutron and Hawker pulled up in the cartoonist's aging Volkswagen Beetle. That surprised me. I assumed they had taken one of the newspaper's staff cars out of the back lot.

"Jesus," Hawker said, "you look worse than before and that's sayin' something."

I just nodded. "Why the vee-dub?" I asked DePutron.

"We tried," he replied. "Got the keys to Car 4, only one left in the lot, and the damned thing was on empty."

That newspaper was going downhill faster than a sumo wrestler on skis.

"That what I think it is?" Hawker asked, pointing to the commotion two blocks away.

"Afraid so."

"Price of poker keeps going up, don't it?"

"It do."

Hawker filled me in on how he and DePutron had spent the past couple of hours. They'd gone straight from the newspaper to the casino. If they were followed, they never spotted the tail. At the casino, DePutron hit on the idea of turning the phone off so they could sneak off without their electronic leash giving them away.

"What?" I was terrified. What if the kidnappers had tried to call? Then I remembered: call forwarding works even when the phone is off.

While DePutron was talking, I was struggling to slip out of his Hawaiian shirt. It split down the back as I did so.

"Just keep it," DePutron said, a disgusted look on his face. But I insisted on trading. If I were spotted by the feds, I wanted to be wearing the same shirt I had on at Kelso's earlier that evening.

"Any luck earlier?" Hawker asked.

"Luck with what?" DePutron interrupted. "Will one of you guys please tell me why I've been drug around the toolies tonight?"

I looked at Hawker. "You tell him?"

Hawker shook his head no.

"No he didn't," DePutron said. "The Sphinx here hasn't told me shit."

That brought a smile to Hawker's face. "Sphinx? I like that. Might change my whole image. Do an Egyptian thing."

"Come on," DePutron continued. "I've been a good sport about this. I gave you the shirt off my back. Literally. Thanks so much for this by the way," he said, pointing to the tattered and bloodstained back of his shirt. "Now what the heck is going on?"

"Well, Garreth, I'm afraid we've drug you into something," I said. "It's complicated."

"I'm listening."

"It's like this. Mohawk, here, is helping me figure out what's been going on with my uncle. Things have kinda spiraled out of control. The FBI's involved and they want to keep tabs on me—just in case I might be in danger, too. I guess that's why they put a tracking virus in my cell phone. I had a tip I needed to check out without any feds snooping around. That's where you came in as my body double."

"There's got to be more to it than that."

"You're right, Garreth, there is. But that's the broad outline of things. I can't go into any more detail. I'm sorry if that pisses you off. I owe you. But for now I just can't say any more."

DePutron lowered his head, dejected. "I thought we were friends."

I knew he was being dramatic, but I played along.

"Garreth…"

He hung his head low for a moment, then peeked at me out of the corner of his eyes. "Great Caesar's Ghost!" he laughed. "You should see the look on your face."

"Jeez, Garreth, you had me worried…"

"Well," he chirped, "my work here is done. It's time to return to the Bat Cave." DePutron whirled theatrically and began strutting back to his car, his discarded shirt lying in the street. "You coming?" he asked Hawker over his shoulder.

"Garreth, wait," I called after him. "We need to swap phones."

DePutron did a 180 and fished my iPhone out of his pocket. First thing, I turned off call forwarding.

Looking at the phone, I found myself marveling how easy it is to snoop on people these days. Once, this was the stuff of science fiction and James Bond movies. Now, stores specializing in spyware could be found everywhere. Bug your husband to see if he's cheating;

trace the keyboard strokes on your kids' computers to see if they're surfing porn sites; wiretap your boss and get the goods on him. Soon, every American would be part of a national registry; every facet of our lives, from financial data to reading habits to DNA would be on file. Nobody was immune from either the prying or the temptation to pry. When Michael Jackson had been arrested on charges of molesting one of the many boys who spent the night with him at his Neverland Ranch, reporters had hidden microphones in the bushes where prosecutors stepped out to smoke. This, of course, was condemned by the journalistic profession as unethical. Never mind we'd been tape recording interviews on the sly for years.

"So, you find anything?" Hawker asked again.

"I managed to get into the garage, but the trunk to Leo's car was empty." That was the truth, but not the whole truth. Not telling the whole truth was becoming a habit.

I turned back to the fire, looking away from the staff car where Leo's planner was hidden under the mat in the trunk.

"I've never seen a house fire like this before," I said. "It was a fucking inferno."

We stood side by side for a few moments, then Hawker broke the silence.

"So now what?"

I turned to him. Hawker's face was impassive.

"I'm going to hang around. Try to see if there's anything that can be recovered. I still have some of my things in there, mostly books, but I'm guessing they're ashes by now."

"You want me to stick around?"

I looked over to the Volkswagen. "No, that's all right. We've been through enough today. We're lucky we're not in jail." I looked back to the smoking ruins of Leo's house. "I don't know how I could have gotten through today without you. Thanks. We'll regroup in the morning."

Hawker nodded. "What are friends for?"

Bevin and Tricia had come and gone. So, too, had Hawker and DePutron. I sat, dumb as a stump, leaning against the trunk of the neighbor's Palo Verde tree, waiting. I knew it was only a matter of time until they found me. I had my story straight. The phone was out of service for a while? So how was I to know? Was I a technician? The "ignorance is bliss" defense.

A voice in the darkness said, "Mr. Strange." It was Agent Collins.

I craned my neck upward and to the left to see the FBI agent hovering over me. Volker, I noticed, was on the right. They'd flanked me, and I hadn't even noticed. If these guys were this sneaky, they could easily have tailed me and I never would have spotted them.

"Mr. Strange, you are under arrest. You have the right to remain silent...."

In a small, remote lobe of my brain, the slice of cortex responsible for out-of-body experiences, I observed the Miranda recitation as if it were someone else being read his rights. I was adrift in a blissful sense of detachment. A subset of that collection of neurons marveled at the quaintness of it all. It was oddly reassuring somehow. Even after the 9-11 hysteria, other terrorist attacks, and the manic efforts to abolish the Bill of Rights, they still had to recite that to me. I recalled that the Supreme Court's Miranda decision was based on an Arizona case. Nice to have a local angle, added a bit of irony to the situation.

Volker, still giving me Miranda, was pulling the handcuffs off his belt. He was smiling. He'd been looking forward to this, the fat little prick.

It was at that moment that my iPhone began vibrating. I raised my index finger to the federal agents, a sign to wait a moment, and put the phone to my ear. Volker stopped in mid-rights reading. Wonder if they trained for that.

"Strange?" It was the voice of Robbie the Robot.

"Yes." I pushed the speakerphone button and tilted the phone outward so the agents could hear.

"What have you got for us?" The kidnapper's voice was tinny but clearly audible. Volker and Collins stood in paralyzed attention.

"What? You afraid you didn't destroy it when you burned down Leo's house?"

Dead air.

"And killing two cops? Are you insane?"

Collins was talking into his cell phone. "You getting this?" he asked, presumably to other bureau agents trying to track the call. What should have been a whisper came out a shout. Can't somebody in the federal government buy this guy a new hearing aid?

"What two cops?'

I glanced at Collins. He was staring at me. The expression on his face was as dumbfounded as I imagined mine was.

"Strange," the voice on the phone said. "You still there?"

I drew a deep breath and continued. "You can catch it on the news. In the meantime, I want to hear from Sarah. Is she all right?"

"Not so much. She spends most of her time crying, wondering why it's taking you so long."

"You shit weasel. Put her on the phone right now."

"I'm afraid I can't do that. She's being held elsewhere." Another pause, then: "So, Strange, do you have what we want or not? We noticed you didn't spill the beans today in your story, the one on your website. That mean we can count on you to cooperate?" He didn't mention my interview with Dani. So much for my televised melodramatics.

"No and yes. No, I don't have what you want. Not yet. But I know where it is. And, yes, I intend to cooperate. But there's one thing…"

"Yes?"

"You're gettin' squat unless I know Sarah's unharmed, you understand? Nada, zero, less than zero." And with that I pushed the END button, killing the connection.

"What'd you do that for?" Volker yelped. "Why'd you cut him off?

That may not have been long enough. We need time to get a trace."
He turned to his partner, who was speaking in into his mobile phone.

Collins begin nodding. "Good," he said. "They got a number."

I dropped back down in the gravel with a crunch. "Won't do you any good," I said. "They told me before they were using burners."

The agents exchanged blank looks. They were good at that.

I extended my wrists, palms up. "Make the call, gentlemen," I said. "You want me Guantanamoed or you want me to get the goods and Sarah's release."

"You know what they're looking for, don't you?' Collins said.

"I don't. But I assume it's the same thing you guys we're hassling Leo about."

"But you know where it is."

"There's that."

Collins was stone faced. He was good at that. We all have our gifts.

"Be a human, Collins, and level with me. Who are these guys? Why is this, whatever it is, so important? Who would go to these lengths?"

His lips started to move, but Volker stepped in between us, still with the cuffs.

"Fine. You gonna arrest me or we gonna walk away from here?"

Collins stepped away a few feet leaving Volker to guard me while he made another call on his mobile phone. I couldn't hear the conversation, but I assumed he needed approval from someone higher in the food chain for whatever would come next. The agent finished talking and turned to me. "When this is done, you and I are going to have a reckoning." He turned and walked away toward the fire trucks and cop cars in front of the remains of Leo's house. Volker lingered a moment, disappointed he wasn't dragging me off to be waterboarded, and then turned to follow his partner.

I exhaled. It was a big gamble and it had worked. For the first time since Sarah was kidnapped, I felt a spark of hope she might be alive. The kidnappers had no other leverage. They needed her for the trade, and I might be able to give them something in exchange.

But I was still boxing with shadows. I had more questions than answers, and I wasn't even sure I had the right questions.

Who was behind this? Since the day Leo was shot at, I'd worried that the sinister hand of the federal government might be involved, maybe even the FBI. I knew it was paranoid, the kind of nonsense that conspiracy theorists thrived on, but I couldn't shake it. After all, Leo was no great friend to Big Brother. He was an outspoken advocate for civil liberties at a time when so many Constitutional protections were being compromised in the name of homeland security. My suspicion was fueled by the cartridges found outside his home after the shooting, bullets favored by the FBI. I knew that wasn't even slightly conclusive, but, still, it was there.

I worried that Volker and Collins might be playing me, since it seemed they were after the same thing as the kidnappers. I realized they had never said why they were about to arrest me. On what grounds? Was it a bluff, trying to rattle me? Good questions. No answers.

While I didn't have a read on Volker—other than he was an ignorant turd—Collins's actions, while not chummy, didn't strike me as conspiratorial. He had seemed genuinely upset when he called from the hospital. Nearly human. Still, I was puzzled why the FBI agents said nothing about the iPhone being offline for a while. What's the point of a good alibi if nobody accuses you of anything?

And Robbie the Robot seemed unaware of the dead bodies hauled out of Leo's house. Maybe the kidnappers were holed up outside the Phoenix metro area, someplace where news like this would take a while to reach.

And what was it about Mohawk that was bugging me? Was it the way he had snatched Leo's business card, or how he was constantly hovering over me? There was something sketchy about his behavior over the past twenty-four hours that nagged at me, breeding a level of—if not distrust—then caution.

Can't I trust anybody? No. Get used to it.

I steadied myself against the trunk of the Palo Verde tree. I felt drained and was in desperate need of sleep. Should have accepted Vicky's offer of coffee. I needed a shower and a few hours of shut-eye. I hadn't been back to my apartment since heading out to meet Dani for breakfast. Probably the place had been tossed by the feds or the bad guys or both. That thought made me uneasy.

Maybe I could catch some Zs on my office couch. But as I hobbled back to the street I noticed Dani's van still parked just outside the yellow caution tape. I looked back toward the ruins of Leo's house and saw her filming beside the hook and ladder truck. Footage for the early-morning newscast, I assumed. On impulse, I limped to the rear of her van and tried the door. It was unlocked. That was careless. The interior was crammed with electronics gear, but there was just room enough to curl up. I started to climb in, then remembered Leo's Day Planner: I had left it in the trunk of the staff car. What an idiot! After all I had gone through to get it, I was about to just leave it sitting out in the street.

I hiked over to the car and popped the trunk. It was there, right where I'd left it, thank God. I really was losing it. If I didn't get some sleep soon I'd have a psychotic break. You can run on fumes for so long. I trudged back over to Dani's van and crawled in, glad to be out of sight, glad to have a place to rest my weary bones. I pulled the iPhone out of my back pocket as I lay down, but before turning it off, I tried one more idea. I launched the Safari browser and Googled AF2. All it showed were references to the Arena Football League's developmental program. Who knew Arena Football had a minor league? That couldn't be it. I powered off the phone and set it on the floor of the van. And closed my eyes.

CHAPTER 32

"*MADRE' DIOS!*"

My eyes snapped open to see Dani Vaquero hovering over me. She was leaning inside the opened double doors at the back of the van, her mouth agape, her hands trembling.

"What the hell are you doing here?" she shouted, her voice cracking.

"Oh, hi, Dani," I mumbled, rolling over on my back and propping myself up on an elbow. "I was waiting on you to finish shooting. Must have dozed off."

She shook her head. "You scared the living piss out of me."

She took two steps backward, bowed her head and brushed her hands through her hair, trying to compose herself. "How'd you get inside the van, anyway?" she demanded.

"Door was unlocked. I decided to lie down for a sec and wait for you." I tried to sound offhand about it, as if sneaking into other people's cars and crashing were an everyday sort of thing.

I peered out the doors past Dani, rubbed the sleep out of my eyes. "Where are we, anyway?"

"We're at my house," she snapped. "And just what am I supposed to do with you now?"

I scuttled out of the van, grabbing Leo's planner on the way. We were standing in the driveway leading to her townhouse.

I looked down at my wristwatch. It was two in the morning. Twelve hours had passed since Leo had been put on a respirator. Thirty-six hours left.

I rubbed my eyes again and stifled a yawn. "Where you been all this time?"

"Having sex in your uncle's front yard… where the hell do you think I've been?" she snorted. "I've been working, which is a lot more than I can say for you." She slammed the doors to the van, and locked them with her remote. She turned and stood facing me, hands on her hips, chin jutting out. She was making a show of being pissed off.

"Dani, I'm sorry I scared you," I said, doing my best to sound contrite, although I didn't feel it. What I was feeling was surprised to find myself at her place. I didn't think TV reporters were allowed to take home company vans, what with all their expensive gear inside. Of course, they're not supposed to leave them unlocked, either. Maybe because it was late? I toyed with quizzing her, but there was enough tension between us. Besides, it gave me an idea. "Look, let me make you a proposition." I said this carefully, calculating her reaction as I rolled out the proposal: "What say you invite me in…"

She started to protest, but I held up my hands. "Hear me out, please, Dani. In exchange for a shower, a couple of hours sleep on your couch, I'll fill you in on everything that's been going on, everything I've held back from you until now—and I admit it, I've not shared everything with you like I should have—but I will."

She eyed me with suspicion for a moment, then strutted to her front door. I leaned against the van wondering if I had overplayed my hand, worried about being abandoned with nowhere to go. It dawned on me that my cell phone was still in the van. Which she had just locked. I couldn't even call a cab. Dani turned to me as she unlocked her front door and stared at me a moment longer, one hand on her hip, the other on the doorknob.

"Well, you coming or no?"

Relieved, I followed her inside. Her condo wasn't any tidier than the last time I'd been there. The sink still overflowed with unwashed dishes, the adjoining living area was littered with magazines, newspapers, and CD jewel cases. How could she live like this? I wondered. Then again, why did I care?

"Come on," she said. "The shower's upstairs. You need to clean up before you crash on my couch."

If I can find it under this mess.

I admired the view as I trailed her up the stairs. She could model for a Buns of Steel ad. Her bedroom was just as untidy as her living room, piles of clothes on the floor, the bed—a handsome oak four-poster—unmade. She caught me critiquing the chaos.

"So, I won't win the *Good Housekeeping* award."

I laughed. "Hey, you should see my place." She should. She might learn how to tidy up.

"Shower's in there," Dani pointed to the bath off the bedroom. "Use any dry towels you can find."

I stripped and left my clothes in a heap on the bathroom floor. I turned the shower up high and let the hot water cascade over my aching body. I reached around my back and soaped the puncture wound from the cactus. I'd need a tetanus booster, but at least it wasn't aching as badly as before. The bathroom became saturated with steam and I luxuriated in the warmth for several minutes, grateful for the chance to relax.

Suddenly, the water turned icy and I almost slipped and fell in astonishment. "What the hell?"

I pulled back the curtain, navy blue, matching the walls—an unusual color scheme for a woman's bathroom. My pile of clothes on the floor was missing. I wrapped a damp towel around my waist and stepped out of the bathroom, beads of moisture still clinging to my legs and back.

Dani wasn't in the bedroom. "Hey, who stole my clothes," I yelled.

"I threw them in the washing machine," Dani's voice rose from the bottom of the stairs. "They were filthy."

That explained the jolt of cold water.

She climbed back up the stairs into the bedroom and sauntered up to me, a provocative gleam in her dark brown eyes. Her gaze swept over me, top to bottom, like Doppler radar, unabashed, unmistakably appraising my physique.

"You clean up all right," she said.

Dani stepped next to me, cocked her head to one side, then reached up and gently ran a fingertip over the wound on my forehead. "This part of the story you're going to tell me?" she asked. Her eyes locked onto mine.

I wasn't expecting this, but I was enjoying it. Her perfume was intoxicating. "Have I ever told you what a turn-on Jessica McClintock is?" I asked, reaching my arms around her narrow waist, drawing her up against me.

"Hmmm."

"Do you know that in Singapore they've outlawed condoms?"

"I'll bet you say that to all the girls."

I leaned down and kissed her. She kissed me back. I let my hands slip down to the arc of her back and pressed her body tightly against mine. Dani's slender arms reached up around my neck, and she kissed me hard, her mouth parting, her tongue playing against mine. She pulled away, gazed into my eyes, and took a deep breath. Then she began kissing me again, this time starting at my chin, then my neck, then my chest. My hands slid up her sides and I gently caressed her breasts as she worked her way down my torso. I felt her hands tugging on the towel, and it fell away.

CHAPTER 33

I AWOKE TO the sound of Dani's purring next to me in her poster bed. Her head was turned toward my face, the air gently whispering in and out of her parted lips, her dark hair splashed across the pillow like an ebony floral arrangement. The digital clock on the nightstand glowed 6:12. It was light outside. The bedroom window faced east, and stripes of sunlight danced across the room through the Venetian blinds. I slipped out of bed, trying not to disturb her.

It was stupid early and I was desperately sleep deprived, but my adrenalin was already pumping. I looked around the cluttered bedroom for my clothes then remembered Dani had washed them. Naked, I padded down the stairs and found the small laundry room off her kitchen. I retrieved my pants, shirt and underwear from the washing machine and tossed them into the dryer, turning the temperature control knob to "High." It would take a while for the clothes to dry. That should give me time for another shower and a shave if I could find a clean razor to borrow. I'd need a new blade.

I noticed a pile of my stuff atop the washer. Dani had emptied my pockets, thankfully. On the top of the heap was Leo's wallet and cell phone. I had forgotten about his phone. Could that be traced? I flipped it open, but the battery had died.

I needed to contact the office. I could imagine the chaotic scene in the newsroom with everyone scrambling to update the story on Leo lapsing into a coma and the mysterious fire that burned his house to the ground. Monday's are always hell at PM papers, anyway, catching up on everything that happened on Sunday when the paper didn't publish.

I had left my cell phone in Dani's van, and I wondered if Edwina Mahoney had tried to reach me. She would be pissed if I didn't check in soon.

I cracked the front door to Dani's condo and peeked out see if the *Arizona Republic* had been delivered yet. It was on the doorstep. I reached out and grabbed it, trying not to flash the neighbors.

A story stripped across the top of the page was datelined out of Uganda. Ravenous Security operatives had secured the uranium deposits in Uganda. Now American Special Forces were pushing into the Congo. No new Ebola deaths in Chicago. CDC officials expressed hope the outbreak had been contained. The Black Canyon Bandito had struck again, hitting two cars with sniper fire. No one injured in the latest attack, which cops said showed signs of increased boldness on the mysterious shooter's part.

There was a tease off the front page to the Local & State section and coverage of the forest fire that was spreading on the Mogollon Rim, now approaching the town of Strawberry. Leo's cabin on the Rim was near there. Could he lose two houses in one week to fire?

There also was a tease to a story about the Tucson family that died in that terrible house fire. The father was an Air Force sergeant named Torres who was in charge of a team that mothballed old planes at Davis-Monthan Air Force Base, the latest of which was the vice president's VC-25A, a modified Boeing 747 that had recently flown to Phoenix during an inspection tour of the new Gitmo on the Rez. The story was accompanied by a picture of the aircraft with dignitaries deplaning. I looked closely and, sure enough, Francis Van Wormer was among the dignitaries, just like the photo we had published earlier.

The story on Leo's condition was the centerpiece of the front page.

It read awkwardly, as if it had been rewritten late in the evening to update it with the news of the fire, which it most certainly had been. There was no photo, not in this edition anyway.

Dani's computer rested on a small desk in the corner of her living room. The screen saver was on. It was a drawing of Wonder Woman. I jiggled the mouse and Diana Prince vanished in favor of her desktop. I clicked on her Internet Explorer icon and navigated to the *Sun's* website. It was packed with stories about Leo. My column was there. There were three photos from the fire. The *Sun* owned the story—online, anyway. I felt a momentary surge of juvenile pride, then felt embarrassed by that. How stupid. Leo was in a coma. His home destroyed. Sarah missing. What a fucking mess. And today, did I really know what the hell I was doing?

I logged onto my Gmail account and dashed out an update for my blog, amplifying on what I'd told Dani in the interview, and emailed it to Edwina, hoping that would keep her off my back for a little while.

Then I climbed back upstairs, hoping to slip into the bathroom unnoticed, but I was surprised to see Dani sitting upright in bed, the sheet bunched at her waist. A silvery band of light from the window painted her naked breasts.

"I like that look," I said, smiling.

"Come here, gringo," she replied, leaning back on the pillow, her eyes locked on mine.

I slipped under the sheet, my torso pressing against her silken skin. My hand caressed her thigh then slowly moved up her body, across her flat belly to her left breast. It was small and firm. I kissed her, gently, on the lips. "This could be habit forming," I said.

"Maybe. If you're lucky."

The first time it had been frenzied; I'd practically torn her clothes off and we had attacked one another. Now, we took our time, exploring one another's bodies, unrushed, tenderly until, finally, she gasped, her hips arching as if shot through with electricity. I held back, determined to satisfy her. Two more times she came, each time with a little gasp like the first, until, finally, panting, she demanded: "Aren't you ever going to come?"

"Wanted to make sure you were OK," I gasped, gazing down into the deep pool of her amber eyes.

She squeezed her strong brown legs even tighter around me. "I'm OK, already."

Later, as we lay entwined, Dani carefully smoothed the matted hair off my forehead and tenderly kissed the C-shaped wound. That seemed to remind her of our bargain, my promise to tell all in exchange for a place to lay my head. I couldn't argue that she hadn't kept up her end of the deal—and more.

"Alex," she said, her voice slipping an octave lower from a tone of endearment to her on-camera persona. "I've enjoyed every minute of this…"

"But?"

"But a deal is a deal."

I considered stringing her along, playing dumb just to make her beg. Taunting had defined our relationship earlier, but it didn't feel right now.

"All right," I said, my stomach churning, fearful about what I might be dragging her into. "But you need to know something in advance…"

"No buts," she insisted. "We made a deal."

"That's right. We're a team, OK?"

She nodded.

"But you need to know something," I persisted. "Once I tell you what's going down, it could be, uh, dangerous for you."

Dani gave me the evil eye.

"I'm not kidding. I'll tell you everything I know, but this is more than just a story, Dani. I'm caught up in something. I'm in in over my head. And once you know what I know you could be, too. I don't mean to be hyperbolic, and I don't want to frighten you, but there it is. You sure?"

"Give it to me."

"Everything?"

"Yeah, everything."

"I'll tell you the whole story on our way downtown."

"Downtown, huh? I'm taking you downtown. Good to know these things. Then what?"

"Then we're going to play Bonnie and Clyde."

"Huh?"

"We're gonna do a bank job."

CHAPTER 34

SHERYL CROW WAS belting out *Steve McQueen* on the van's radio as Dani exited the Papago Freeway and turned south on Seventh Street toward the center of Phoenix. I had just finished telling my story, ending with crashing in the back of the TV van the night before. I had left nothing out. She now knew everything I knew.

Dani was smart; she understood the implications.

"So, let me see if I got this," she said, changing lanes to pass a slow moving Lincoln. I checked for a vanity plate. I wasn't disappointed. "EZ RDER" it said. The blue-haired woman behind the wheel looked nothing like Dennis Hopper. Then again, Dennis Hopper didn't look like Dennis Hopper anymore.

"We got some bad guys who've kidnapped Mrs. Strano and her dog, and they expect you to deliver something to them or, she's gonna get iced. Right?"

I nodded.

"And somebody burned down your uncle's house and killed two cops, to boot. Maybe the same bad guys, maybe not. The kidnapper— you call him, what, Robbie the Robot?—seemed surprised, but of course, he could be lying.

"You may, or may not, be under FBI surveillance, which means *I* may, or may not be under surveillance, too. And since we don't know who the bad guys are, and since, paranoid or not, you think there's a chance the government may somehow be hooked up in this fucking can of worms because of that bullet you found, the fact that the FBI may be tailing us shouldn't make us feel all warm and fuzzy."

Dani looked over at me for confirmation.

"So far. so good," I said. "And the bad guys may be tailing us, too, I suppose, though I hope we've given them the slip, traveling in this van instead of my car." While she was talking I was chowing down on a granola bar I'd liberated from her kitchen. It was the only edible food I could find in there. She had been out of coffee, too, and if I didn't find some soon I'd get the DTs.

"All right, then," she continued. "If I'm linked to you, then I might be in danger, too. That's what you were warning me about back at my place. Got that right?"

"Yeah, Dani, I'm afraid so."

"Oh, don't look so glum, Strange," she said.

Strange?

"I mean, what the hell. This may be a story that makes my career, or I could be dead by sunset. Gotta roll the dice, right?"

"Look, Dani, there's a very good chance nobody knows where we are right now," I said, looking at the exterior rear view mirror. The old lady in the Lincoln was drifting further behind in the other lane. A blue Ford pickup truck was two car-lengths to our rear.

"Your cell phone has built-in GPS, right?" she asked.

I slipped out my iPhone and waggled it. "Sure." I hadn't mentioned the virus the FBI had loaded into my phone. Wasn't being coy, but with all I had to unload, I'd zoned out on that detail. "Thing is, my phone's been turned off. Unless somebody spotted me crawling into the van last night, I'm off their radar screen and you're in the clear."

"If some Peeping Tom wasn't tailing you, yeah."

"Let's assume that for now," I said. "If things go south for me, you've got a hell of a story to tell."

I slipped on my Oakleys. Even though it was early, it was already bright and it looked like it would be another scorcher. Dani had ditched her Eltons for contact lenses. It was a better look. I shifted my weight in the seat to take the pressure off my back where it had been pierced the night before by the prickly pear cactus.

"Listen, Dani, we're still a few blocks from my office. Why don't you just drop me off and I can hoof it in. That way if anyone is staking out the newspaper, you won't be seen with me."

She gave me a hard look.

"What?"

"We're partners, you know."

"Sure. But this way is safer..."

"No. We're in this together." She waited a beat or two then glanced sideways at me. "Besides, you said I could rob a bank. What's that about?"

I shrugged. "Yeah. I need to get into my safe deposit box and find out what Leo's hidden there."

"So what's the plan?"

I cleared my throat. "Well, it's a simple plan, an elegant plan, really. When the bank opens, I'll go over there, empty the safe deposit box, and take it all back to the office and see what's what."

"That's it? That's your plan?" Dani was incredulous. "And if you're followed when you leave the newspaper you think you'll just walk out of that bank. How far you think you'll get, Alex?"

I liked that she was calling me Alex again. She sounded worried about me, too. That was reassuring.

"Hmm." I cleared my throat again. "There is one more itsy bitsy little thing I suppose I should tell you. Nobody outside my family—which would be Leo—knows this, but, uh, how can I say this..."

"*Habla ingles.*"

"When I was born, and my mom filled out the birth certificate, she didn't name me Alexander. She was stoned, you understand, and not altogether in her right mind."

"So..."

"You have to understand, I loved my mom, but she was a world class drug addict."

"So?"

"So, my uncle—Leo—when he adopted me, the first thing he did was get my name legally changed."

"Is there a punch line here?"

"Uh, yeah. My original name. No longer my name, mind you, was Alice."

"*¡Qué!*" The van swerved halfway into the next lane before she regained control. "What do you mean your real name is *Alice*?"

"Was. No more. It was my mother's name. There was a mix-up on the birth certificate. She never bothered to get it fixed, in part, I think, because she thought it would be cool, you know, like Alice Cooper. Never asked what I thought."

Dani shot me a "What the fuck?" look. If a Martian had landed on the hood of the van and started pissing gasoline, I don't think she could have been more dumbfounded.

"Anyway," I said, "I still have that original birth certificate. And sometimes I use it to, uh, you know, obfuscate my identity, cover my tracks."

"So is Strange your real last name?"

"Well, yeah, although Mom's last name was Strano, like Leo's, but she never liked it. Went by Alice Sunshine. When I was born—I mentioned she was stoned, right?—she not only fucked up my first name but also went with Sunshine as my last name."

"Not your father's last name?"

"She didn't know his name."

"Your mother was an asshole."

That pissed me off.

"And your name is Vaquero? Really? A cowboy?"

"Yeah, it is. And I know who *my* father is."

"That's special."

A few minutes passed, and then it eventually dawned on her that maybe she should say something if she wanted to know more about my plan. I was too annoyed to volunteer it. The word pissy comes to mind.

"All right, Alex. So where were you going with this?"

"The name on the safe deposit box. It's registered to Alice Sunshine."

Dani shook her head as if that would clear out the confusion. I marveled at the way her hair swirled around when she did that.

"Soooo… I've just slept with an Alice. Girl gone wild. How nice for me. Now tell me, what's this got to do with our bank job?"

"Well, um, it occurred to me that when I went to the bank I might go, you know, in disguise."

Dani burst into laughter.

"Don't tell me," she said, trying to catch her breath and keep the van in the road at the same time. "You're going in drag?"

I felt the blood rush to my face. "That's what I was thinking. It's been more than a year since I've gotten anything out of the box. Doubt anyone at the bank would recognize me. So I show up, sign for it as Alice, slip out."

"Slip out. Underneath the radar screen?" She was parroting a line from Sheryl Crow's song.

"Right."

"What, you gonna wear a wig? And a dress?" She was tittering now. "You shave your legs lately, sweetie?"

I raised my knee, the uninjured one, and pulled up my pants exposing a cleanly shaved calf. "Used your razor this morning."

Dani stared at my leg in disbelief. I frantically grabbed the steering wheel to keep us from drifting into the curb.

Dani shook her head again. It was becoming a habit.

"I slept with a cross-dresser."

CHAPTER 35

As WE APPROACHED the *Phoenix Daily Sun* building on Adams Street, we could see a crowd gathered outside the front entrance. Dozens of staff members were picketing the building, waving signs demanding that the management bargain with the Newspaper Guild.

"This Newspaper is Edited by Rats," one sign read. I wondered how Edwina Mahoney felt about that. Another said: "Guild Local 55446." Simplicity defines elegance. Yet another: "Boycott the Sun." That was unacceptable. Now was not the time to drive off readers, for crying out loud.

Dani edged to the curb and stopped the van. We were getting a lot of smiles from the picketers. Took me a moment to realize why. Of course: We were in the television station van. The strikers thought they were going to get some TV coverage, earn their fifteen seconds of fame. Standing curbside was Elmore James, the ringleader of the insurrection. He turned toward the van, a wide grin cracking his pockmarked face, confident that the strike was going to receive the media attention the union organizers craved. His idiotic smile vanished when I stepped out the door

"Hello, Elmore," I said cheerfully. "Fine day for a strike."

"Strange," he sputtered.

"Very good. Your powers of observation are as keen as ever."

James was looking up at me, blocking the front entrance to the newspaper. I heard a door slam, and Dani strode around the van to stand beside me.

"Move it, pinhead," I said.

James blinked, briskly stepped to one side, and we crossed the picket line.

"Scab!" I heard him yell at my back.

"Who was that pussy?" Dani asked as we walked into the building.

I really liked this girl.

After negotiating the security desk and walking up the stairs to the second floor, we stepped into the newsroom. It was quiet for a Monday, what with half the staff boycotting the place. Edwina was on the phone at the City Desk, her back to us. Eduardo was hammering madly away at a keyboard. Abigail Conwest and a handful of editors were over at the Copy Desk, their faces glued to their computer screens. That, at least, was a helpful sign: We might not have many stories in the paper with all the reporters skulking on the sidewalk, but at least with the Copy Desk hard at work we could get a newspaper out.

I led Dani along the back wall of the newsroom, taking a wide detour around the City Desk, hoping to avoid Edwina's gaze. We slipped into my office. I knew we wouldn't have long before she spotted us and I ended up shanghaied into helping write for the first edition. The deadline was 9 a.m. Bank didn't open until then anyway.

"Let me just check for messages," I said, spying the blinking red light on my phone. I slipped into my chair, setting Leo's planner on my desk. I wasn't sure when I'd have time to start digging through it again. While I punched in my voicemail pass code, I also turned on my desktop computer. I wanted to check my email, too.

There were the usual circulation complaints on voice mail, a handful of crank calls including yet another from Dr. Omar Franken demanding a retraction of my column debunking his Stealth Car Wax, and a message from Hawker, already up after a late night and checking in, wondering what the plan was for the day. He'd slept fast, too.

The last message was from Sarah's sister, Rebecca, in Ogden. Sarah hadn't arrived on her flight. She'd heard the news about the judge. She couldn't think of anyone else to call. Her voice sounded nervous, if not downright panicky. She said I needed to know something, and would I please pass it along to Sarah (if only I could): She had filed a motion in juvenile court to remove their mother as the guardian of their little sister. The judge had granted her temporary custody.

"I don't know if you know what's happening, if Sarah has shared this with you, but Jacoby's attorneys have filed an appeal, and it's scheduled to be heard next week." There was a pause. "Listen, you should know that I've heard from a friend in the church that he's, Jacoby's, furious about this. He's going on about vengeance, burning in hell, and such. I'm worried. This guy's crazy. I need to get out of here for a little while. Please let Sarah know I'm taking our sister away and I'll call back in a few days."

I tried returning the call, but there was no answer.

Terrific. Like I didn't have enough to worry about already.

I noticed a pink phone message slip on my desk blotter. It was from a Mr. Akin at the Akin Bowdy Funeral Home. I punched in the number. I was surprised when a voice answered after the second ring.

Akin: This is the Akin Bowdy Funeral Home. How may we be of service to you and yours?

Me: Yes, this is Alexander Strange, I was returning your phone call.

Akin: Oh, certainly, Mr. Strange. My sincerest condolences. Akin Bowdy stands ready to assist you in any way we can.

Me: Thank you, I guess. But what's this about?

Akin: Your uncle, of course. Judge Strano. We have specific instructions from him to contact you.

Me: Uh, you do know he's not dead?

Akin: Yes, of course. But we can't be too prepared, can we? Should his condition worsen, we want you to know we are here to assist you and to provide you any support we can.

Me: Uh…

Akin: Mr. Strange, you should know that Judge Strano has taken care of all the paperwork in advance. Our 'Golden Hereafter Plan' makes this so much easier on the bereaved. You needn't do anything other than select the date.

Me: Maybe sometime after he's actually dead?

Akin: There are upgrades available at a small additional charge…

I hung up, puzzled, and looked up to see Edwina Mahoney in my doorway.

"Where the hell have you been?" she demanded, whipping her glasses off. "We've been trying to get hold of you all night."

"Hi, Ed, good seeing you, too," I replied in my best effort to sound chipper. "Edwina Mahoney, Dani Vaquero. I don't know if the two of you have met yet."

Edwina turned to see Dani rising from the couch, her hand extended in greeting. Edwina ignored her and turned back to me.

"What's she doing here?"

"Uh, you know, media convergence partners…"

Dani remained standing, her hand still extended. Edwina turned to her, took her hand, and shook it.

"I'm sorry," she said. "That was rude. How do you do?"

Dani kept her cool. "It's chill. We're all stressed right now."

"Sit down, Ed," I told her. "We need to talk."

I brought her up to date on what had happened since we had spoken last, filling her in on everything except Dani and me: I lied, told her I slept on the couch, but I didn't think she was fooled. Edwina gave Dani the hairy eyeball, but had sense enough not to press it.

"So you dragged DePutron into this, too?"

"Yeah, I was desperate."

"What about Hawker?" she asked. "You still—what was it you said? —you still think he's sketchy?"

"Don't know," I replied. "He gives me the jibblies sometimes."

That earned a curious look, like she wanted to hear more about that, but there wasn't time. I glanced at my watch and realized we needed to get going before I lost my resolve.

"Look, Ed, I know we've got an edition to publish and you're as busy as a one-armed paper-hanger, but I need a favor."

"What is it?"

"I need you to talk Conwest into letting me borrow her wig."

"*Her wig?*"

"Yeah." I leaned to one side to peer out my door toward the Copy Desk. "Oh, good, she's got that new platinum job."

I turned back to my boss. "One more thing, Ed."

Edwina shook her head, as if somehow that would reorder the words she had just heard into something that made sense.

"There's more?"

"Yeah." I plugged my iPhone into its charger.

"I'll need her dress, too."

CHAPTER 36

"I think I'm having a hot flash."

I turned to my companion, hoping for a little girl-to-girl sympathy. All I got was a scowl.

"Believe me," Edwina said, "you'd know it if you were."

I tugged on the wig, making sure it was snug. "OK, you ready?" I asked.

"Ready."

We opened the doors to Edwina's car and stepped out into the Wells Fargo parking garage. We were on the seventh level overlooking the bank below. A circular glass dome pierced the flat roof of the bank. I knew that underneath that dome was the spacious, circular lobby, with its concentric rings of black terrazzo flooring creating a bulls-eye motif. Seemed a strange decor for a bank, painting a target, as it were, but nobody's ever paid me to be an interior designer. Our immediate destination was the elevator that opened to an outdoor plaza below, next to the Wells Fargo History Museum, the centerpiece of which was a beautifully restored stagecoach that once carried the mail in these parts.

Plan A called for me to follow Edwina into the bank. She would linger in the lobby, maybe hang around at one of the information kiosks or pretend to fill out a deposit slip or something—anything to stall for time—while I went to the safe deposit vault. Dani would be along soon and would park across the street from the bank's main entrance on Washington Street.

The plan assumed that even if the newspaper were staked out, my wig and dress would throw off any trackers and I could get in and out of the bank unnoticed. Because we had to cross an outdoor plaza to get from the parking garage to the actual bank building, we agreed, outrageous as it seemed, I would need to stay in disguise the entire time; it wasn't enough to just leave the newspaper undetected.

Plan A also assumed, in the alternative, that in the event I were spotted, that I still would be able to enter the bank, but would be intercepted only when I tried to leave. After all, there would be no point nabbing me until I got the goods. That's where Dani and Edwina would come in. I would empty the contents of my safe deposit box into Edwina's brown handbag, which I was carrying. As I left, I would discretely hand off the bag to Edwina in the bank lobby and exit via the front door where Dani would be waiting inside the TV van with her camera rolling. If anyone tried to grab me, she'd get it on videotape and put it on the air right away. If not, we'd meet back at the newspaper where, Plan A assumed, Edwina would return unnoticed with the goods from the safe deposit box. That was it. Basically.

There was no Plan B.

"How are the shoes?" Edwina asked, glancing down at my borrowed high heels. They were white, matching the red and white belted shift Conwest had been coerced into donating.

"I'm going to break my freaking neck. Would you believe they're too big for me? What an Amazon. Why do women put up with these things, anyway?"

"Wheels, baby, wheels. Gotta look good for the sperm donors," she replied. Edwina reached out and made an adjustment to my silvery wig, brushing a few strands down over the horseshoe-shaped scab on my forehead. The makeup she had applied didn't quite conceal it. She handed me a cell phone. "Don't forget this."

I took it and clipped it on the dress's white belt.

"You do look flushed," Edwina said. "Stage fright?"

"I feel like a complete ass. I've never been more embarrassed in my life. Why did I believe this was a good idea? I'll need therapy—if I survive."

Edwina laughed. "You think you're embarrassed, think about poor Abigail, locked in my office. We'll never convince her this isn't some sort of elaborate practical joke. She'll end up suing the company."

Conwest was shocked when Edwina called her into her office. "Abigail, I know this sounds preposterous, but it's urgent," Edwina said straight-faced.

"You're setting me up," Conwest blurted. "What's next? A photographer storms in here and takes a picture of me in my underwear? I'm being punked, right?" She began to tear up. "I can't believe you, of all people, would pull a stunt like this," she screeched at Edwina. "This is sexual harassment!"

It had taken a few minutes to talk her off the ledge, to calm her hysteria, to persuade her that, as bizarre as it sounded, the request that she disrobe was on the level and a matter of utmost urgency; that by doing this she was playing a key role in an investigation that had life and death implications; yadda, yadda, yadda. Eventually, she relented when Edwina pointed out that no photographer could storm into her office to snap Conwest's picture—they were all outside on strike.

"And what the hell am I supposed to do while you're off gallivanting about town with my clothes? Just sit around in your office in my bra and panties?"

"Here's a copy of *Fowler's Modern English Usage*," Edwina said, deadpan. "Amuse yourself."

Edwina turned to leave, then paused. "Oh, one more thing. Monitor my calls when they come in, would you? Might be something important."

"I'm not your fucking secretary," Conwest pouted.

"Good girl."

Edwina gave me one last look-over and adjusted something on the wig.

"You looks tense," she said.

"No shit."

"Come on, Alex, where's that smartass we know and love?"

"Your mom."

"That's better."

I was so nervous, I forgot I was in the confined space of an elevator. Maybe you can't be paranoid about more than one thing at a time.

Edwina exited the elevator and made a beeline for the bank's entrance. I trailed a few steps behind, stumbling in the high heels. When we entered, she meandered across the lobby to join a line waiting for a teller as I haltingly walked toward the vault holding the safe deposit boxes. At any moment, I would fall out of the damned heels and make an even bigger fool of myself. I was sweating. With every click of my high heels I imagined a hundred suspicious eyes trained on me.

I'm as conspicuous as a fart in church.

I hobbled over to the desk at the gate dividing the lobby from the safe deposit vault and presented my key to the receptionist, a slight young man in a dark coat, white shirt and rep tie.

"Name, please," he asked without looking up from his paperwork.

"Alice Sunshine," I replied softly, feeling my face grow hot. The receptionist glanced up.

His right eyebrow rose perceptibly and he cocked his head fractionally.

"I've undergone some changes." Alexander Strange, master of disguise. I felt like melting into the cracks in the terrazzo floor.

"Step over here, please," the receptionist said, officiously. I noticed the brass nametag on his lapel.

"Certainly, Robert," I replied, my voice pinched.

The "here" to which Robert referred was a fingerprint scanner, installed as an extra security measure. It was the reason I knew I had to personally make the trip to the safe deposit box. I had considered dispatching Dani, having her forge my signature, hoping that since the account was in Alice Sunshine's name she could bamboozle a bank clerk. But she couldn't fool a machine.

"Place your right index finger on the screen, please," Robert said. I did as I was told. A blue light moved up then down the screen. Robert looked up from a desktop computer attached to the scanning device, an expression of faint surprise on his face.

"Thank you, uh, Alice," he stammered. "Please follow me."

I turned to follow him into the vault and almost fell on my face as the heel of my right shoe slipped on the polished floor.

"Dammit!"

Robert stopped and turned to me. "Beg your pardon?"

"It's nothing. Just a little hitch in my giddy up."

That earned me another raised eyebrow, but Robert turned back toward the vault.

Hitch in my giddy up? You can take the boy out of Texas...

My stomach was churning and my right knee was beginning to throb again. What would I find in the safe deposit box? Would there be anything at all? Would I make it out of the bank alive? Will they find a cure for paranoia?

Robert inserted his key, then mine, into the matching locks of the small steel door to the safe deposit box. He twisted them in a simultaneous motion, tugged the door open, and then turned to me to finish the job. I stood motionless for a moment, transfixed. "Well?" he said, a tone of impatience in his voice. I grabbed the handle and slid the box out of its snug compartment, then allowed Robert to guide me to an alcove with a small countertop. He closed the curtain to the booth as he exited. With nervous fingers, I opened the lid to the box.

Lying on top was a manila envelope with AF2 scrawled in Leo's green ink. As I lifted it out of the box, I noticed another document underneath. I set the manila envelope aside and opened the sheaf of papers. It was Leo's living will and durable power of attorney. I checked the date. It was only a month old. Leo had updated his end-of-life instructions. Nervously, I thumbed through the document until I got to the page where he listed his power of attorney. He had changed the name to Sarah Strano. But he had added a second name: Alexander Strange.

Oh My God. I had the power all along to forestall Leo's DNR and didn't know it.

I folded the document and shoved it into Edwina's purse. I had to get out of the bank and head straight to the hospital. But first, I had to examine the contents of the manila envelope.

Inside was a small memory card and a letter addressed to Leo. I opened it and pulled out a sheaf of typewritten pages stapled together. In the opening sentence, the writer identified himself, and when I read the name I paused for a moment, realizing it was familiar. Then it hit me and I began sweating. I had to set the letter down. I gripped the counter and forced myself to calm my breathing. It took at least a full minute to regain my composure to read the letter in full. Then I took out my cell phone, not the one Edwina had given me, but my own, which I had tucked under Conwest's dress.

I was surprised to see Edwina still waiting in line for a teller as I wobbled back into the main lobby. Things must be moving slowly this morning. At that moment, to my right, I heard shoes slapping rapidly on the hard floor. Out of the corner of my eye I saw a man in a dark suit lumbering toward me. It was Volker.

"You! Halt!"

I broke into a sprint toward the door and felt myself falling as the high heels buckled underneath me. I hit the terrazzo hard on my left shoulder, rolled and jumped up, the wig and high heels flying free. I raced for the revolving door in my bare feet, glancing back to see Edwina throw herself on the floor in front of the Volker, who stumbled over her and fell flat on his face. If she ever burned out in the newspaper biz she could play tackle for the Cardinals.

A frail, elderly woman, gray haired, hobbling with a cane, was just clearing the slowly turning revolving door as I smashed into it in full stride. I burst onto the sidewalk.

I looked across the street, expecting to see Dani and her TV van, but she wasn't there.

Another dark suit appeared around the corner to my left and began running toward me. I wheeled to the right and 20 yards away were yet another two suits, dark like the others, heading my way.

Somebody in this town was making a killing in menswear.

Tires screeched on the pavement behind me and a black Chrysler 300 with a custom panoramic glass top lurched to the curb. I whirled to see Morrison Hawker leaning out the passenger window.

"Get in," he barked.

The side door opened. and I dove in.

CHAPTER 37

"Nice ride," I said, gasping. "The cavalry to the…"

I looked around the interior of the Chrysler and clammed up. Mohawk's great bald head was brushing the glass-top ceiling over the seat rest in front of me. The driver was a white guy with close-cropped black hair and sunglasses. The guy in the back seat next to me was also wearing sunglasses and a very large gun that was resting in his lap. The barrel was pointed at me. No suppressor.

"Those Ray Bans?" I asked. "They're styling."

He gave me a tough-guy sneer, but said nothing.

"Uh, Mohawk, who are your friends?"

Hawker lowered his sun visor and slid open the mirror. "Nice dress," he said.

I grabbed the door handle and tugged at it frantically. Locked. Childproof, prisoner-proof.

I turned, determined to do something, anything, to fight back, and found myself staring into the blank eye of Backseat Thug's gun.

"Mr. Strange, please," he said, extending the open palm of his other hand. His acne-scarred face and raspy voice were unfamiliar, but there were just three people who called me mister. Bevin, Collins, and…

"Robbie the Robot! You're even uglier than I imagined. What's with your face? You fall on a hand grenade?"

He speared the barrel of the gun into my solar plexus, and suddenly I couldn't breathe. Was I shot? I looked down, but there was no blood. I still couldn't breathe. With his free hand, Robbie shoved me over to my side of the seat, where I collapsed. I crouched there, like a beached flounder, desperately trying to force air into my lungs. My head was swirling. I choked back an upsurge of vomit. I sensed more than felt Edwina's purse being pulled from my hand. It entered my line of sight as Robbie the Robot passed it forward to Hawker. Then I could feel him tugging at the belt of my dress.

"Robbie, I didn't know you cared." I croaked. Then he punched me in the gut again with the muzzle.

"We'll take that too," he said, unclipping the cell phone Edwina had given me. He handed it to the driver, who rolled down his window and tossed it into the street.

"No need," Hawker said.

The driver glanced at Hawker. "What's in there?"

Hawker began digging through the purse. "There's some papers. Looks like medical forms. Oh, the judge's DNR."

"What else?"

"Let's see. Some keys, lipstick, a camera, notebook, pens, a compact, Kleenex…"

"Come on."

"Ah." Hawker removed the manila envelope with AF2 scribbled in green ink on the outside. He opened the envelope and extracted the letter inside. Then he shook the envelope and out of the corner of my eye I saw a tiny black SD memory card fall into his lap.

"Well lookie here," Hawker said.

He picked up the SD card and waved it for Robbie to see. It was smaller than his fingernail.

Robbie kept the gun pointed at me as he reached over the front seat with his free hand. Hawker handed him the memory card and papers. Robbie glanced at them, then turned to me.

"Who knows about this?"

"Is it true robots have no dicks?"

He was shouting now: "Who knows?"

"Me, myself and I."

He let the papers and the SD card drop to the floor mat, turned to face me, and put both hands on the submachine gun.

"Dude," I blurted. "I told you I would play ball. What more do you want from me?"

Hawker looked at me in his sun visor mirror. "You read the letter?"

It took me a moment to grasp the significance of that. I shook my head. "Of course not."

The driver glanced at Robbie in his rear view mirror. "It don't matter."

"He didn't read…" Hawker started.

The driver persisted. "It don't matter."

Hawker exhaled, said nothing.

I was unnerved by the exchange. "Mohawk, you're making your friend very anxious. What's going on here?"

A sign, "Black Canyon Freeway 1 Mile," loomed through the Chrysler's windshield.

"Mohawk, where're you taking me, anyway?"

Nothing.

I repeated the question: "Come on, Mohawk." A lesser man would have experienced anxiety in that moment.

Hawker grabbed the back of his seat with his massive right hand and swiveled around to look me in the eye. But it wasn't his eyes that I noticed. It was his ring, the oversized gold one, his bling. But for the first time I noticed it had a raised horseshoe in the center. The arrogant son of a bitch had been wearing it all along, even when we were at Kelso's talking about the shape of the wound on my forehead.

"What's the 'C' stand for, Mohawk? Cocksucker?"

That earned me a raised eyebrow. He raised his hand and admired the ring.

"Kelso was right. Not a 'C.' A horseshoe. Won it at Binon's."

At least now I knew how they got my cell phone number to call me the night Sarah was snatched. How they had Leo's number to threaten him. Mohawk had been on my short list, but I hadn't wanted to believe it.

"Tell me about Sarah. Where is she? She all right?"

Nothing.

"Goddammit, Mohawk, enough of the silent treatment. Level with me."

Mohawk shook his head before answering. "Sorry," he said, turning to stare straight ahead.

Sorry? What the hell did that mean?

"You working with the feds I saw in the bank?" I asked.

The driver snorted.

"What?"

"How the hell did you ever get to be a reporter?" Robbie asked.

My uncle arranged it, and I'm not a reporter, I'm a columnist. So there. But, I still had a trick up my sleeve. More or less literally.

"OK, not government. Private, right?"

Hawker turned in his seat, as if he were about to say something, but Robbie cut him off. "Turn around Hawker."

The driver steered the Chrysler onto the Black Canyon Freeway on-ramp. I leaned back against the door and turned my head so the glare from the sun shining through the car's custom glass roof didn't blind me.

"Just out of curiosity," I asked Robbie, "is that a Heckler and Koch MP5 slash 10?"

Robbie cocked his head in surprise.

"I've never handled one of those before," I continued. "Mind if I try?" I reached out, but he jabbed me in the ribs with the barrel and leaned back to his side of the car, raising the weapon and aiming it at my forehead.

"Don't get too cute, Mr. Strange. This car may be boosted, but I still don't want to get it messy. Now sit back and put your seatbelt on."

I pushed my back to the door and swiveled to face him. "I don't wear seatbelts. Makes me claustrophobic."

"So will a coffin."

The Chrysler was barreling north, heading out of town. The big sedan's AC was struggling to cool the car with the sun baking the interior through the glass top.

"Mohawk, talk to me."

Hawker looked at the driver. He shrugged. "Doesn't matter," he said.

"Tell you what," Robbie said. "We've got a bit of a drive ahead of us. Why don't you tell us what you know and I'll fill in the blanks, satisfy your curiosity, not that it will do you any good."

If there were a downside to that proposition, I didn't see it. I had nothing to bargain with. He had the gun. Maybe I'd learn something; maybe the trick I had up my sleeve would work.

"OK, well I guess there's no point bluffing now," I said, trying to sound contrite, resigned to my fate. "I did read the letter in the bank. I wonder if you guys even know the extent of what you're involved in. No offense, but I can't imagine any of you, especially you Mohawk, being too high in the food chain."

I looked to see if that got any reaction. Robbie just nodded, offered a paternalistic smile and said, "Go on."

"Here's the Reader's Digest version. I'll try to use small words: That document is a letter from an Air Force sergeant in Tucson named Manuel Torres. He refers to a recording, the memory card you're after, I presume. Torres says in the letter that it's an audio clip between two men aboard Air Force Two, the vice president's plane."

At that, Hawker turned in his seat, his eyes wide.

"Easy, Hawker," Robbie said. "Let him finish his little story."

"The sergeant was part of a team assigned to decommission the aircraft. The VP's got a swankier new plane now with updated electronics and stuff. Anyway, they flew it down to Phoenix before heading over to Davis-Monthan in Tucson where they mothball old Air Force planes. The Secretary of Homeland Security hitched a ride to check out the new Guantanamo they built out on the Rez.

"What they didn't know is that the VP, paranoid douche bag that he is, had the plane bugged, like Nixon's White House. A conversation between the secretary and another man was captured on the recording system. Torres stumbled across it during the decommissioning."

At that, the driver's eyes left the road and were for a long moment trained on me in his rear view mirror.

"The other guy appears to have been a high ranking executive of an energy conglomerate. You will recall that before joining the government, our esteemed Secretary of Homeland Security was CEO of Ravenous Unlimited Global Holdings."

The car swerved and there was a thump. I was thrown toward Robbie. He jabbed me in the ribs again with the barrel, hard.

"Watch it," he barked.

I looked out the back window. The remains of a dog were in the lane behind us. From the looks of the carcass, it was a German shepherd, and ours wasn't the first car to run over it. I wondered if it could have been the same bad boy who attacked me the other night.

The Chrysler continued northward on the Black Canyon Freeway leaving the city behind. We were in the passing lane, going fast, closing on a pickup truck in front of us. I checked the plates.

RALPH.

Another shot to the ribs and that might just be me all over the back seat.

"You were saying," Robbie prompted.

"Yeah, well, during the conversation captured on the recording, the secretary and the greed head from the energy company are yakking about how political unrest in the Congo was spreading to the borderlands of Uganda where American mining companies have major lease holdings. The skirmish in Uganda, by the way, fellows, has been in the news quite a bit if you haven't been keeping up. What with all your running around, shooting up innocent people's houses and kidnapping helpless women and puppies, I know it's got to be a struggle to stay current..."

"Just get on with it," Robbie snarled.

"And the mining, it's for uranium. You know, the stuff that makes atom bombs."

Robbie wagged the gun in my face.

"Right. Well, the upshot is that Mr. Homeland Security and Mr. Greed Head agree something must be done. The unrest in that region of Africa would prove threatening to our national security. After all, the business of America is business and ain't no bidness like the atom bomb bidness, right, fellas? They chat a bit about public reaction, political polls, and stuff. Then there's some mention of the Ebola virus outbreak in Chicago, something about how convenient that might be, and then the recording goes dead.

"Our sergeant knew he was holding a hot potato. And he didn't know what to do with it. If he turned it over to his superiors, it could end up in a black hole. Uncle Leo had represented his older brother some years before when he was a trial lawyer. Torres said in his letter that he remembered how hard Leo had worked to get his brother off. Armed robbery or something. He'd been reminded of Leo after reading in the papers a while back how he had blocked the federal government from building a new Gitmo in Mesa. Figured Leo might be somebody not in The Man's pocket. So he contacted him.

"The night before you fuckers shot up his house, Leo arranged to have me meet with someone. Wouldn't say who. It's pretty clear, now, that it was that sergeant. He never made it. He and his family burned to death in their house."

A green highway sign flashed overhead blocking the sun for an instant.

"I gotta ask you," I said to Robbie. "Did you have to kill his entire family?"

The driver was watching me in the rear view mirror. Robbie and Hawker both had their eyes glued on me.

"You down with that, Mohawk?"

He shook his head, started to speak, but the driver snapped, "Don't say anything."

I looked at Hawker. "Tell me, Mohawk, I'm dying to know this—you'll excuse the expression. You're the inside guy. You told these clowns about Torres. Had to be you. But how'd you know I'd be at the bank this morning?"

Hawker shook his massive head. "You just like the judge. Predictable." His voice was raspy, as usual, but there was something off in the tone. Remorse? Guilt?

"I am not predictable," I said. "I'm reliable. There's a difference."

"Well," Hawker said, exhaling, "I relied on you to go to the bank. Tailed the judge there Friday. He went in with an envelope. Came out empty-handed. Figured you'd get there after a while."

"Nice," I said. "So you knew all along."

"No. But I knew when I saw 727."

"How?"

"Told you I'm devious. Judge had the safe deposit number in his planner."

"Which you read. Which is how you knew about the meeting."

Hawker said nothing.

"That how these assholes were able to get into Leo's house. You give them a key? You steal that from Leo?"

Hawker's mouth opened then closed. Then he did it again, like a guppy struggling for air. I had my answer. It wasn't Sarah's fault after all. An unlatched gate and an unlocked door? It was always too easy.

"Well, good to solve that mystery. There's just one more thing, isn't there? Now we know the truth. How the American people have been lied to. The lengths some people will go to cover up the truth.

This is a massive conspiracy. Americans have died. This is murder. This is treason."

Nobody said anything.

"What, cat got your tongue?" I said to Robbie. "How about you, Mohawk?"

I took a breath. Then another. Nobody was talking. Robbie was staring at the back of the driver's head, though the MP5 was still trained at my midsection. Does a pro ever take his eyes off a captive? Why hadn't they cuffed me? Or thrown me in the trunk? Or shot me, already?

"Satisfy my curiosity on one more thing, would you?" I was looking at Robbie and he turned back to me and met my gaze. The creases on his forehead and around his eyes had become cavernous.

"Why'd you try to kill Leo? Why not just snatch Sarah in the first place? How'd you know he hadn't made provisions to have this stuff released in case something happened?"

Robbie grinned. "If I wanted the judge dead, he would have been dead. That was just a warning."

A warning? A hugely public warning when they were trying to keep this covered up? That was idiotic.

"Who are you guys?" I asked.

Robbie slipped his finger inside the trigger guard. I felt a sudden need to urinate. If I'd been smarter, I'd have felt a sudden need to shut up.

I was keeping my eyes low, avoiding the sun's glare through the glass roof. But, out of a corner of my eye, I spotted something high in the sky. Not a jet. Maybe a chopper. It was there, then it was gone.

"You guys are private, right? You Ravenous Security? That would fit. Same mercenaries guarding the uranium mines. That you?"

"Shut up," Robbie barked. "Just shut the fuck up."

Bingo.

"Let me repeat the question I asked you last night," I said. "You the pyromaniac that burned down Leo's house, killed those cops?"

"That wasn't us," he said, his voice strained.

"By 'us' who do you mean?"

Nothing.

"How about you, Mr. Driver Man? You know who the cop killers are?"

Still nothing.

"You kill that family in Tucson, or was that somebody else, too?"

Nobody said a word, but Robbie blinked. Twice. His face was drawn, a bead of sweat ran down the side of his face.

"I'll take your silence as a no, too." I shook my head. "You poor saps. You don't have a fucking clue. You're just the errand boys. Get the recording, that's what you were told, right? You think the guys who burned down Leo's house, who killed those cops, who murdered that family, you think they're going to let you live? Knowing what you know now?"

"Except for one thing," said Robbie, his voice hoarse. "No one knows we know." He'd addressed the statement to his fellow co-conspirators. The driver nodded, obviously understanding the implications.

"Too late for that now," I said.

"And why is that?" he asked, irritated.

"Because of this."

Ignoring the gun in my ribs, I dug into the top of the dress and pulled out my iPhone. The phone Abigail Conwest was listening to and recording. The phone that I had used inside the safe deposit vault to photograph the documents. The phone I used to dictate to Conwest a summary of what the documents showed. And because it was on, the phone the FBI would no doubt be tracking.

My original plan had been to use Edwina's phone and to leave mine turned off, but she had an older model and the camera's resolution was inadequate to get good images of the documents. So I'd activated my iPhone, hoping its signal would be shielded by the vault. But to email my pictures of the documents, I had to leave the vault area, and when I did, I knew the FBI tracking virus would be onto to me. At the time, I hated that, but there was no choice. Now, it seemed genius.

Hawker released his grip on the seatback and snatched the phone out of my hands.

I enjoyed a fleeting moment of feeling very smart, very superior. Then Hawker turned the phone's screen to face me.

"Notice a problem?" he asked.

I stared at the screen in disbelief. "No Service," it said.

I was stunned, and for a moment said nothing.

"I told you guys it works," Hawker said.

"What?" I asked, dumfounded.

"Stealth Car Wax. Stops radar, Also stops radio signals, like cell phone signals."

I sat there numb for a moment, then finally recovered enough to ask: "But it doesn't work, Mohawk. We proved that. Right?"

"Nah. You didn't prove shit."

"Huh?"

"You put it on your convertible, right?"

I nodded, still dazed.

"But you didn't put it on the top."

"Top's canvas."

"God, you dumb. Steel frame's inside the canvas. How you think it holds together? Your test was flawed."

"You knew this? You didn't say anything? What's with that?"

"I was just the driver. You didn't ask my opinion. Took the extra can. Figured it might come in handy. This whole car's smeared with it, even the glass."

The driver had been following our conversation in the rear view mirror and lost sight of the road ahead. There was a huge traffic jam. Cars were at a dead stop. Too late, he realized his mistake and slammed on the brakes.

I was thrown forward into Hawker's seat-back. Robbie's seatbelt locked and held him in place, but the momentum flung the submachine gun he was holding forward toward the driver's seat back. I lurched for the gun, grabbing it in both hands, and hurled myself across the back seat, ramming my head into the man's jaw as hard as I could. A series of deafening explosions rocked the car's interior and the Chrysler spun out of control. The MP5 had been set on full auto. The gun swung around out of control blasting away in the car's interior, blowing out the windows. The car hit the shoulder of the road and the world began tumbling. I was thrown against the glass roof, back down into the seat, and then up again. The roof shattered and I was airborne. There was a brief flash of desert sky. I was floating in a sea of sparkling, shattered glass. Then I wasn't.

CHAPTER 38

THE SKY WAS black and blue. I lay stunned for a moment, staring upward, marveling at the furious swirls of indigo smudging the clear, azure sky. Below me there was a turbulent flapping, like sheets on a clothesline. The desert breeze was whipping the fire, propelling those streams of dark smoke into the air above me. My eyes burned and the coppery taste of blood filled my mouth. The pungent odor of gasoline and burning rubber permeated the air.

Then I noticed another sound, this one a steady chop, growing louder, up the embankment from behind. I glimpsed a bit of movement and it gained shape and focus, growing larger. It was a helicopter and it was hovering over the roadway.

I eased myself up on my elbows. Gingerly. I ached all over. The sky wasn't the only thing that was black and blue. The Chrysler had furrowed a gully into the gravel of the hillside. The back half of the car was a raging inferno, its wheels pointed skyward like an overturned tortoise. Pillars of smoke boiled off its blazing undercarriage. The downdraft from the chopper swept overhead, kicking up sand and pebbles and enraging the flames below, hurling the roiling smoke across the desert.

I pushed myself upright and discovered I could stand in a wobbly sort of way. I began descending the embankment toward the fiery wreckage, taking baby steps, trying to walk upright. But it was pointless. The gravel burned my bare feet and in no time I lost my balance and fell backwards on my butt, sliding the rest of the way down the slope, stopping just short of the burning car. For the first time since flying out of my high heels, I longed for shoes.

Robbie and the driver were dead. The machine gun blast had torn through the back of the driver's seat. The rear seat was in flames and Robbie's body was hideously charred. If I hadn't been thrown out of the car, I would have been trapped there with him.

I crabbed over to the other side of the car, shielding my face from the heat of the burning sedan. Hawker was sprawled halfway out the passenger window, feebly struggling to unlatch his seatbelt.

I reached in to help him. The buckle was scalding and flames were licking at Hawker's legs. The latch came free and I began to pull. He moaned as I yanked on his arms. It was then that I noticed that a bullet had torn through his shoulder. Blood was pouring out.

"Come on, Mohawk," I shouted. "Help me here." He managed to move one of his feet and push against the driver's bloody corpse. It was just enough leverage, and I pulled him the rest of the way out of the car.

He was face up in the gravel, his eyes fluttering, taking shallow gasps of air.

"Where is she, Mohawk?" I yelled. "Where's Sarah?"

He blinked and mouthed something. I couldn't hear, so I leaned closer.

"Strawberry," he whispered. His eyes seemed to bulge, then turned glassy.

Strawberry?

It took me a moment to process that. It was the town, not the fruit. Leo's cabin on the Mogollon Rim, it was just outside the town of Strawberry. The bastards. What a clever place to hide Sarah. In Leo's own summer cabin.

I heard approaching footsteps crunching on the graveled slope above me.

"Hey. You all right?"

It was Special Agent Collins.

I stood up, too fast, and my head went swimming. Collins caught me before I fell on my face.

"Steady there, big guy," he said, "Looks like you banged your head again." Collins looked past me toward the wreckage and spotted Hawker's limp body beside the car.

"What took you so long?" I asked, a feeble attempt at humor. But he took it at face value.

"We got tied up in that traffic jam on the freeway," he said. "They caught him."

"Him? Who?"

"The Black Canyon Bandito. That's why the traffic's backed up. He was on the overpass, taking aim, when some old guy in an antique car saw what he was up to and rammed him, knocked him clear off the bridge into the highway below."

"Dead?"

"Yes, sir."

The Chrysler was now completely engulfed in flames.

"Let me guess," Collins said, nodding toward the car. "It's in there."

"It's what you guys wanted from Leo, right?"

He nodded.

"Collins, you have any idea what was on that memory card?"

"I didn't until I talked to your boss. She gave me the broad outline of what you phoned in."

That surprised me. "Why'd she do that?"

Collins was still holding me steady. He let go and appraised me. "My young friend," he said. "Do you have any idea how close you've come to being killed? If not by these...these...*people*"—he spit the word out—"or by us, for that matter?"

"By you?" I was feeling very stupid and not understanding where he was going with that.

"He grabbed my shoulder again and gave it a squeeze. "Not me. I knew you were trying to do the right thing. But some of my colleagues didn't see it that way."

"Volker."

Collins let me go and slid down the hillside to Hawker. He pushed his palms against Hawker's ruined shoulder to staunch the bleeding "Medics are on the way," he said.

"That wasn't the only thing burned up in the car," I said.

Collins continued to apply pressure to Hawker's shoulder, but looked up at me, curious.

"I found a medical directive of Leo's. It allows me or Sarah to countermand his DNR."

"What's that?"

"Leo gave explicit instructions that if he were ever intubated, put on a respirator, that the plug be pulled after forty-eight hours. Time's running out. We only have a few hours left."

Collins's eyes grew wide. "We need to get you to the hospital."

"You don't get it. I can't do anything. His revised directive just burned up. We have to find Sarah."

I kneeled down next to the agent and gestured toward Hawker. "He going to make it?"

"He's got a pulse."

I sighed. "Bastard."

Collins looked up at me and shook his head. "Things aren't always as they seem."

I could hear a siren in the distance, growing louder. Collins continued to press on Hawker's wound. He was sweating and starting to breath heavily from the exertion. I nudged him out of the way. "I'll take over."

While I kept pressure on Hawker's shoulder, Collins filled me in: Mohawk was, indeed, working with the kidnappers, but not voluntarily.

After Leo's Gitmo ruling, a man matching Robbie's description, a guy with an acne-scarred face, had approached Mohawk. He represented an organization that had acquired Mohawk's marker from some not very nice people in Vegas. Hawker was deeply in debt. His debt could be erased if he would just keep an eye on the judge. Certain people did not want any more surprises from the maverick jurist.

But when Hawker reported that the judge had received an unusual letter in the mail, things began to spiral out of control. When they shot up Leo's house and kidnapped Sarah, panic set in. He spilled his guts when Collins found him in Leo's office.

"He knew he was in trouble," Collins said. "He promised to help us find Mrs. Strano."

"And I was kept in the dark, why?"

Collins shrugged. "You were bait."

"And Mohawk slugged me at Leo's house why?"

"They came back to search the house. You and Mrs. Strano surprised them when you showed up. They stepped outside, hoping you wouldn't discover them, but Mrs. Strano's dog gave them away. Or so he said."

"So he hit me?"

"He probably saved your life. They might have shot you if you hadn't been knocked out."

"And grabbing Sarah? That wasn't planned?"

"My guess is they were winging it at that point. Figured they'd use her. Again, oddly, that may have been fortunate. They could have just as easily killed her and you both."

"They plant the bug?"

"I can neither confirm nor deny."

That was as close to an admission as I was going to get.

"Shooter told me he missed on purpose."

"You believe that?"

"No. Killing Uncle Leo would have been ham-handed, but it might have worked. I think he just missed and didn't want to admit it."

Hawker's breathing was shallow, but the pressure on his shoulder had slowed the flow of blood.

"Collins, you figure them for the murdered family in Tucson?"

"Them," he said nodding at the car, "or somebody else working with them."

"Ravenous Security," I said.

Collins cocked his head. "They tell you that?"

"Not exactly. But they got agitated when I mentioned the name."

"That might make some sense. Probably their top people are in Africa. These guys might have been last-minute hires. Muscle from Vegas. Not too bright."

"Mohawk, he have anything to do with burning down Leo's house?"

"No. We tracked him and your cartoonist pal. They were nowhere near when that happened."

"You *were* tailing them, then."

"You, too."

"Me? You guys follow me to the airport?"

"Yes, but then we lost you. Got caught up in the traffic jam entering the airport."

"Hoisted on your own petard?"

"Something like that."

An ambulance rolled to a stop at the top of the hill. Two paramedics carrying a folding stretcher appeared at the top of the embankment and scrambled down the hillside.

"Come on, Collins, " I said, "we've got to get out of here. I know where Sarah's being held."

I turned and started up the hillside, trying to ignore the sharp, hot gravel grinding under my bare feet. Collins raced to catch up.

"Where?"

"Hawker told me. Right before he passed out. Strawberry. My uncle has a cabin there."

I stopped and whirled on Collins. "Did you know all along where Sarah was being held?"

"Hell, no."

"Well, Hawker knew. He didn't say?"

"No."

My legs were leaden and my knee was beginning to throb again. My feet were on fire. When this was over, I intended to crawl into a jar of Motrin and live there for a while, maybe with a bottle of Bushmills to wash it all down. I felt Collins' arm wrap around my waist, steadying me as we struggled up the grade.

"Come on," he encouraged. "We can make it."

I just hate it when guys I've pegged as bastards turn out to be OK.

Never assume, I reminded myself as we pushed our way uphill, slipping and stumbling through the gravel to the roadside above. Never assume.

"Look," Collins said. "No love lost between me and Tonto, but I seriously doubt he knew where Mrs. Strano was being held. He has his flaws. Heaven knows. But I had the sense that, despite being caught up in all of this, he was seriously concerned about finding her. If he found out the location, it must have been recently."

Off to my right, another suit edged his way down the hillside toward us. It was Volker. He swept past us and tromped down the embankment to the car while Collins and I trudged upward. Never said a word, which was fine with me.

"He's dirty, isn't he," I said.

Collins shot me a look and said, "Keep walking."

We watched our steps as we struggled to the top of the embankment, avoiding the outgrowths of cholla and prickly pear. Off to my left, something shiny glinted in the sun. My iPhone. Like me, it had been thrown free of the tumbling Chrysler. I stepped over, retrieved it, and pushed the power button. Amazing. It worked. But I noticed it still showed "NO SERVICE." Had it been the Stealth Car Wax, or had we just been out of the cell phone's coverage area?

A few feet away was Edwina's purse. I stepped over, looked inside, and a wave of relief swept over me.

"What is it?" Collins asked. "That the paperwork you need to save the judge?"

"No, something else. I'll tell you about it later."

I sat down and tore off the bottom half of the dress I was wearing and ripped it again into two pieces. Then I wrapped the cloth around my feet. "I think I can make it the rest of the way, now." Collins helped me to my feet and we continued trudging up the embankment.

"Hey, Collins," I said.

"Yeah?"

"I just killed a man. Maybe two."

We stopped walking. He nodded.

"How am I supposed to feel about that?"

"Don't know," he said. "I've never shot anyone, let alone killed somebody. How *does* it feel?"

"That's the thing. I don't feel anything at all."

CHAPTER 39

THE CHOPPER WAS perched on the interstate blocking both lanes. Dani Vaquero burst out of the cockpit. She ducked to avoid the sweeping rotors and charged across the road, throwing herself into my arms.

"Dios mio. Dios mio."

She went on incomprehensively for a full minute and I have no idea what she said but I knew what she meant.

I hugged her and when I pulled back I could see blood smudged on her face—mine. "Come on," I said, grabbing her hand and turning toward the chopper, "we gotta get out of here."

She sprinted and I hobbled across the two lanes of burning asphalt. The drivers stalled in traffic were laying on their horns. One daring soul tried to drive around the chopper through the median and sank into the gravel. I checked the plates:

BRN2RUN.

Not today, pal.

Dani and I climbed aboard the helicopter, clambering into the back seat behind the pilot. Collins jumped into the front passenger seat. Without waiting for orders, the pilot revved up the powerful engine, yanked the cyclic and we lifted off, nose down, kicking up a whirlwind of dust in our wake. The pilot aimed the chopper north up the freeway, gaining altitude. I looked through the Perspex window to see Volker scrambling up the hill. Fat fuck, it would probably give him a heart attack. He was carrying something, long and black, but I couldn't quite make it out.

Just then we passed above the overpass. An old cuss with white hair and goatee was surrounded by cops next to a plumb colored antique roadster. Must have been the guy who ran the Bandito off the bridge.

"Tighten up the Jesus Nut," I yelled at the pilot.

"What nut?" Dani shouted, her voice barely audible in the cacophony in the cabin.

"It's the nut on top of the rotor," I shouted. "It holds the blades on. If it goes, the next guy we meet is Jesus."

I gave her my best 200 watt smile and a wink, but she just stared at me, bewildered. I knew what she was thinking: What have I gotten myself into?

"Where we heading?" the pilot asked.

"Got enough fuel to get to Strawberry?" I asked.

"Sure, from here it's maybe sixty miles as the crow flies."

"Collins," I shouted over the clatter of the chopper's blades, "can you call ahead, have somebody meet us on the ground, and I'll lead us to Leo's cabin?"

He gave me the thumbs up and swept his jacket back to unclip his cell phone. As he did so, I saw the nine millimeter on his hip.

I hoped we wouldn't need it.

"No signal," he said.

"Hang on," the pilot said. "We get a little more altitude and you should be able to call."

"Oh, Collins, one more thing," I shouted.

He looked back at me. "What?" he said, turning up the volume of his hearing aid.

"Any chance they could find me some clothes? This dress was swell when I bought it, but I think it's gone out of style."

CHAPTER 40

THE ASPHALT PARKING lot of a shopping center rose to greet us as the helicopter kicked up a storm of dust and debris, adding to the haze clouding the air. The front line of the forest fire was less than a mile away down Route 87. From the air, we saw the tops of pine trees bursting into flames, like so many burning matchsticks, a line of flaming soldiers marching relentlessly in our direction. A trio of sheriff's deputies shielded their eyes and grabbed their hats as the chopper descended. The deputies were standing beside two marked sheriff's cars and a van. A chain gang—all women, just like the crew I'd seen earlier in Phoenix near Dani's place—stood there with them, turning away from the down blast of the rotors. The deputies must have been supervising the chain gang and were dragooned into helping us. They were doubtlessly up here on the rim supporting the firefighting efforts.

"Dani," I shouted over the din in the cockpit, "grab your camera gear."

She reached into a space behind our seats where she had stashed the bulky equipment after filming an aerial of the dramatic end to the Bandito's reign of highway terror.

Dani told me during the flight that after Edwina and I left for the Wells Fargo Bank building, it dawned on her she might have better luck staking out the bank from the air rather than from the ground across the street from the bank. The station's chopper was already up doing morning traffic reports. She'd called in and sweet-talked her assignment editor into commandeering the aircraft. She had been airborne over the city, watching the bank, and caught everything on film as I came charging out the front door. She and the pilot had tracked the Chrysler up the highway, staying behind us to avoid detection. When the car flew off the road and burst into flames, she was certain I was dead. But as happy as she was to see me alive, she was positively ecstatic over the footage she'd shot. "Best thing since O.J.'s ride through L.A."

The chopper touched down with a bump. Dani and Collins sprinted over to the deputies, ducking under the chopper's blades. I hobbled behind them, the bottoms of my feet so raw I could barely walk. I had hoped for a S.W.A.T. team, but this was the best the Sheriff's Office could muster on short notice, three chain-gang guards. And what were we supposed to do with their prisoners? The deputies were giving me the once over. So were the female prisoners. What? Never seen a guy in a dress limp out of a chopper in the middle of a forest fire before?

Collins took charge.

"Mr. Strange, if you will show us on the map the location of Judge Strano's cabin, we'll take it from here."

"Forget it, Collins," I said. "I'm coming."

"And so am I," Dani said.

"Don't even try to argue," I said before Collins could object. "Besides, I got an idea I think you're going to like." There was nothing about a guy half his age horning in on his authority that Collins liked, but he listened to my plan and after a bit of fussing finally agreed.

I was full of plans today. This one was even more elegant than the bank job: Dani and I would walk down to the cabin, which was a hundred yards away. I would man the camera, she the microphone, and we would proceed to do a fake stand-up television report outside the front door as a diversion to distract anyone inside. Heck, it didn't have to be fake. There was an honest-to-God forest fire cascading down the Rim upon us. It occurred to me that it would be a good thing if the chopper still had some gas.

If we were confronted outside the cabin, we'd just tell the truth, that we were from KPX-TV in Phoenix—Dani had ID—and that we were doing a report on the fire. The idea was to give Collins and the deputies time to work their way to the rear of the cabin and then do their cop thing.

What they were going to do with the chain gang ladies, I didn't know. Couldn't just leave them, not with the fire raging.

"What about them?" I asked.

"What about them?" Collins asked.

"Jesus, you can't just leave them here chained up with the fire heading this way."

Collins winced at the J-man reference, but I was past caring about his religious sensibilities. There were about a half-dozen women, all in the sheriff's black and white striped outfits.

"Hey, he's right," said a woman at the back of the group. I caught a glimpse of a tall redhead with her hair drawn up in a ponytail. A wave of smoke washed over us, and we could hardly see one another, as if in a dense fog. "This is a dangerous situation," she said. "You can't just abandon us here. We might die."

I peered through the haze to get a better view of her features, but she was hidden behind the other prisoners. There was something about how she had spoken that seemed out of place—well-articulated, educated. What would such a woman be doing on a chain gang? And the tone of her voice was a little deeper than that of most women. Contralto, I think it's called.

"You've heard us talking," I said to the women, "so you know we've got a kidnapping, someone's life is in danger, and we're short on time. We have to go, but we'll be back. Can you huddle in one of those stores? You're in a shopping center, buildings are concrete block, you're surrounded by asphalt. Fire can't jump across this pavement. You'll be safe until we get back. Can you do that?"

I turned to Collins, Dani, and the deputies.

Collins's mouth opened then closed. The deputies began jabbering at one another.

"We just can't leave them here. They're our responsibility," one of them argued.

I wasn't sure if he was more concerned about their safety or his job if they bolted.

"Dammit, Frank, ain't one of these women got serious felonies."

The third deputy jumped in. "I ain't leavin' 'em. Y'all go ahead, help these guys. I'll stay with 'em."

They yakked for a few more seconds and it was decided. Two deputies would accompany Collins, the third would watch over the prisoners, make sure they didn't escape, make sure they were safe.

He ushered them toward one of the stores in the shopping center. I saw him removing his keys, which I hoped meant he would unshackle them. If things went south, they would need to run.

Dani and I waited after Collins and the deputies left before we headed out, which gave me a few minutes to change into the jeans, shirt, and boots they had found for me. Probably looted from one of the stores. Surprisingly, they fit. We wanted to give Collins and the deputies time to get into position. That would involve hiking up a ridge a hundred yards away and sneaking down the slope to the cabin below. The pungent scent of burning wood was choking. A slight shift in the fire's direction and we could be in a world of hurt, especially Collins and the deputies, upwind from us, nearer the blaze.

Leo's cabin was built on the edge of a small streambed that meandered its way down the rim to the forest floor below. This time of year, the creek would be dry and provide an easy and secluded trail right to the cabin's back door for Collins and the cops.

There was no sign of activity when Dani and I walked up. She quickly showed me how to hold the camera, sight it, what buttons to push. For the purposes of our plan, it didn't matter if I knew what I was doing, of course, but if I got some useable video for her that would be a bonus.

"You nervous?" I asked her.

"Scared to death," she said.

I nodded.

"What? You too macho to admit you're scared, too."

"In brightest day, in blackest night, no evil shall escape my sight…"

She punched me in the arm.

"…Let those who worship evil's might…"

"Shut up, already."

I shut up.

Dani positioned herself before the front door, her back to the cabin. I was about fifteen feet away, the camera hoisted on my shoulder aimed at her. She started doing her TV thing.

"We're here in Strawberry, not far from the line of the forest fire bearing down on this vacation community at the edge of the Mogollon Rim…"

I manipulated the zoom on the camera to peer inside through the front window, but it was dark and I could detect no movement. Dani kept talking, I kept recording, wondering what, if anything, was going to happen. Suddenly there was the sound of splintering wood and daylight burst into the living room from a shattered door at the rear of the cabin.

"Dani, down!"

She hit the dirt. I ran over, wrapped my arm around her and we scuttled toward a towering pine tree by the side of the house. "Stay here," I ordered. She didn't argue. I set the camera down in the grass beside her and dashed back to the front door. I grabbed the handle and it turned effortlessly in my hand. I swing it open and lurched into the house.

"Sarah!" I yelled.

"She's not here," Collins shouted, entering the living room from the kitchen, the shattered back door to the cabin backlighting him. He held his pistol in front of him, scanning the room. "We checked the bedrooms upstairs, the kitchen, the closets. Place has been occupied, no doubt about that. Don't touch anything. We'll have to send in a team to get prints, assuming it survives this fire. But there's no evidence of Sarah Strano, no personal belongings, no signs of violence, nothing."

He was shouting, which wasn't unusual, and jabbering, which was. Dani and I weren't the only ones in a state of high anxiety. She was at the door now with the camera. Its strobe light flooded the room.

I felt deflated. All this effort for nothing. I just knew Sarah would be here. What else could "Strawberry" have meant? I glanced at my watch. Time was running out.

"We'll take a look around outside," Collins said, "see if we can find anything."

Outside?

"Oh, my God," I shouted. "Outside. The cellar. There's a storm cellar. Off the side of the cabin."

I ran out the door.

The cabin was a two-story, log-sided box built on the hillside leading down to the creek. On the northern end of the structure, there was an entryway to a small cellar that extended for a short distance under the house. It was only accessible from the exterior. As far as I knew, there was nothing down there; Leo never used it for anything.

The metal cellar doors abutted the house at a forty-five degree angle. They were closed, a section of rebar was jammed in the hasp to prevent entry. Or escape.

Collins, gun drawn, removed the rebar and threw open one of the doors. The light from Dani's camera illuminated the darkened interior. I jumped down into the cellar. There, propped against the far corner was Sarah, hands and ankles tied, a cloth gag tightly wrapped around her mouth. She'd been left to die, abandoned to the fire rampaging down the Rim. At her feet was Fred, whimpering.

She looked up and squinted at me. I was backlit by Dani's strobe light. Light wasn't the only thing invading this space. The sharp scent of burning wood enveloped us.

"She alive?" Collins yelled from above.

"Yes!" I shouted back to him.

"Then let's get her out. We're running out of time."

I turned back to Sarah. She was crying. Fred turned to Sarah, then me, then bounded up the stairs and ran out into the woods.

CHAPTER 41

MY HEART FROZE when I saw Sarah tied up in the basement. I couldn't believe it. I never really expected to see her again.

And there she was: Alive.

And there I was, holding her in my arms: Leo's wife. I'd saved her. I hadn't fucked up.

Sarah begged me not to let her go, and she clung to me as I carried her in my arms up to the shopping center parking lot where the helicopter was waiting. I realized that for the first time in my life I was responsible for another person's well-being. I had always been the one being bailed out. Now I had done my part to hold our little family together.

It was Leo's turn, now. He had to live. Which meant we needed to get Sarah back to Phoenix, pronto.

"Find Freddie," she cried.

"Sarah," I said, too loud, but I needed her to pay attention. "I know you've been through hell, but there is something you need to know."

"Please, find Freddie."

"Sarah, pay attention. Leo's in a coma. They are going to pull the plug. Only you can stop it. You have to get to the hospital and countermand his DNR. Do you understand me?"

She gave me confused.

"Collins, explain it to her on the flight back."

"Count on me."

I turned Sarah over to Collins—inconceivable just a few hours before—and I watched as he helped her aboard the chopper. Dani had videoed all of that, then turned to me, a question on her face.

"Go on," I said. "Get out of here."

She blurted something in *Espanol*, then stopped, took a breath, then said, "Tell me you are not going into that"—she waved at the flames approaching us—"to look for a fucking dog."

"Go on."

She turned to the helicopter, then turned back to me.

"You're doing this for her."

"Take off."

Some more *Espanol*, then she thrust the camera into my hands. "Give me thirty seconds," she shouted to Collins. He was still busy securing Sarah aboard the chopper and it would be a few moments before the pilot could crank up the aircraft.

Dani began talking into the camera. I wasn't paying attention to what she was saying, just aiming the camera in her direction.

Let's go, people. Time is running out.

The pilot began to rev up the engine and I handed the camera back to Dani. "Get out of here," I said. She started to turn toward the chopper. "One more thing, Dani. Behind my seat. Edwina's purse is there. Give it to her, please."

She looked at me like I was nuts. Like why would I be worried about that right then.

"Just do it."

She stopped and stared at me. "Since when are you a fucking hero?"

I turned away and ran back toward the cabin and the approaching fire.

"Fred!" I shouted as I neared the cabin. The smoke was getting thick and the acrid smell of burning wood was irritating my sinuses and burning my eyes.

I sprinted behind the cabin in the direction I had seen Fred run and screamed his name again. The fire was marching relentlessly my way and the sound of trees exploding was deafening. How would Fred hear me over the cacophony?

I slogged up the dry creek bed, hoping Fred might have used that as a pathway, while I continued to shout his name. Now the smoke was so thick I could barely see where to step. I began coughing and realized if I didn't find Fred in the next few moments all would be lost.

Suddenly, there was a thundering roar and the helicopter appeared overhead, blowing the area free of smoke, like a giant airborne fan. And then I saw him. Fred was standing next to a bolder. He was taking a whiz. No wonder he'd bolted out of the basement.

I stumbled over to him.

"Good boy, Fred. Now, let's *vamoose.*"

The chopper lifted higher, and the smoke re-engulfed us.

I heard movement to my left and turned. Fifteen feet away stood a black bear and two cubs. Momma bear was down on all fours. The fur on side of her face was scorched. Her cubs were huddled at her feet.

"Easy there," I said.

She snorted something back.

I reached down to pick up Fred, but he slipped from my grasp and bounded over toward the bears.

"Oh, no. Fred! Come on, guy. Get back here."

Momma bear bent down and stuck her snout in Fred's face. I just knew she was going to bite his head off. Instead, she sniffed and grunted. Fred looked up and paused for a moment, as if interpreting her bear-speak. Baby bears squealed. Momma bear grunted again. Then Fred licked her nose.

There was a thunderous crack behind the bear as the top of a pine tree burst into flame just a few yards away. Momma bear rose on her hind feet, turned to look, then dropped down on all fours and bounded away.

Her squealing cubs followed.

Fred followed the bears.

I followed Fred.

"Jesus Christ, Fred. Stop!"

For once, he actually paid attention. I ran over, scooped him in my arms, and tucked him under my shirt to protect him. For a brief moment, I felt smart: Alexander Strange, dog rescuer. But as I prepared to flee, I realized I was utterly disoriented. I knew the fire was racing down the mountainside in a ribbon of flame, a fiery line of death.

To survive, Fred and I had to stay ahead of that line. On one side was safety—if I could move fast enough. On the other, nothing lived. I'd always hated deadlines. Now this gave an entirely new meaning to the word, a real deadline.

The smoke was so thick I could barely breathe, let alone see more than a few feet, and spot fires, ignited by flying embers, were breaking out all around us. It was impossible to tell which direction to run. We would have been better off following the bears.

I had to decide quickly. Which way was the road? It led to the shopping center and safety. I began coughing. The smoke would kill me before the fire ever arrived. I slipped and dropped to one knee. My bad knee. And the pain radiated up my spine.

"Dammit!" I shouted.

A female voice responded: "Over here."

I struggled toward the direction of the sound. Did I see a shadow of a woman ahead? Was there a flash of red hair? Wasn't that voice familiar? Or was I just imagining it? I kept moving in that direction.

"Where are you?" I shouted.

No answer.

I continued in the direction of the voice, scrambling uphill, slipping on loose rock and underbrush. Fred was whimpering. I would have whimpered, too, but I was too out of breath. Had I imagined that voice? Had a woman really called out to me? Was I hallucinating? Nothing for it, I had to push forward. Uphill. Stumbling. Trying to take shallow breaths, as if that would help. Visibility was now reduced to inches. My lungs were on fire and I was starting to feel lightheaded. I kept climbing, one foot after the other. Then, suddenly, my foot landed on pavement.

As I stepped onto the road, I looked around for the woman who had called to me. But if she had been real, and if I hadn't simply imagined her voice, she had vanished in the haze.

CHAPTER 42

IT WAS AFTERNOON by the time I arrived back at the newspaper, Fred tucked under my arm like a football. He didn't seem to mind. The picket line blocking the front entrance had long since evaporated. Hard to keep that up in 100-plus heat. It took two calls upstairs to get clearance to enter the building. The guards were under strict orders not to allow any of the staff inside without approval.

Edwina was waiting for me. I'd called Abigail Conwest from the back of a sheriff's van, traveling with the female inmates as we evacuated the shopping center. I dictated a short story from there about Sarah's kidnapping, including how one of the prisoners had disappeared in the fire.

The red headed woman who spoke out for the prisoners, wasn't in the van. The guard who stayed with them was befuddled. He had no idea how she slipped away. Was she the woman who called out to me? And who was she, anyway? I asked the guard if he had a list of prisoners and he surprised me by not only acknowledging that he did but by handing it to me.

"Which one is missing?" I'd asked.

He checked off the inmates assembled in the truck. "This shows all present and accounted for."

"But we know there was one more," I protested.

He shrugged his shoulders. "My list's good and we gotta get out of here." And that was that.

I'd just finished dictating the story to Conwest when my cell phone rang. Caller ID showed it was Collins.

"Did you get Sarah to the hospital? Did she stop the DNR?" I blurted.

"I'm afraid there was a mixup," Collins said, his voice weary. "The hospital medical records department got the time wrong. It was twenty-four hours, not forty eight."

"Oh, God."

"But there's good news. They pulled the tube, but your uncle continued breathing on his own. Everyone's buzzing about it. They say it's a miracle."

"He's awake?" I felt like a bolder had been lifted from my chest.

"No. But he's alive. Mrs. Strano is by his side."

Edwina and Abigail Conwest had posted the brief story I'd dictated to them on the newspaper's website. That, at least, was still a going operation. The newspaper was not. For the first time in the paper's history, the *Phoenix Daily Sun* missed a publication date. Francis Van Wormer ordered the presses idled and, in a brief statement to the news media (allowing his own paper to be scooped), he announced that management was shuttering the newspaper due to unprofitability and labor difficulties and that there were no plans to resume publication.

"Can he do that? Just shut the doors, not even try to sell it to someone else?" I asked.

"He owns it," Edwina said.

"Yeah, but that makes no sense."

"Really?" she asked, an edge in her voice. "We were going under, anyway. Why not pull the plug, before we can publish a story that will embarrass his pals?"

"Christ."

"Yeah, but maybe God's on our side this time," she said. "That asshole turned off the presses but he forgot to turn off the electricity.

The dead tree edition may be extinct, but we've still got the website. She had a look of grim determination on her face. "I haven't spent a lifetime in this racket to let a cretin like Wormhole stop me from doing my job."

"You got your purse, right?" I asked.

Edwina smiled. "Yes, Dani said you insisted that she give it to me."

"So you found the SD card…"

"Yeah, that was clever. Hiding it in my compact. But I'm surprised they didn't tear the purse apart trying to find it."

I nodded. "When I was in the bank, I swapped the SD card in your little camera with the one in the envelope. Not sure why, really. I just had this incredible sense of foreboding when I left the vault."

"And you were right."

"Yeah. Anyway, I was feeling pretty good about hiding the real card in your camera, then it hit me that it could get overwritten in there. So I decided to hide it in your compact."

"Clever."

"Nice tackle, by the way, Ed. That took some courage to throw yourself in front of that asshole."

She waved it off.

"I'm surprised he didn't arrest you. Interfering with a law enforcement officer or some such."

She shook her head. "He didn't stick around. He bolted out the door after you. Didn't have time to mess with me."

"Well, thanks for that. You saved the day."

She nodded. "Let's get to work."

I banged out a first-person column detailing everything that had happened that morning, how I had gone to the bank hoping to find the key to Sarah's release only to end up being kidnapped myself. I wrote everything, every detail. There were no length restraints writing online unlike in the newspaper with its limited amount of space for news, crammed between the advertisements. The only restriction was the attention span of the readers.

When that was done, we began work on the Air Force Two story. I had phoned Abigail Conwest from the safe deposit vault and asked her to check out the article about the death of Sgt. Manuel Torres and his wife and two children that had been in the *Republic* that morning. Ponitz, who had been online rummaging through Leo's court records at my request, shelved that and jumped on the story, gathering additional background information from the *Tucson Citizen*. He also tracked down a copy of the police report on the Tucson fire. Collins confirmed that the FBI was looking into the deaths, but would say no more on the record.

The names of the police officers who had burned to death at Leo's house had been released—Lt. Janice Warren and Officer Susan Valdez. Both had agreed to overtime duty guarding the house.

I placed a call to the Medical Examiner's Office and was patched through to one of the pathologists.

"Can you tell me anything about two cops found at Judge Leonard Strano's house?" I asked.

"Yeah. They're very dead. But not my case. There'll be a press briefing tomorrow, I'm told. Now I gotta go. I'm in the middle of someone."

He hung up.

I found a ceramic bowl near the microwave and fridge in the back of the newsroom and filled it with water for Fred. Abigail Conwest, wearing a new dress Edwina had scored for her, showed up with a ham sandwich from a vending machine and she tore it into little bits for him and spread the feast on a newspaper on the floor by my feet. I faced the blank screen of my computer, hands balanced over the keyboard. I felt a trickle of blood seeping from my head wound.

For a brief, whimsical moment, I was reminded of another of my favorite Gene Fowler quotations:

"Writing is easy: All you do is sit staring at a blank sheet of paper until drops of blood form on your forehead."

They were forming. I began typing:

By Alexander Strange

Phoenix Daily Sun

A plot to destroy a secret audio recording made aboard Air Force Two appears to be behind the attempted murder of Maricopa County Superior Court Judge Leonard Dwayne Strano, the kidnapping of his wife, the deaths of a Tucson Air Force sergeant and his family, the murders of two Scottsdale police officers and the subsequent abduction of this reporter.

The audio recording, which was discovered by an Air Force sergeant involved in decommissioning the aircraft that is used by the vice president, also suggests that the U.S. military involvement in Uganda may have been a ploy to protect the financial interests of an American energy company.

According to a letter that was delivered to Judge Strano and discovered today in a Phoenix Wells Fargo Bank safe deposit box, the sergeant said the aircraft contained a hidden recording system. A letter that the sergeant wrote to Judge Strano summarized the audio recording and alleged that an energy company executive and the Secretary of Homeland Security could be heard "talking about how the Ebola outbreak in Chicago could be used as an excuse to invade Uganda."

The letter indicated that the Administration's decision to send troops to Uganda may have been designed not to combat terrorism, as the American people have been told, but to ensure that uranium mining leases near the Congolese border remained secure.

The assassination attempt on Judge Strano and the kidnapping of his wife were conducted by a handful of men employed to retrieve the damaging recording.

The sergeant, his wife and two children were found dead in their home, which had been destroyed by fire. The FBI is now investigating those deaths…

CHAPTER 43

EDWINA WALKED INTO my office as I was writing. She held a little doohickey in her hand and offered it to me. On one end was a slot for an SD memory card. On the other, a USB connector.

"Took forever to find this," she said. "The photo department looks like it's been looted, almost all of the gear is gone. Guess they cleaned house when they went on strike."

I slipped the memory card into the device then plugged it into my computer. A file folder came to life on my computer desktop and I clicked on it, eager to play the recording. Our plan was to post the audio file verbatim on our website along with the news story.

I looked at the file.

"Houston, we have a problem."

"What?" Edwina asked, walking around behind my desk to see the screen.

"The folder is empty."

"How can that be?"

"You sure this is the right SD card? The one I hid in your compact?"

"Yes, yes," she said. "Could you have gotten them mixed up?"

I doublechecked the brand on the card. It was a SanDisk. "No, this is the right card. The SD in your camera was a Lexar."

"Well, fuck. Without that recording we don't have a story."

I turned in my chair and looked up at her. "Sure we do. It's a weaker story, but we have loads of hard facts."

She was scowling so I pressed on. "We know Sarah and I were both kidnapped. We know Leo was shot at and his house burned down. I know firsthand that the goons who did all that were looking for the recording. We have the sergeant's summary…"

"But we don't have the actual words that were recorded," she interrupted.

"No but we still have a lot. The letter from Torres is powerful. We know he and his family were killed."

"We know they died in a fire, we don't know they were killed."

"OK. But still."

"I don't like it."

"You saying I should stop writing?"

She hesitated for a moment then said: "No, finish it up. Just give me a minute to process this."

Before I could resume typing, the phone on my desk lit up and I saw the call was from the security desk downstairs.

"You got incoming," the guard said. "FBI with a search warrant coming up."

I pulled the SD card out of the computer and slid it under a magazine on my desk. The elevator door opened and Special Agent Volker and two other men in suits stepped out. I couldn't be positive, but they looked like the guys I spotted outside the bank earlier in the day.

Volker spotted us and walked into my office brandishing a piece of paper. Edwina took it from him.

"Hand it over," Volker said.

"Hand what over?" I asked, innocently.

"I've about had it with you Strange," he sneered. "The SD card. Where is it?"

Edwina interrupted. "The warrant looks legitimate," she said, turning her attention to me. "Give it to him."

"But boss…"

"No buts," she said, her tone harsh. "We are a law-abiding business."

It was everything I could do to keep from laughing out loud, but I contained myself.

"Edwina, if we give up the SD card, we have no way of proving what Sgt. Torres said in his letter is true," I said to her then turned to Volker. "You can't do this. The world will never know what's on this recording."

Volker sneered: "Why do you think I'm here, genius?"

"Well, Volker, what can I say?" I pulled the SD card out from under the magazine and handed it to him.

"I'll take that, too," he said, nodding at my iMac.

"In a pig's eye."

Edwina jumped in. "This warrant is narrowly drawn. It says nothing about computer equipment. You've gotten what you came for. You want more, get another warrant." She moved from behind my chair to confront him. She'd already tackled him once today. Somewhere in the back of his itty bitty brain it had to register that she wasn't to be messed with.

"You download the recording?" Volker asked.

"I was just about to. Your timing is perfect, damn you. No, we do not have the recording downloaded on this computer or anywhere else."

He spun on his heels and headed out the door. "If you're lying to me," he said over his shoulder, "I'll see to it that you'll spend the rest of your life in prison."

Edwina and I watched the elevator door close.

"Nicely played," I said.

She nodded. "I'd say that blowhard has just given us the confirmation we needed about the memory card. Make sure you quote him in his entirety, especially that bit about sending you to prison."

I was already scribbling on my note pad, making sure I got it down.

"Keep writing," Edwina said. "We won't have much time before he discovers the card is blank."

I was about to start pounding away on the keyboard again when I heard a clacking sound at my feet. It was Fred, lapping some water out of the bowl under my desk. Fred's dog tags always rattled against his dog dish at Leo's, but this wasn't the usual metallic sound, more like plastic.

I scooped him up and examined his collar. Hidden under his long fur, an unfamiliar ornament dangled next to his ID and rabies tags. It was small, thin, and ivory, hard to see against his white chest fur. My first thought was that it must be one of those radio devices used to help find missing animals. But I quickly realized how stupid that notion was. If Fred had a radio tag, Sarah wouldn't have been so frantic about finding him. She wouldn't have been asking me to print up flyers, she would have been on the computer tracking him down. The little plastic rectangle had a seam and a very small clip. I detached it from Fred's collar.

"Edwina, you've got nails. Can you pop this open?"

She took it from me and a moment later something black fell out and landed on my keyboard.

It was an SD memory card.

"Well, merry fucking Christmas."

I loaded it into the SD card reader, plugged it into the back of my computer, then clicked on the folder that appeared on my desktop. There was a single file inside: AirForceTwo.wav.

The recording wasn't great quality, but you could hear the voices, and they validated what Sgt. Torres had written. We were in business.

No wonder Leo was so concerned about Fred. When had he done this? If he ever woke up from his coma, we had things to talk about.

I began hammering away on the keyboard again. The story was telling itself. Then the overhead lights flickered.

"Hey, we got an issue." It was Abigail Conwest sitting at the Copy Desk.

"What was that, Abby?" Edwina yelled out my door.

"Motherfuckers!"

Edwina and I turned to one another. "Did I just hear Conwest say…"

"Yeah. It's got to be bad."

"The fucking website is offline," Conwest shouted. "The bastards have hacked us."

Edwina squeezed my shoulder. "Keep writing."

"Cigarette me," I said in my best Jack Lemmon imitation, his famous line from the movie *The Front Page*.

Edwina stopped halfway out the door and turned back to me and smiled. She got the joke. I was her Hildy Johnson and she was my Walter Burns.

"Dammit," she said. "This can't be the end. It's just too much fun."

CHAPTER 44

IT WAS LATE and I was sitting at the bar in Kelso's drinking Bushmills and popping Motrin like I promised myself. After all I had been through, I should have gone straight home and crashed. But I knew I couldn't sleep.

The television over the bar was on and Dani Vaquero was doing a talk-back with a CNN anchor from outside the *Phoenix Daily Sun* building. The network showed a clip of Dani in front of the helicopter while Collins loaded Sarah inside. Not a bad shot, if I say so myself. Maybe I'd win an Emmy.

Dani chatted for a bit with the guy in the CNN studio, then they aired another clip, this one of me climbing out of the cellar holding a sobbing Sarah Strano in my arms, her hands wrapped tightly around my neck. She had been screaming at me:

"Find Freddie, find Freddie."

"So, who's Freddie?" Stormy Sheetz asked. She pulled up a bar stool and sat down beside me.

I nodded at the television. "Sarah's dog."

"Sarah. I remember her. She was in here with you, right?"

I nodded.

"She had her head in your lap."

"She'd fainted."

Stormy pulled back a little and her nose scrunched. "Jesus, you smell like smoke."

"No shit."

She looked back to the TV then returned her gaze to me. "Huh."

Stormy grabbed the remote and turned up the volume. The CNN anchor was quoting from my story. A week ago, I might have bitched about the TV pukes stealing newspaper material. But this was exactly what we wanted.

Earlier, while I was in my office writing, Edwina and Conwest worked the phones and email. With our website down, it was vital that the story receive widespread attention. It was critical not only for the questions it raised about the integrity of the Administration and why we had gone to war in Uganda, but also for our own safety. Once word was out that the attempt on Leo's life and Sarah's kidnapping were linked to a plot to destroy the Air Force Two recording, we would be inoculated against further harm. At least we hoped so.

Edwina first called the Associated Press and alerted them to the story, then started working her contacts at other newspapers around the country. Conwest called the local television stations, then started pestering the assignment editors at the networks including CNN, MSNBC, and FOX.

Having primed the pump, we began sending the story out via email as soon as I was finished writing. It was accompanied by my first-person column about being kidnapped and copies of the audio file off the SD card. I also posted all of that on my personal website, www.thestrangefiles.com.

I emailed copies of the stories and the Air Force Two recording to Collins, along with a message that we had just discovered the real SD card. If he wanted to come by, we'd be happy to give it to him. Or he could just listen to it on the web.

CNN flashed my mugshot, the one that ran with my column in the paper, and Dani was saying something about me. I didn't quite catch it as Jake Kelso wandered over, his brow furrowed in concern. "Alex, you look like hell," he said. He grabbed a bottle of Bushmills from behind the bar and refilled my glass. Then he poured himself one.

"It's been a long day."

He looked up at the TV. "So, you're famous now."

"For fifteen seconds."

He nodded and appraised me for a moment. "Sorry about the paper."

"Yeah, looks like I need to start looking for a job."

He nodded, understanding. "You know what I always loved about newspapering?"

I smiled at him. "Tell me."

"I just loved the fact that every day was a do-over. You know what I mean?"

I shook my head no.

"No? Well, I guess it's different now. But in the days of hot type, when I started out, it was a very physical experience. Every day we would come into the newsroom, pound out our stories on our Remingtons and our Underwoods and we'd send those pages to the Linotype operators."

He nodded at the ancient Linotype machine across the room. I turned to look. It was an engineering marvel, standing taller than a man, with its ninety character keyboard and other contraptions used to cast, as the name implies, lines of type.

"They'd mold our words into molten lead," he continued. "And those thin strips of lead would be assembled into pages. And those pages would be pressed into huge, curved lead plates to be bolted onto presses. And at the end of every day, after the papers had been printed, you know what we did? We took all those words set in type, all those pages formed into plates for the presses, all that lead—and we threw it all into the hell box."

"The what box?"

"The hell box. We were the original recyclers. At the end of every edition, all that lead in the hell box was melted down and reused. Every word I'd ever written was recycled and molded into new words the next day. Every day you started over fresh. Every day, there was no telling what the newspaper might read like. The lead that formed the words for yesterday's top story could be tomorrow's wedding announcement. Who could predict? If the world were a predictable place, there'd be no need for newspapers, right?"

I had to agree with that.

"So you get the metaphor, don't you?"

I shook my head no. Maybe I was tired. Maybe I just wasn't the sharpest pencil in the drawer.

Kelso leaned over, grabbed me by my shoulders and pulled me so close to him our foreheads were nearly touching.

"Yeah you do," he said. "I'm sorry the *Sun* has folded. Damn shame. But every day is a do-over. Throw the past into the hell box and keep going."

EPILOGUE

I watched, transfixed, as the baseball flew high overhead. There was the briefest of instants, as the ball reached its apogee, that it appeared it might not make it out of the park or that it might stray foul into the stands. But, no. It plummeted across the left field fence, just inside the yellow pole in fair territory, a home run. The Cincinnati Reds were now up 4-3 over the Diamondbacks with one inning left to play.

I turned to Bevin Darcy. "How about that, Redlegs fans?"

We high-fived.

I turned to his aunt, Vicky, and she smiled back at me. I had promised Bevin I would take him to a ball game and it was important that I didn't disappoint him. It was a somewhat less special moment for all the D-Backs fans surrounding us who failed to appreciate our enthusiasm for the Reds' inching ahead of the hometown team. Some people can be so parochial.

I'd put together a checklist of things I had to do, issues that needed to be resolved, so that I could bring closure to all that had happened to me, to Leo, to Sarah, to Dani, to everyone whose lives had been impacted by the events that past August. Fred's, too. I knew Leo would appreciate my attention to detail.

Making good on my promise to Bevin was one of those items.

The story of Sarah's kidnapping and rescue got big play on the wire services and networks. Our account of who was behind the assassination attempt, the arsons, the kidnapping, and murders was controversial, however, even with the recording. With Sgt. Torres dead, there was no way to prove where the audio recording came from. The quality was too poor to do an authoritative voice analysis. And with Leo still in a coma, he couldn't explain how the recording came into his possession.

We turned to Hawker, who was hospitalized with a gunshot wound. Unfortunately, he couldn't pin Ravenous Security. He identified the guys blackmailing him as Robbie and the driver, but he didn't know their names or background.

But the FBI figured that out. They got clean prints from their corpses. Robbie had done time for forgery; the driver for armed robbery and assault. Both men were from Las Vegas. No connection could be established, however, between the men and Ravenous Security. While that was disappointing, the police took me at my word about the circumstances of my abduction. I had been caught on security cameras leaving the bank. Which meant questions about how the driver of the car had been machine-gunned to death fit nicely into that narrative, a clear case of self-defense.

The story fascinated bloggers and conspiracy websites. Especially intriguing was the missing gun. My account told how I had grappled with Robbie in the back seat of the Chrysler and how his MP5/10 discharged killing the driver and causing the catastrophic wreck on the Black Canyon Freeway.

Because the accident occurred on a state highway, jurisdiction for investigating the crash immediately was delegated to the Arizona Highway Patrol. State forensics analysists found the 10-millimeter Auto slugs in the car. Further analysis showed the barreling on the slugs matched those plucked from the exterior stucco and living room bookcases of Uncle Leo's house.

There was only one problem: No gun was found in the wreckage.

I recalled seeing Volker climbing up the embankment from the burning Chrysler with something in his hand. Could he have been carting off the weapon? I asked Collins to inventory the Phoenix FBI's armory. He already had. All eight MP5/10s in the bureau's arsenal were present and accounted for with one anomaly: One of the guns serial numbers didn't match the inventory records. The official line was that it was a clerical error. I didn't buy it. And I don't think Collins did either.

The Administration said it was preposterous to suggest that the federal government of the United States of America would go to war under false pretenses. And it turned out to be a moot issue. Three days after our stories were posted, victory was declared, the uranium mines were secured, and the troops began deploying back home.

While the FBI promised a thorough investigation, its authority was yanked by the Department of Homeland Security, which convened a secret tribunal to review our accusations. I was permitted to issue a written statement. Hawker testified in a closed-door meeting, as did agents Collins and Volker. And then…nothing.

We may have been right about inoculating ourselves, though. We're all still alive. As of this writing, anyway.

Two weeks to the day after Leo was admitted to Good Sam, he awoke from his coma. The first person he saw when he opened his eyes was Sarah. She had been reading to him, one of his old favorites: Edgar Rice Burroughs's *A Princess of Mars*. John Carter and Dejah Thoris, a love story for the ages.

As soon as Leo regained consciousness, federal investigators queried him about the letter from Torres, the interview he had scheduled with him, and the contents of the audio recording.

They didn't get much. Doctors said it was not uncommon for coma victims—especially in cases resulting from head injuries—to have memory gaps. Leo remembered only bits and pieces from two weeks before the assassination attempt until he woke up. He couldn't recall talking to me at the hospital, of his painful erection (which by then had subsided), his trip with Sarah to the airport, or the phone call he received at Kelso's. As a corroborator, he was useless.

He did, however, remember having his secretary make a copy of the SD card that Sgt. Torres had mailed to him and hiding the copy on Fred's collar. I talked with a computer tech about this later, and her best guess is that the original must have been accidentally erased during the copying process. If we hadn't found Fred, not only would we have lost a world-class puppy, we would have lost the only copy of the recording, too.

A week later, Leo was released from the hospital. He took a leave of absence from the bench, and he and Sarah flew to Naples, Florida to spend some time on his fishing trawler, the *Miss Demeanor*. I agreed to watch Fred for them while they were gone. Before they left, I asked Leo about the letter he had mailed the afternoon I had met him at the courthouse. He had no clue.

Brett Barfield tried, but failed, to find the identity of the person behind the wheel who had driven by Leo's house when I had it staked out—the one with the U.S. Government license plate. It was a pool car and there was no record of who had checked it out.

Sarah had recovered from her ordeal. Physically, anyway. It could have been much worse: Leo's cabin was among the last structures claimed by the fire before it was brought under control. We'd gotten to Sarah and Fred just in time. She had never seen the faces of the men who had thrown her in the trunk of a car and hauled her up to the cabin in Strawberry. They had been wearing stocking masks when they barged into the house after slugging me. She had been blindfolded during the trip and immediately locked in the cellar along with Fred, and, incongruously, her suitcase.

So while those maniacs were burning down Leo's house and kidnapping me, they had what they wanted right under their noses—literally. In the cellar, on Fred's collar.

Sarah's sister, Rebecca, contacted her with troubling news shortly before Sarah and Leo left for Florida. Rebecca had persuaded a Utah juvenile court judge to grant her temporary custody of their younger sister, but then the girl disappeared. Sarah's sister had pleaded with authorities to issue an Amber Alert. But the cops were dragging their feet. There was no evidence of an abduction, which was necessary to issue an Amber Alert. Sixteen-year-olds ran away all the time.

Hawker caught a break. The bullet wound was a through-and-through—no bones broken, no arteries severed. It would take time and therapy, but he was expected to make a full recovery. But he would be doing it in prison.

The U.S. district attorney, a recent presidential appointee, wasn't interested in pressing any federal charges related to the theft of the Air Force Two recording—ostensibly because of his cooperation with the FBI. A trial would keep the story in the news and, call me cynical, I had to believe that played into the calculation.

But the Maricopa County Attorney filed kidnapping charges against him and he copped a plea to a Class Four Felony. Because he cooperated with police and aided in Sarah's rescue, he got six months in jail and three years' probation.

Hawker's recovery from his bullet wound, oddly, was a disappointment to Garreth DePutron, who imagined compressing Hawker's cremated remains into a diamond and selling it on eBay.

The Centers for Disease Control eventually determined that the Ebola virus outbreak in Chicago was caused by viral hemorrhagic septicemia, a fish virus similar to Ebola that had been believed unable to infect humans. It had mutated. The Department of Homeland Security challenged the finding and put the entire Great Lakes coastline on Orange Alert. Former Vice President Al Gore declared this revelation to be further evidence of global warming. The Rev. Lee Roy Chitango, the president's spiritual adviser, divined it to be God's wrath on "America's hedonistic, homosexual agenda."

The mail had been accumulating, both at work and at my apartment, and one afternoon I sat down to sort through it. One letter was addressed to me in green ink. I checked the postmark. It

314 | J.C. Bruce

was stamped the Monday after I had met Leo at the courthouse. This had to be the letter he had dropped down the mail chute.

Dear Nephew,

I write on the anniversary of your mother's—and my sister's—death. I know this is always a painful date for you. I just want you to know that she would be proud of you. As am I.

Were she alive, she would urge you to be your own person, not a docile member of the mindless herd. She blessed you, oddly enough, with the opportunity to literally make a name for yourself.

Embrace it. It's good to be Strange.

Leo

I also heard from Dr. Omar Franken. He called to say he was not going to sue me. His formula for Stealth Car Wax needed improvement, he acknowledged. I had learned from Collins that my iPhone's signal had gone in and out of service during the ride up the Black Canyon freeway; it had nothing to do with Franken's invention. Why Hawker made such a big deal out of it was a puzzle. I'd have to ask him about that. But giving him the benefit of the doubt, it could have been his way to flimflam his partners to allow my phone to stay on. I wanted to believe that.

Franken also told me he was investing in a hot new internet concept called the Nightie News. Stormy Sheetz had called Franken with a business proposition. He could get in on the ground floor of what she believed would soon be a hot syndicated news program. Was he interested? But of course. It helped that she made the sales call in person.

I had asked Dani if she'd like to help Stormy get started—as a consultant, of course—but she gave that idea the cold shoulder. I got pretty much the same treatment. Her star was rising. The video she'd captured of the race up the Black Canyon Freeway and of Sarah's rescue had been broadcast nationally. She had an offer from a TV station in Los Angeles. CNN was sniffing around, too. She wasn't long for Phoenix.

With the demise of the *Phoenix Daily Sun*, I was out of work and my career was on ice. I agreed to help Stormy with some of the basics of how to set up a rudimentary news gathering operation. None of the women had any journalism training, but that's not what they were hired for, was it? It was something to do while I figured out my next moves.

The next move came sooner than I expected. Edwina Mahoney had cobbled together a handful of investors and some grant money and was launching a new online news service. Did I want in? Sure, I told her, but I was heading to Florida. Leo had offered me the use of the *Miss Demeanor*, and the idea of living on a boat for a while was appealing. Edwina agreed. She wanted me to keep writing *The Strange Files*. What better place to cover weird news than the Gunshine State?

Leo and Sarah had returned to Phoenix and rented an apartment while their house was being rebuilt. But there was a catch: no pets were allowed. They asked if I would keep Fred for them for the time being. At least that was their cover story. I suspected that given all both Leo and Sarah had been though, they just couldn't handle the responsibility of caring for a dog, too. They could barely take care of themselves.

But it was fine with me. Fred's a great roommate. I think he was happy with the arrangement, too. Nothing like a death-defying race through a forest fire to draw a boy and his dog closer.

And, no, that lottery ticket I bought when I was making my way to the airport to find Leo's planner, it wasn't a winner. Otherwise, repairing Leo's boat would have taken much less time. But that's another story.

It turned out not to be such a great day for Reds fans, after all. In the bottom of the ninth the Diamondbacks scored two runs, all on walks. An ignominious ending. But there's a reason space is a vacuum—the Reds' bullpen sucks.

We were leaving the ballpark, Bevin holding hands with Vicky and me. He looked up: "Hey Alex," he said, not bothering to see if his aunt would give him a disapproving look. "You never did see my room. Wanna?"

I glanced at Vicky.

"Perhaps *Mr. Strange* would like to stay for dinner," she said.

I did.

AUTHOR'S NOTE

Alexander Strange and I were colleagues at the *Phoenix Daily Sun*, our columns running on alternate days in the newspaper. I wrote about politics. He wrote about weirdness. During the events described in this book, I was on vacation, hiking in the Grand Canyon. I returned to find my newspaper had folded and my friend making headlines instead of writing them. Weird had become more than a topic for him; he was living it.

Shortly thereafter, Alex turned over to me a box of audio recordings, his comprehensive oral history of these events. He said he needed someone beside himself to tell this story and to independently verify the facts.

It is from those recordings that I have constructed this book, and it is through them that I have endeavored to tell this story in Alex's voice. In addition, I have turned to published accounts, police reports, sources in the federal government, interviews, and, I will confess, some extrapolation to fill in the blanks. I am especially grateful for the cooperation given to me by Dani Vaquero, Superior Court Judge Leonard D. Strano, Sarah Strano, Edwina Mahoney, Garreth DePutron, Harold Ponitz, the late Jake Kelso, and Michelle "Stormy" Sheetz.

While many of the events in this book may seem familiar to readers after the explosion of news coverage that followed Alex's revelations, in this account the names of some individuals and corporations have been changed. Several people, including the "Darcy" family, asked that their son's real name not be used. Similarly for his aunt. And others. I conjured "Ravenous" as a pseudonym for the energy company and subsidiary security firm. And I made up other names, events, and descriptions for a variety of reasons—to protect the innocent, to safeguard confidential sources, to avoid tedious lawsuits—things like that. I also took a few liberties interpreting Alex's inner thoughts. He, of course, had the chance to review this manuscript before publication, and offered no objections. Some nitpicky details may be slightly off despite my best efforts to faithfully describe locations, vehicles, courthouses, bullets, etc. Any errors are strictly the fault of the internet and certainly not those of any of my generous readers and editors who trusted me to get my facts straight.

One final note: Alex had given me a key to his apartment to check on Fred from time to time when he was out and about. When I hadn't heard from him for several days, I dropped by. Alex was gone. Fred's food and water bowls were missing, too. Looking around, I discovered a black leather journal with the initials L.D.S. engraved on a brass plate on the cover—Leonard D. Strano's planner. I recalled Alex telling me that when Leo and Sarah Strano flew to Florida, the judge had left the journal behind. Alex said his uncle wanted to reinvent his life, to be less rigid, to spend more time on things that were important "like Sarah, and drinking, and chess."

I picked up the planner and thumbed through the pages. Alex had been using it as his own. But not in his uncle's signature green ink. All of his entries were in red. Every one. I assumed that was his way of differentiating himself, but, actually, it was revealing of how alike Alexander Strange and Leonard D. Strano really were.

On one of the diary pages, he logged a phone call from Brett Barfield. While the notes accompanying this entry were cryptic, it appears Barfield and Strange had been working together to find Sarah Strano's missing younger sister.

Barfield had resigned from the Scottsdale Police Department shortly after the events described in this book and had joined the Third Eye Investigators detective agency.

In red ink, clearly pressed harder into the page than any other note, was this final entry:

"Gone hunting."

— **J.C Bruce**

POSTSCRIPT

Tropic ☉ Press

BOSTON—Controversial polygamist leader John Jacoby was listed in critical condition today after being hospitalized with a gunshot wound sustained during a confrontation with an Arizona private detective at a local motel.

Jacoby, who had been scheduled to speak here at a convention of Christians for Polygamy, was rushed to Massachusetts General Hospital with a wound to the "groin" following the shootout at the Del Mar Resort and Lakefront Spa.

Witnesses said a 16-year-old girl was found tied to a bed in Jacoby's motel room after the incident and was released into the custody of a relative.

The Arizona detective involved in the shooting, Brett Barfield, was detained, but police said no charges are likely to be filed…

ACKNOWLEDGMENTS

WRITING CAN BE lonesome work, but getting that work published requires a team effort. This story would never have been shared were it not for the generous contributions of many people to whom I am deeply grateful.

Foremost among them are Sandy Bruce—my skillful, patient, and insightful first reader who refused to allow me to quit on this project. Logan Bruce, an extraordinary editor and accomplished writer in his own right. And Kacey Bruce, my talented web designer and marketing advisor.

I would also like to thank the feedback I received from trusted readers Mark Stange, Barbara Estes, Ron Rollins, the late Dr. Benjamin Schuster, Dr. Melissa Spirek, and authors Karna Bodman, Howard Giordano, Jean Harrington, and John Wayne Falbey.

Special thanks to my master's degree faculty, Dr. Jon Saari, Bill Roorback, Debra Spark, and Nina de Gramont, and to my friend Marv Meyerson for his expertise on the Phoenix underworld.

And a big shout-out to my International Thriller Writers teachers Meg Gardiner, F. Paul Wilson, Gayle Lynds, and Donald Maass. And all my Master Craft classmates.

Of course, none of this would be possible were it not for Alexander Strange's willingness to allow me to share this with you.

ABOUT THE AUTHOR

J.C. BRUCE IS a journalist, teacher, and author living in Naples, Florida. A lengthy newspaper career included serving as an editor, managing editor, or reporter at the *Naples Daily News*, the *Dayton Daily News, Tribune* Newspapers in suburban Phoenix, the Longview, Texas *News Journal,* the *Austin American-Statesman.* the *Miami Herald,* the *Palm Beach Post*, the *St. Petersburg Times* (now the *Tampa Bay Times*) and the *Tampa Times* (now deceased).

As the journalist-in-residence at Wright State University, young impressionable minds were subjected to instruction in the basics of reporting, editing, and feature writing. Some of those students are now committing journalism for a living.

A brief foray into politics as a press secretary in Washington, D.C. turned disillusioning when the FBI showed up with handcuffs and hauled the congressman for Florida's fourth congressional district off to jail for bribery.

Affiliations, present and past include: Mystery Writers of America, International Thriller Writers, Sisters in Crime, the American Society of News Editors, the Society of Professional Journalists, Investigative Reporters and Editors, the Press Club of Southwest Florida, the League of Women Voters, NAACP, the Dayton Literary Peace Prize, and juries for the National Journalism Awards and the Pulitzer prizes.

Made in United States
Orlando, FL
05 November 2021